When the Drum Major Died

Seasons in Purdah

Keeper of Secrets ... Translations of an Incident

The House

NOJ Publications
Berkeley, California

ISBN 978-1-938070-01-3

Published by NOJ Publications
P.O. Box 9405
Berkeley, CA 94709
www.anjuellefloyd.com

Cover by:
Iryna Spica of SpicaBookDesign
www.spicabookdesign.com

Deb Tremper of Six Penny Graphics
http://www.sixpennygraphics.com/

Hydrangea Image
by Kevin Sherman

Bond Chapel
by Rick Seidel

Edited by:
Jenny Grace Editorial
www.jennygrace-editorial.com

Cindy Bauer/Authors Express Promotion
www.cindybauerbooks.com

Printed in the United States of America

•.•.•.•.•.•.•.•.•.•

When the Drum Major Died

•.•.•.•.•.•.•.•.•.•

Anjuelle Floyd

You are the beat of my heart.
~ ~ Tan Jun Yong, celebrated Asian florist speaking of the
flower, hydrangea

*"If you want to say that I was a drum major, say that I was a drum
major for justice. ...Say that I was a drum major for peace. ... I
was a drum major for righteousness. And all of the other shallow
things will not matter."*

--Dr. Martin Luther King Jr.
<u>Drum Major Instinct</u>, sermon, February 4, 1968

•.•..•..•..•..•..•..•

When the Drum Major Died

•.•..•..•..•..•..•

Anjuelle Floyd

Chapter 1

Voices raised in disagreement flowed from the study and pulled Florina from her ruminations on the intricate weavings of the tablecloth.

"It's time for me to make my own way," said Redmond. "You and Mother have done enough."

"You've never had to go without," said Hammond, his father. "You speak as if what we've given you has caused us strain."

"All for which I'm grateful."

"Then stay here in Poinsettia, and make a life for yourself. It's a privilege and a gift to be able to do so."

"Particularly, when so many don't have that chance."

"Please, God," said Hammond. "Tell me you haven't been thinking about that again."

Florina traced the stitching once more. It appeared to match the one in the ivory tablecloth she had received as a wedding gift.

She struggled to comprehend the swift transition of her life from widow to bride.

Even now the words from October, two months earlier,

held an eerie echo. "I'd like to marry you. Your father has given his permission," Redmond had said. "As long as you agree."

Everything within her had stopped. I'm married. Florina had thought. *But, no.* She remembered. *He's dead. Ennis.*

The argument continued in the study across the hall. "Would it be so bad for me to work as an Army surgeon?" Redmond asked.

"I don't want my son dying in a war that both you and I know is evil, senseless and impossible to win."

"You sound like Dr. King."

"On that the man is right," said Hammond.

The potential of losing another person she loved, to a war defying sensibilities, exhumed an old pain. Florina's first husband, Army Lt. Ennis McCreary had been killed in Vietnam during April 1966. She had never told her parents of Ennis, nor of her marriage to him. Neither had she told her new husband, Redmond.

The exchange from the study across the hall grew louder. "I'd be an Army surgeon," said Redmond establishing points.

"As if bullets will steer themselves in another direction because you hold a scalpel." Hammond refuted.

"I hate this war too," Redmond said. "But that doesn't help any of our boys over in Vietnam. With me operating in a MASH unit, Negro soldiers will have at least one surgeon seeing to their--"

"Barely three days married and you're seeking to make your bride a widow. Good god, son. Are you out of your mind?" The ache of fear and possible loss resounded in his voice. "I won't hear of it!"

Hammond Austin loved his only child. Florina had witnessed that when first meeting Redmond and his parents four months earlier in late July. She touched the tablecloth, again examined the intricacies of its weaving.

Florina lived and died once more, this time gaining and losing Redmond as she had Ennis.

Against the flow of the embittered conversation mounting in the study, she left the dining room and made her way to the closet by the front door. On gathering her coat, twenty-four year-old Florina Gavin Austin lifted her suitcase, and left.

The eighteen months since Ennis' death in Vietnam had been surreal and painful at best. In the worst sort of way, Florina's life had taken on the quality of a fugitive enslaved in her own home.

Devastated by the loss of her husband, Florina lacked the strength to return to college. That she had married Ennis in secret, a man her parents and godparents had neither met nor knew existed, placed Florina in the precarious position of having to explain why an honor student, who denied being pregnant, had withdrawn from college.

Her announcement made in August, when others were returning to their respective institutions as she had in previous years, shocked Florina's family-- none more so than her mother and godmother. That Florina would not be joining them in the ranks of alumna sent a crushing blow to their dreams one year from their realization. She might not return to college, and she could never escape their demand for answers. Florina's mother, Helen, pushed and prodded, and Florina's father, came short of demanding she return to college and graduate.

Kay Reynolds, Florina's godmother, attempted a more passive approach, talking in an effort to feel Florina out and uncover the root of her decision.
Fearful that her emotions would overtake the best of her, Florina withdrew. Her bedroom and the woodlands behind her house where she played as a child became her refuge.

The arrival of a letter from the professor who was to have advised her in writing her senior thesis perplexed them even more. His high praise and his offer to assist her in re-entering college in her own time placed her mother and father at odds. The professor's letter moved Florina's father, Major

11

Gavin, towards concluding that Florina would return to college when and if she decided.

Major's decision left Florina feeling both cherished and

guilty for having failed him and her mother. Despite the constancy of his love, Florina would need to move forward, either by returning to school or revealing her secret.

As ensuing months evidenced that Florina was not pregnant, interactions between Florina and Helen grew quietly strained. In the absence of questions, Helen took on an interrogating demeanor. Her every move and gaze seemed to ask Florina, *"Why have you done this?"* An English major, Florina had studied to become a teacher like both Helen and Ava Reynolds.

May 1967 marked not only what should have been Florina's commencement from college into life, but also a year since her husband had died. While riots and fires enveloped many of America's large cities, Florina spent the summer of 1967 ruminating on what to do with life. Unable to openly mourn the loss her husband of one year, and with whom she had never lived, Florina approached the encroaching end of summer emotionally fatigued, and lacking hope of mustering the strength to ever leaving home, much less resuming college.

She entered the dog days of summer afloat on the sea of life without a sail or compass. Withstanding their prying eyes and interrogating voices, her mother and godmother stole what little energy that remained.

And then one afternoon late in July Florina drove to Ava Reynolds to deliver strawberries.

•.•.•.•.•.•.•.•.•.•

Chapter 2

•.•.•.•.•.•.•.•.•.•

Florina fingered the key to the front door in the pocket of her wool coat as she walked against the brisk cold. With suitcase in hand, she pressed towards the house where she and Redmond would live. They had driven past it on their arrival in Poinsettia moments after dawn. The sun, piercing remnant clouds of the previous evening, had delivered sufficient light for Florina to view the new coat of white paint Redmond had commissioned glistening against the December morn three days in the wake of Christmas.

Eager to forget the conversation she overheard between Redmond and his father, Florina's thoughts now slipped to hopes of making good on the new lease life had granted in her efforts to survive.

Hydrangeas.
Pink hydrangeas.

She had considered them when passing the house hours earlier. The hope of nurturing them to bloom in spring, maintaining their presence through summer until autumn, offered respite from the hurt of her loss amid yearnings to move

13

forward. Yet desires alone might not sustain and make them real.

Hydrangeas.

Florina continued down the street, buoyed by the image, towards her new home. With each step she pictured how the hydrangeas might encase the verandah, adorn and bring dimension to the home in which she would begin a new life aching from a loss she had yet with which to make peace.

And then she saw her ... a woman sitting upon the steps leading up to the veranda. She held a cigarette between her fingers, the woman.

She flicked ashes into the space between the shrubbery and the veranda, the space where Florina had silently proposed to plant the pink hydrangeas.

Florina cringed.

Florina viewed it strange *this woman* sitting on the steps of Florina and Redmond's house, and smoking *in public*. Many things were changing for women around the nation, but upstanding Negroes of North Carolina still deemed a woman smoking as lurid, something engaged in by those who were loose, or of ill repute.

She entered the walkway leading to the porch, and the woman stood. "Hello. I'm your neighbor." She extended her hand, "Our house is next door." The woman, with a tight, almost sculpted hour-glass waist, turned towards the brown house with the green trim, then brought the cigarette to her lips, inhaled and released a ring of smoke. Again she flicked ashes into the space between the shrubbery and the veranda.

Florina was put off. She observed her neighbor, who like herself was fair, extremely fair. On a clear day she could have passed for white.

"Aren't you cold?" Florina asked. The woman wore but a cropped, black sweater against a red, wool dress and black heels.

14

"Oh, me." The woman brushed her dress revealing her manicured nails with glistening with red polish. "Like I said. I live just next door." Holding her hand with the cigarette as if balancing a tray, she walked toward Florina and took Florina's suitcase. "There's lot of talk about you around Poinsettia," the woman said on her way up the steps.

Florina followed hesitantly. She was unaccustomed to such displays of openness, especially from people she had newly met, and whose name she did not know.

"You're Redmond's new wife?" The woman turned back on reaching the front door.

Like the woman, Florina too, had failed to introduce herself.

"Where is he, Redmond?" The woman inhaled from her cigarette.

"Back at Mama and Papa Austin's." Florina glanced in the direction of the Austin home from where she had walked five houses down.

Remnants of the heated discussion flooded Florina's thoughts. *Please God, I can't lose another husband to this filthy war.* She prayed.

The woman pushed open the door, entered the house and dropped the suitcase on the floor. "Let's get some heat on in here." She grasped her shoulders then rubbed palms together.

Florina closed the door as the woman then across the room, lit the heater that once lit, displayed thriving flames. "And don't feel the need to do that again." The woman eyed Florina's suitcase. "Struggle with those bags, or with anything else for that matter."

"It wasn't heavy." Florina removed her red coat and brown leather gloves, sliding them into her coat pocket--a gift; she didn't want to lose them.

The woman strutted down the hall, entered the kitchen and returned with a round glass ashtray. "This is a really nice house," she said. "Carolyn and Hammond have kept it in good shape." The woman's accent reflected bits of northern and southern flavor.

15

"You mean Dr. and Mrs. Hammond?" Southern custom required you attach "*a handle*" to the names of the elders, address them as '*Mr.*' and '*Mrs.*', or '*Miss.*'

Florina looked into the woman's eyes, blue-gray, like Ennis', an aspect she had avoided since spotting her perched upon the steps. Memories of the attraction she felt toward Ennis when first meeting him came alive.

"I love you, Florina."

Now as with Ennis, words remained glued to the roof of her mouth. He had needed Florina's permission to enlist. As a college student, he had avoided the draft, but upon graduation he saw a military stint clearing the way for him. After returning from Vietnam, he planned to secure a loan to start an engineering business.

He had it all planned. Ennis.

Regret filled Florina's heart. "*I should have told him, 'no, don't go.'*"

Cigarette in one hand and ashtray the other, the woman started back down the hall. Florina followed. Memories surfaced.

"*I'll be back*," Ennis had promised.

"*And I'll be here ... waiting*," Florina had said. A roar of guilt for having married Redmond but three months after their acquaintance tore through Florina.

Upon reaching the back of the house, the woman, whose name Florina did not know, pushed opened a door. "Now this is the sun room, as Grandma Austin likes to call it." The woman looked out onto the back yard displayed through the windows. "This was originally an open back porch before Grandfather Austin enclosed it. He died a year after it was completed." A wisp of sadness traipsed across the woman's face.

The woman's crème colored face bordered on white, like Florina's aunts, her father's sisters. Florina surmised that white Americans failed to recognize the woman, as they did Ennis, and Florina's aunts, for being Negro.

Florina regretted having lacked the strength to ask her parents', most particularly her mother's, permission to marry Ennis.

16

She had asked that Ennis to send his military pay to his mother, Melinda McCreary. "*I don't need it. She can use it to buy a house.*" Florina never considered he might not return. Her thoughts had instead settled upon how to explain to her parents their marrying without having told them.

Ennis thought her suggestion kind. "She'll be forever thankful. *"* He had smiled. "As am I."

Florina thanked God that she had instructed Ennis to send his military pay to Melinda, who while working as a domestic throughout his childhood, had raised him alone, and struggling to make ends meet. Melinda being the beneficiary of her son's military pay had kept secret their marriage. Military officers delivering the news of Ennis' death had gone to Melinda instead of Florina.

The woman remained focused on the backyard. "With Grandpa Austin gone Grandma Austin moved in with Redmond's parents."

"I know," Florina finally spoke. Redmond's Grandmother had given Florina a quick history of her life hours earlier over breakfast.

The sadness in the woman's eyes intensified, and Florina witnessing it sank farther into her pit of loneliness. She had yet to comprehend making a new life with Redmond, whose attraction towards Florina, much like Ennis', mystified her.

The woman walked past Florina back into the hall. "And here we have the bedroom," she said looking to the window facing the doorway. Florina followed her inside.

"Our bedrooms face each other." The woman nodded towards the brown house displayed through the window, then plopped onto the bed Florina and Redmond would occupy that night. She lowered the ashtray onto the bedspread and exhaled a circle of smoke that dissipated into the air as Ennis' life had in the Vietnam War.

Florina grew angry and was about to speak when the woman said. "You know he's planning Poor People's March. Dr. Martin Luther King, Jr." The woman gave a haunting smile. "It's going to be like the March on Washington, but more serious this time."

17

Florina frowned.

The woman continued. "The Poor People's March is going to be longer. There's going to be a tent city on the White House lawn."

"How do you know these things? Florina asked completely confused, but also intrigued.

"A friend of mine is a follower of Dr. King. When Malcolm was killed we turned to him. No one was left."

Florina again knitted her brows.

A dark shadow overtook the woman's gaze. "I was there when those men killed Malcolm. I saw it all. Him lying there. Blood streaming from his chest. It was ..." Her voice caught. The woman's shoulders trembled.

Florina thought her about to cry.

The woman lifted the ashtray and stood. "It's been nice meeting you, but I need to go and prepare dinner for Macon," she announced and strutted back to the front of the house, sitting the ashtray on the coffee table before the sofa. "Macon is my husband," she said blowing out more rings of smoke.

"Macon and Redmond are childhood friends. They grew up together." The woman flashed a smiled. "I'm sure we'll become good friends too."

Florina didn't know of Macon Elder.

The woman walked to the front door, grasped the knob then turned back. "Oh, and by the way, I almost forgot. In fact, forgive me." She extended her hand and with a smile said, "My name is Agnes. *Agnes Elder*."

Eager to rid herself and their home of Agnes, but now even more mystified, Florina accepted her palm.

"My husband, Macon, is the other doctor in town along with Redmond and his father, Hammond," said Agnes.

"Is he a surgeon?" Florina asked.

Agnes' melancholy again came forth, Florina sensing that despite her smiles it had found permanent residence within Agnes. "No. There's only one Negro surgeon in Poinsettia, and that's Redmond. And there's only one Redmond Austin." Her voice trailed into the half-smile, losing shape upon her lips.

Her gaze receded, she reflecting upon a past Florina was both curious and cautious to understand. The cigarette between her fingers all but gone, Agnes opened the door and left.

She had been thinking of Ennis when she looked up and he was standing in the doorway to their bedroom. Redmond. But Florina saw Ennis.

"Why didn't you tell me you were leaving?" said Redmond.

"You said you'd come back." She spoke to Redmond as if he were Ennis.

"After my talk with grandmother, Father called me into the study."

"I don't want you signing up for this war," Florina said to Redmond, who for her had become Ennis.

"You overheard." Redmond glanced at Florina's suitcase unopened and standing by the bed.

"I'll go back home if you enlist, wait in Laurel for news that you've been killed." She stood and looked to her suitcase.

Redmond grasped her arms. "I'm not going away."

"But you told your father it was time to--"

"Strike out on my own," Redmond said.

Ennis has spoken similar words when stating his intention to enlist. He had then asked Florina to marry him. "I'll be back," he had promised when she said, "Yes."

Again Redmond eyed the suitcase. "Father found my enlistment papers, began to question me." Redmond explained. "It's been nearly fifteen years since I left for college, then medical school and residency. Since I came home last spring I've barely had room to breathe."

Florina met the gaze of Redmond's brown eyes and saw herself. "I wish mama could understand," she said. She was speaking of the loss of Ennis.

Redmond enveloped her into his chest and caressed her

head. "You know what it is to love someone, but to also need to be free of them."

"I don't want to be free of you," Florina said still speaking to Ennis. She relaxed her head upon his chest and closed her eyes.

"I never intend to be free of you. That's why I married you. I love you."

Those words resounding in Redmond's chest jolted Florina into the present.

Chapter 3

They returned that evening to Redmond's parents' for dinner.

Hammond greeted them at the door. "Long time, no see, or was it just this morning?" He embraced Florina with open arms and patted Redmond's shoulder, "Glad you made it back, son." Florina heard sincere regret in her father-in-law's voice for having argued with his son.

She entered the hallway that stretched from the front door to the back of the house and all seemed clearer. Florina sensed the red scarf draping the bottom of the Christmas tree emitting a vibrancy absent during the morning. The blue of the walls cast a crisp coolness. Florina's arms prickled underneath her sweater.

Her body was alive with intimacies of the afternoon. She recalled Redmond's face morphing into Ennis' the latter now a *Diaspora* having surrendered to safekeeping within present moments of the former.

Florina lifted her head to the mistletoe hanging over the dining room entryway then turned to Redmond talking with Hammond by the front door. She caught Redmond's gaze He started towards her. He was Redmond, now and forever, his face as it was and would always be, brown and dark and full of love.

Hammond hung their coats in the closet, said, "Mrs. Brooks has prepared a special meal for tonight." Redmond's favorite. Roasted duck with rice pilaf and some of the collard greens my mother blanched and froze back in the summer."

Lyla Austin appeared on the second floor landing.

"Grandmother, you've outdone us again," Redmond said. He walked up and escorted her down.

"I agree," Florina said. "You look stunning."

The sequins of Lyla Austin's black tea-length dress shimmered within in the soft light of the long hallway on her approach.

"I had a feeling we might have an addition to our family- -when Redmond returned to see Florina in Laurel that first weekend after vacationing there with Ava and Bill," Lyla said. She gave Florina a wink.

"Your earrings are lovely," Florina said.

"A gift from Hammond," said Redmond's grandmother. She lifted Florina's hand, a sign for her to bend and accept a kiss. "I have a loving son." Lyla then flashed Hammond a smile of approval. "No one could have made me prouder. Just as Redmond has done with Hammond, all of us."

The eighty-one year-old woman, barely four-and-a-half feet, and with hair soft as cotton, reached up to Redmond. He bent over, and availed his cheek to her palm, and Lyla caressed it much like Redmond's palm had greeted Florina's earlier that afternoon.

Redmond's mother walked down the hall from the back of the house. "Oh good, everyone is here," she said.

Redmond gave his mother a kiss after which she hugged Florina, and whispered, "Thank you for getting Redmond to come back," a sign that Carolyn, too, had overheard the argument.

Florina smiled softly.

"Mrs. Brooks has prepared everything," Carolyn said,

22

"All we need do is bring it out to the table."

"On that note I'm ready to eat." Hammond rubbed his palms together and joined Carolyn in returning to the kitchen.

Redmond drew close to Florina. His gaze intensified above his smile. She felt his desire to kiss her. Her breasts tingled in recalling the touch of his hand hours earlier, his lips meeting hers, the breath of his soul. Then as if remembering they were not alone, he relinquished her hand. The passion pouring into his eyes amplified.

Earlier that afternoon Redmond had explained his stance in the argument with his father.

"I just need to know that he respects me for being my own man. I've lived on my on for over a decade. I'm a surgeon," Redmond had said.

"But he loves you. You're his only child and son," Florina said. She knew what it was to be a couple's only offspring. "If he loses you, he'll have ..."

"He's not going to lose me," Redmond said. He had then caressed Florina's cheeks, bringing his lips to hers where they lingered until he had moved to undress her.

They had not been intimate since the ceremony that took place in Florina's home.

Redmond said, "Your parents were very respectful, but I just kept feeling like your father would walk in at any moment and catch me in the ..."

Florina flashed a bittersweet smile. Thankful that he had waited she now felt petulant about physically consecrating their vows.

Oh God, help me to do this.

He touched her chest. They were lying in bed. Redmond kissed one nipple then the other.

As when he had stood in the bedroom doorway, Redmond's dark brown face morphed into that of Ennis McCreary, now dead, and whose cheeks had been fair as butter.

23

Florina closed her eyes. Tears formed underneath her eyelids, but she willed them to remain hidden.

Redmond kissed her cheek and forehead, touched his lips to her neck.

Florina's body tightened.

Lifting the chalice of her breasts, Redmond supped.

Florina's eyes remained close. But unlike in early autumn when Redmond planted his first kiss her upon her cheek, and moments earlier, her defenses now deferred to the desires of his body requesting full sway.

Florina's body, made empty of clothes by Redmond's skilled hands, slipped under the waters of a reality, though familiar and known, that reeked of pain and rage.

Redmond entered the dwelling place of her suffering, treaded upon her pain.

Undulations of recognition and remembrance encompassed Florina's body. The rhythm of her heartbeat hastened. The wish of Redmond's soul to merge with Florina's eclipsed that of hers seeking atonement. A wave of energy rippled about the room. Her breathing grew full. With the grace of a dove Redmond dispensed his passion.
Darkness exploded into a light. A blinding flash shot forth claiming all it touched and shattered the perpetual stream of thoughts clouding Florina's head. All that remained in resistance faded into nothingness.

"*Oh.*" She clutched Redmond's sturdy shoulders.
Florina's heart slowed.
Peace as she had never known settled upon her soul and sped throughout her body.

She opened her eyes.

Redmond, his hearty, brown face had lain over her.

The consummation of their love had come once, twice, thrice.

And with each coming and going Florina had sunk deeper and deeper into a place where no traces of Ennis ever existed.

Dinner bestowed a calm--all but erasing memories of Redmond's and Hammond's argument following breakfast. After promising to convey to Mrs.
Brooks everyone's compliments for the meal, Carolyn went to the kitchen to
prepare coffee and dessert. With their arms entwined as they had been following breakfast,
Redmond and Lyla headed for the family room. Florina was about to join
them, as Redmond and his Grandmother disappeared around the corner, but Hammond said, "I'd like to speak with you for a moment." He
extended his hand towards the study. She followed him down the hall and into the room where earlier that morning he and Redmond had exchanged heated words. "Please have a seat," Hammond said and closed the door. He gestured for her to sit in the leather chair facing the desk. Florina observed the carefulness with which her father-in-law, donning a gray striped suit, leaned half-standing, upon the front edge of his desk. "You've clearly made Redmond very happy," Hammond began. "Both Carolyn and I thank you for that. A good woman is hard to find. And we believe you to be a sincere person, someone who will stand behind and beside Redmond in the years to come, whatever the difficulties."

Florina rested her hands upon the lap of her dress.

"You're probably thinking that what I said is a preface to my adding that
we were against Redmond marrying you," Hammond said. He gave a wry
smile. "Everything has happened so quickly. You two meet in July, really August.
Redmond makes, let's see--" Hammond lifted his fingers, "--how many trips
back to Laurel following our vacation with the Ava and Ben," he began
counting.

"Six," Florina said, "--before he asked me to marry him."

"You're a smart girl, excuse me ... young woman," said Hammond. He braced his palms upon the edge of the desk on which he leaned.
"I had considered that you and Mother Austin might not want Redmond
to marry me."

Hammond arched his brows. "Quite the contrary," he said. His eyes grew
alert and focused, revealing the roots of the same gesture displayed by
Redmond. "I've been practicing medicine for over thirty years. Trust me; I'm a fairly decent judge of character. You're just the person
Redmond needs." Hammond stood from leaning upon the desk and walked
behind it. "My job, as your father-in-law, is to see that you get what you need." Redmond's father opened a drawer and lifted out two small leather folders. He returned from behind the desk and handed them to Florina. "In one you'll find checks to an account I opened for you. The other lists all the stores where I have established accounts for you to purchase things you need."

Florina flipped through the latter and read the names of a dress shop,
the local grocery store, a pharmacy. "But I'm married to *Redmond*," she
said.

"And Redmond's my son. I want him to stay happy. And with you happy
here in Poinsettia ..." he gestured, "... well it certainly won't make
Redmond any less happy."

"This is very nice, but ... " Florina observed the folders, recalled seeing
Redmond in the doorway of their bedroom, thinking him Ennis then speaking
a truth she wished to have said to her first husband; however, her words had also born intentions for Redmond. "I'll go home,

26

wait to hear you've been killed." Unlike with
Ennis, "I won't have to lie and hide my sadness this time."
Florina read the names of stores listed within the leather folders
once more. She said to her father-in-law,"I told Redmond I don't
want him to enlist. I'll go back home if he does."

"I see you've gone to the root of it," said Hammond.

"I aim to make Redmond a good wife. That's not possible
with him dead. I love your son. As for where we'll eventually
live ... "Florina stood. "Redmond will decide." She handed
the leather folders back to Hammond and left.

The five of them were half-way through eating dessert
when the doorbell rang.

"I'll see to it." Hammond rose from the armchair and
went to the front door. Moments later he returned with Agnes.

"We meet again," Agnes said to Florina and smiled.

Redmond turned to Florina, sitting beside her on the
couch. She dabbed her lips with the white linen napkin.

"I greeted Florina when she arrived at the house this
afternoon, gave her a tour of the place," Agnes said to
Redmond.

Redmond and his father, standing beside Agnes,
exchanged glances.

"And, Grandma Austin, aren't you looking well?"

"Thank you, my dear," Lyla said.

"I heard you didn't attend the wedding." Agnes threw a
wink at Florina. "Had I known you were remaining here in
Poinsettia, I would have I come to visit. Looked in on you."

"Oh, I was quite fine. Mrs. Brooks was here every day as
usual," Lyla said.

Agnes then said to Florina, "I hope I didn't stoke the fire
too much. The heater looks simple like it can't do that much.
Left unattended it can make the house feel like the tropi--"

Carolyn stood. "Would you like some fruit cake? Slices
to take home for you and Macon," she directed towards Agnes.

27

"I'd ask you to join us for dessert but," Hammond chimed in, "--but as you can see we're nearly finished eating."

"Not to worry," said Agnes. "I didn't come to stay." She touched Hammond's shoulder as if to ease the mounting anxiety. "Macon's having some problems with the administrators at Poinsettia General." The pleasant cordiality that had accompanied her entrance vanished. "I thought you'd be the best person to address the issue."

"Of course," Hammond said hesitant and dismayed. "Let's go into the study." He bid Florina excuse him. "If I'm not here when you and Redmond leave, please know we had a lovely time." Florina nodded. Hammond gave her a fatherly kiss. "Carolyn and I look forward to seeing you in church," he said, and left.

Agnes had yet to leave the study when Florina and Redmond left his parent's house and they headed home. They had barely cleared the steps when Redmond said, "You didn't tell me that Agnes had been over."

"She was sitting on the steps when I reached the house."

Redmond massaged his temple, touched the bridge of his nose.

"I didn't think about it until she arrived tonight," Florina said.

Seeing Agnes, her blue-gray eyes had brought back memories of Ennis, awakened his spirit sent sleeping in the wake of Redmond making love to Florina.

A year and a half and I'm still haunted. This has got to stop. I'm married now. And Redmond loves me.

She said to Redmond as they walked against the midnight cold, "Agnes asked me where I was when Medgar Evers was killed, told me she saw Malcolm X when he was shot. She said they were nearly the same age. Malcolm born in May, Medgar in July, both in the same year."

"Nineteen twenty-five," Redmond said. His gaze receded against the light of the streetlamps illuminating the darkness. Sadness seemed to overtake him.

28

She also asked me about Emmett Till."

Redmond turned to her.

"I was eleven when it happened," Florina said. "I didn't remember where I was when Malcolm and Medgar were killed. I'll always remember when Emmett died."

"I think we all will," said Redmond.

They resumed walking.

As they neared the house soft lights aglow within, Florina recalled her first glimpse of Agnes, perched upon the steps of the verandah, cigarette between her fingers. Agnes had taken Florina's suitcase and...

"Agnes said you were nineteen when it happened, that she had been seventeen, and Macon, her husband, twenty-one," Florina said.

"Did she say anything else?" Redmond asked.

Florina shook her head. Then ... "I almost forgot. She's planning to go to Dr. King's Poor People's March in Washington, D. C."

"What march?" Redmond looked to her, moonlight revealing the anxiety in his gaze. "How does she know about this?"

"Agnes says she has a friend who works with the movement. It seems they correspond, perhaps by letters. This friend tells her about the marches and rallies that are coming up." Florina asked, "Does her husband know about her involvement?"

"Macon? No. He'd be furious." Redmond shook his head clearly frustrated. "She needs to give all this up. She's married now."

"How long have they been married, she and Macon?"

"Since April."

Eight months, Florina thought.

"They're newlyweds. Like us."

"Agnes and Macon are nothing like us. You the least of all like Agnes."

Redmond sighed as they climbed the steps of the verandah. On reaching the door, Redmond placed his key in the knob.

"The door was open," Florina said. Redmond turned to her, his eyes again searching hers for meaning. "Agnes lifted my suitcase, opened the door and brought me inside the house," Florina explained. "The door was unlocked. I never used my key."

Later that night as they prepared for bed, Redmond said, "I'll call Mr. Phillips tomorrow morning and have him put in new locks."

Now in her nightgown, Florina pulled back the covers then bolstered their pillows. "Agnes said her husband is a physician," Florina spoke.

"Macon," Redmond said. His back was to Florina as he stood to the armoire hanging his trousers. "We grew up together."

"I suppose he has patients at the Poinsettia General. It's the white hospital," said Florina. She was now in bed.

"Macon has white patients, poor and with no money. White doctors refuse them because they owe money and can't pay."

Florina tried to reconcile how southern whites persecuted her people with Macon caring for their illnesses.

"He needs to be able to admit his to Poinsettia General since White patients can't or won't go to Charlotte Negro Hospital," Redmond said. He crawled in bed.

"His white patients." Florina turned the idea over in her mind.

"They pay him what little they can," Redmond said. "Certainly not what they owe the white doctors. A hospital stay is expensive."

Again, Florina reflected on what she had learned of Macon. She asked Redmond, "Do you have any white patients?"

"I saw them when I was in Washington, D. C."

"But here, down south?"

"No."

30

"Would you treat them if they came to you?"

"I have no interest in turning away anyone who's sick and suffering," Redmond said.

"But what if the patient dies and his family blames you?"

Again, his gaze retreated, though this time with what appeared less anguish.

"Do you want to admit your patients, Negro patients, to Poinsettia General?" Florina asked.

"I'd like access to their technology, the ability to have my patients undergo tests that Charlotte Negro Hospital lacks. My hope is that if enough Negro patients gain the option of entering Poinsettia, the administrators of Charlotte Negro will have evidence that Negro patients want the same level of care."

"Why would they think any differently?" Florina frowned.

"Perhaps I should send you to speak with the trustees and administrators of Charlotte Negro." Redmond smiled for the first time since Agnes' arrival at his parent's home during dessert.

"And what about the white patients who can't pay?"

Redmond kissed the top of her head, and eased his hand under her back. "You're a good person," he said. His words echoed Hammond's statement. He drew Florina closer, their shoulders touching, and enfolded her into his chest, she wondering from what he wanted to protect her.

31

Chapter 4

A farm girl, Florina was accustomed to rising at five am, and helping her mother prepare breakfast. The death of Ennis sent her home the summer of 1966 a different person.

She dreaded awakening in the morning to the reality of Ennis' death, the person she had married and vowed to spend the rest of her life with. Florina had planned to tell her parents of Ennis and that he was her husband on graduating college. Ennis had promised to return, "*I'll come home somehow*," and witness Florina receive her degree.

By Florina's estimation, Helen Gavin could not dislike a First Lieutenant in the United States Army who had survived Vietnam, even if some thought him a white man. Ennis' mother was of both Negro and Cherokee heritage, but she had grown up Cherokee.

Ennis' death prior at the end of her junior year stole Florina's confidence to reveal her actions. She lost the strength to explain that she had loved someone who looked like Florina's aunts, her father's sisters, who so despised Helen for her dark skin and made plain their disdain of their brother having married her.

Florina had the coloring of her aunts, a curse that in her mind left her unsure of Helen's love. Seeing Agnes brought it all back--the shame and fear of having fallen in love and married a man who looked like the enemy--both whites and pale Negroes who counted themselves better than their brown and darker relatives. The emotional torture that Florina had witnessed throughout her childhood her mother endure under the bitter derision of Gavin's sisters, assured Florina that Helen would have never forgiven her daughter in presenting a son-in-law who many assumed was white.

These worries imprisoned Florina and her thoughts during the summer of 1966 following her junior year. During the fall when others had returned to college, Florina entered a dark tunnel reflecting no light, or hope of day with an end through which either might enter.

A year later, the summer of 1967 and all that occurred during the fall were as unexpected as seeing Agnes sitting on the steps leading up to the verandah of the home Florina now shared with Redmond. Meeting Redmond in late July 1967, his proposal in October, and their marrying in December, ejected Florina from the cave of sorrow made worse by hidden mourning. The unending days of summer, with little darkness within which to silently cry, ebbed into the fall equinox which displayed a balance of daylight and nighttime hours.

The two times, she had seen Agnes, reminded Florina of what fate had delivered. But if Agnes symbolized all Florina had left behind, Redmond, and their making love, was now living proof of her present, which was attached to a vibrant future.

Florina and Redmond went to bed in a house absent of others, the topic of Macon, his patients and Poinsettia General directing their words. The light out and Redmond's arms around her, sent them on another journey of intimacies that superseded anything Florina had experienced with Ennis. She loved Ennis. But Redmond's skilled hands played a song that spoke directly to Florina's body. Memories of Ennis, what they had shared, and all that had died with him on a battlefield half-way around the world Florina had yet to conceive or imagine, deferred to the

34

immediacy of Redmond's lovemaking, and receded from her present thoughts.

After a year and a half of dreading the dawn of a new day wherein some parts of Florina still sought to deny Ennis' death, Florina awoke the first morning in her new home as Redmond's wife grateful for the melody of his passion that had touched her soul. She went down to the kitchen buoyed by the present moment that offered possibility and hope.

The following morning Florina returned from emptying the trash out back to find Redmond standing at the kitchen table and scanning the front page of *The Poinsettia Times*. "Something smells good," he said with one hand to his waist, the forefinger of his other upon the newspaper lying upon the kitchen table.

She brought two plates of eggs, bacon and toast to the table, poured two cups of coffee and joined him in sitting.

Redmond folded the paper and began to eat. Even from upside down she recognized the obituary section.

"We're losing a lot of our boys over there," said Florina.

"*Mmmm.*" Redmond continued reading.

"Last I read the US had nearly five hundred thousand soldiers in Vietnam."

Redmond lifted his head and caught her staring. "I'm not going anywhere," he said, then touched her hand, and stilled its trembling. "I tore up my enlistment papers after you left the house yesterday." He smiled. "I didn't need Father to make me see what there is to lose--all I have to live for."

The warmth of his palm on hers reminded Florina of their lovemaking last night. Florina spoke softly. "I have a lot to live for too."

The newlyweds finished breakfast. Redmond had put on his coat and was headed for the front room when Florina handed him his lunch. "Two turkey sandwiches. Your mother gave them to me last night said they were your favorite."

"I suppose like the eggs and bacon this morning," Redmond said. He arched his eyebrows.

35

"We have to eat. You know that, Dr. Austin."

Warmth filled Redmond's face softened his angular cheeks. He leaned forward and kissed her. He moved to open the door, said, "By the way, I spoke with Mr. Phillips this morning. He'll be here around noon to change the locks."

Florina nodded and agreed she would be home.

Redmond gave her one more kiss. He then opened the door and there stood Agnes on the verandah, a cigarette between her fingers, and she donning a red coat.

"Well you two are up early this morning," Agnes said. Wearing black patent leather heels as if for a night on the town, she strutted through the door. "Being so newlywed I thought you might have slept in." She flashed a mischievous grin.

"That being your conclusion then why are you here?" said Redmond.

"You're looking spiffy." Agnes eyed Redmond's black wool coat, and touched its lapel. "Haven't seen that one before. Must have bought it in anticipation of becoming a married man."

"Perhaps I did. I'd introduce you to my wife, but it seems the two of you already met."

"Caught you by surprise," Agnes said. "My being here yesterday."

"May I take your coat?" Florina asked. She found it odd that Agnes was wearing one this morning unlike yesterday when sitting outside.

"Thank you. It's good to see someone still has some manners." Agnes shed her red coat and handed it to Florina. The pearls about her neck softened the austerity of her black dress. Twice Agnes had presented herself dressed in high quality and on a weekday like Florina had never witnessed any woman in Laurel, not even Florina's god mother, Ava Reynolds, the wife Laurel's only Negro physician.

36

Florina looked down upon her dress and wondered if she should change clothes. She would have also have to observe the way Redmond's mother dressed.

Agnes said, "For a newly married man he's in a bad mood. Things not go well in this big ole' lonely house all by yourselves last night?"

"Redmond took the cigarette from between Agnes' fingers. "Everything is fine. But I don't allow smoking in my home. These things kill." He walked out the front door, discarding the cigarette in dirt between the shrubberies encasing the veranda.

"Redmond Austin, I do believe you have become an ogre," Agnes said and turned to Florina. "What have you done to him?"

"Nothing that you could ever accomplish," Redmond said. His words were not lost on Florina. "Have a good day," Redmond said. The haze of sadness draped his eyes as if to offer an apology.

But to whom and for what? Florina thought.

Redmond turned and started down the steps then quickly returned. "Don't forget Mr. Phillips at noon," he said to Florina.

Again she nodded.

Redmond started down the steps and out to the car as Florina closed the door.

"So Redmond's got Ole' Man Phillips sprucing up the place a bit," Agnes said. She whipped around and settled one hand upon her hourglass waist. Her black patent leather heels shone in the morning sunlight.

"He's changing the locks," said Florina. She started down the hall towards the kitchen in the back of the house.

"Redmond wants to keep you safe." Agnes followed her into the kitchen.

"I suppose." She had begun clearing away the breakfast dishes when Agnes, peering inside the refrigerator said, "Looks like you need to make a trip to the grocery store. Today's my day for buying groceries." She closed the refrigerator door. "Come with me. I'll show you around."

37

Redmond had said last evening, "Macon's parents own the local market. My mother does pretty much all her shopping there."

"That's really nice that we have one of our own to patronize." Florina had said, excited at the entrepreneurship of the Elders.

Florina washed the last of the breakfast dishes, and Agnes, grabbing a towel, dried them.

As the wives of two of Poinsettia's three Negro doctors, Florina felt the core of her relationship with Agnes stood upon supporting the financial independence of not only each other, but also Macon, and his parents, along with any other Negroes of the community who sought their livelihood by starting their own businesses.

"Now about those groceries," Florina said to Agnes. "I do need to get some."

"Then let's head out." Agnes said. She strutted towards the door as if they were going to a party.

Florina made a list and the two set out with Agnes' housekeeper in tow. Not knowing the layout of the town, Florina was shocked when Agnes led them into the local A&P instead of the Elder's Grocery owned by Agnes' in-laws.

Florina continued inside, dismayed, as Leena, the young woman who cleaned and cooked for Agnes, and whom Florina considered a girl, followed.

"This place is really busy," Florina said. She removed her gloves.

"Does it bother you?" Agnes turned.

"I thought that we might go to your in-law's market."

"That place is so behind the times. They don't carry half the things I need." Agnes directed Leena to get a basket.

The three moved down each aisle, Agnes pointing to various items, and Leena lifting cans from the shelf and placing them in the basket.

Florina carried her own basket. When Leena had gone to another aisle to get detergent, Florina asked Agnes, "Isn't she a bit young working for you? She can't be over eighteen."

"She could never please Macon sexually," Agnes said with a smirk.

"I didn't mean *that*. Shouldn't she be in school?"

On Leena's return Agnes asked her, "How old are you?"

"Nineteen, ma'am."

"And where would you be if I hadn't hired you?"

"Cleaning ole Missy Hanson's house."

"And how clean is old Missy Hanson's house?"

"It ain't no cleaner than a pigsty."

Agnes smiled at Florina. "By my estimation, I'm doing Leena a favor by employing her."

A dull cast spread across Leena's almond face.

Florina gathered some milk, dishwashing liquid and soap. She then entered the line at the register.

Agnes and Leena joined her. "Is that all you're going to get?" Agnes knitted her brows and surveyed the few items in Florina's grocery basket, all appearing lost.

"I'll get the rest later."

"Don't tell me you're one of those who only patronizes Negroes," Agnes said.

The customer in front of them, a white woman wearing a tan hat and plaid coat, began placing her items on the conveyor belt.

"And what if I am?" said Florina. She refused to look at Agnes.

"I would say to each his ow--"

The white, male cashier with black hair yelled at the older Negro man bagging groceries. "If I've told you once I've said it a thousand times Jonah, two bags in one for Mrs. Greene. Or else the bag's gonna' break then she's back in here with her food all mixed up with glass, and I'm out of product and money." He turned to the woman in front of Florina and Agnes, presumably Mrs. Greene, and whose items he was ringing up.

"*Niggers*," said the cashier with black hair. He shook his head. "Dumb as nails and stupid as horses."

"Make that mules, Mickey," said Mrs. Greene. "My horse, Rose, was smart as a whip. Then, of course, she knew who cracked it." The woman's lips, lipstick bleeding into their cracks, flashed a crooked smile.

Florina cringed.

"Now don't go and do something foolish," Agnes chided in a whisper. "From the looks of it, one might think you lived all your life up north in New York City."

"I've certainly never had anyone use that offensive word in front of m--"

"Well, how you doing, Mrs. Elder?" asked the cashier. He greeted Agnes with warmth--absent his criticism and condescension at Jonah bagging groceries.

"Fine as I've ever been, Mickey," said Agnes. She assisted Leena lifting the last of the items from the shopping cart onto the conveyor.

"Let me see if I can help ya' there." Mickey stretched his arm down the length of the conveyor belt as Agnes pushed box of detergent towards him. "There we go," he said and began ringing up items.

"How's your mother doing?" Agnes asked Mickey. She stepped forward as Leena took the basket towards Jonah.

"Just fine now that Dr. Elder came by to see her."

Florina forced herself to remain calm.

"That medicine he gave her did just the trick," the cashier continued.

"Glad to hear it," said Agnes. "I'll tell Macon. He'll be glad to know."

"Now that'll be $65.30 cents," Mickey said.

"Can we put it on the bill?" asked Agnes.

"Of course," Mickey said. He lifted a black book from behind the cash register and jotted down the amount. "Just let Dr. Elder know he can send payment at any time."

"Oh, he hasn't paid the bill yet?" Agnes said with a measure of surprise.

"No, ma'am," the cashier said. He appeared bewildered.

"I'll speak to him," Agnes said. "In the meantime you give your mother my regards." She turned to Florina and shrugged. "And by the way I've brought you a new customer, Dr. Redmond Austin's new bride." Agnes extended her palm towards Florina then touched Florina's shoulder as if to bolster and direct her to speak. "Florina, this is Mickey, head cashier here at our local A &P."

"Pleased to meet you, Mickey," Florina said. She extended her gloved hand and shook Mickey's palm.

"Glad to have you come in. I heard young Dr. Redmond had taken himself a wife," the cashier said. "I hope you found all you needed." His eyes widened in what appeared anticipation of her answer. Surely the man had not mistaken Florina for being whit--

Florina gazed upon the conveyor belt where Leena had placed the few items Florina had purchased then to Jonah, his head hung. Her cheeks grew hot. She wanted to scream, then cry.

"She'll be buying more," Agnes said with an exaggerated Southern drawl. "You know how it is with these newly *marrieds*. Honeymooners, I call them." She turned to Florina. "They're not thinking so much of food, but ... "

Mickey nodded and grinned revealing his crooked, yellow teeth. With everything itemized he turned to Florina.

Having opened her purse she lifted out her wallet.

Mickey asked, "Which account would you like me to place this on?" He reached for the black book behind the cash register. "Seems like both your husband and father-in-law have opened accounts with us just for you."

"How much are my items?" Florina asked.

"Five dollars and fifty cent to the penny."

Florina handed the man a five dollar bill and two quarters.

"Sure you don't want to put this one of your accounts?" Mickey asked. "They've been set up just for you."

"Perhaps later when I need more things," Florina said. She lifted her bag and indicated to Agnes and Leena that she was ready to leave.

Outside Agnes seemed bothered. "Mickey's a nice man," Agnes said.

"He's also a store owner who probably charges interest on any bills he carries over. Never mind he's racist," Florina said low and with restraint. Leena walked but five steps behind them.

"Find me one white person who isn't."

Florina turned to Agnes, stunned at what seemed her turnabout in thought and behavior.

"Besides, money shouldn't be an issue for you," Agnes said.

"It's not my money we're speaking of."

"You're Redmond's wife. What's his is yours."

"And we won't have any if I spend it all at the A &P," said Florina. She was furious.

Florina grew anxious when reaching home and seeing a man sitting on the steps leading up to the verandah. His faded blue overalls and brown plaid coat, identified him as Mr. Phillips. "Oh, my goodness. I totally forgot." She left Agnes and Leena, and hurried towards him.

"I'm so sorry," Florina said. The man stood, gray hair peeking from underneath his cap. "Redmond told me this morning you were coming at noon," said Florina. She removed her gloves and extended her hand.

"Don't worry, ma'am," Mr. Phillips said. He removed his cap, dipped his head, and shook her palm. "I just arrived. Was just sitting here and taking a rest." Phillips gazed back upon his black lunch pail. "Just finished off the last bite of one of my Sarah's turkey sandwiches. She'd be mighty glad I had this moment to eat and sit a spell instead working through lunch. So would Dr. Redmond. He told me to slow down."

Agnes said on approach, "Well, Mr. Phillips. I see you're on the beat." Leena had gone into Agnes' house. "Out working four days after Christmas."

"Bills keep-a-comin'. And we all eatin' right on through Christmas," said Phillips. He turned to Florina. "Best be getting 'bout changing those locks. I'll take those groceries." He reached out to Florina. "Put 'em inside if you like. "

"Thank you," Florina said. She handed over her bag of groceries. "Here are the keys."

"Oh, I've got my own. Mr. Redmond gave me a set, asked me to hold 'em in case he got locked out." The white-haired man went up the stairs onto the veranda. Observing him unlock the door stirred the memory of how on her arrival yesterday Agnes had opened the door with no key.

Agnes said, "I'd watch that man if I were you. He comes on as simple. But--"

Florina turned to Agnes and hit her with a pointed gaze.

"But those are the ones who cause trouble," said Agnes.

"Like Mickey, I supposed," Florina said. Ever more frustrated by what appears as one more reversal in Agnes' ideals, Florina left Agnes and went inside the house.

Mr. Phillips changed the locks to the front and back doors in less than an hour. Florina then called Redmond's mother, and asked for directions to the Elders' Market.

"I'll take you," Carolyn said. "Then I can introduce you to Macon's parents."

Florina thought it interesting that you she would meet Macon's mother and father before him.

Along with a variety of fresh vegetables, meats and fish, Elders' Market served as gathering place for the old men of the community. Two pairs of gray-haired men sat inside the market, a table between each pair—one pair playing checkers, the other chess.

After exchanging pleasantries Carolyn made introductions. "Mr. Hampton. Mr. Timmons. This is Redmond's new wife."

"Please to meet ya' ma'am," said Greenwith Hampton. He stood, three others joining him and they shook Florina's hand.

Otis Timmons tipped his hat, and dipped his head at Carolyn, said, "Young Mr. Redmond's got him a might fine lookin' wife, if I may say so."

"Well thank you, Mr. Timmons. Mother Austin, Hammond, and I agree," Carolyn said.

Two of the four men had known Redmond's grandfather, Louis Austin.

Papa Austin knew your mother," Carolyn said to Greenwith Hampton.

"He delivered me into this world."

"Otis Timmons said, "Louis Austin was the first person to touch all of us when we left our mother's wombs. Poinsettia's had midwives. But it won't cause we didn't have no doctor."

Each indicated pride in that Redmond had returned to follow in his father's footsteps. "I can't remember a time when Poinsettia hasn't had an Austin doctoring on us," said Greenwith Hampton.

The men, ranging in age from mid-eighties to as old as ninety-two, were proud that the Austin doctors saw fit to establish their presence in Poinsettia and not seek greater heights elsewhere.

Though he had promised it would not include enlisting in the military, Redmond had expressed a desire to leave Poinsettia. The crests of change encircled Florina and the country. Progress rarely accompanied the constant motion of life without sacrifice and mourning.

Hearing the old men speak heartily of a legacy to which she now belonged warmed Florina's heart and offered a sense of rootedness she longed to claim in having left her home in Laurel. Yet she did not know how long it would last.

Increasing demands concerning Civil Rights for Negroes, Equality for Women and the persistent cry to end the War in Vietnam stirred the hearts and minds of every American citizen. The summer of nineteen sixty-seven had poured over with violence. Riots and looting had pulled the country's every bone and nerve.

The two pairs of gray and white-haired men, their smooth, brown faces, softened and not hardened by time, bid, "Good day," to Carolyn and Florina, and returned to their activities of checkers and chess. Observing them, Florina wondered what further changes the New Year, only days away,

44

would deliver, lurching them forward, or where they all might land.

An amiable and kind couple, Florina wondered how Franklin and Irene Elder could have permitted Macon to marry Agnes. So touched by them, Florina made good on the account Hammond had established at the Elders' Market in her name.

"Never a borrower or a lender be, " Florina's father always advised. Major Gavin despised bankers. Regarding credit, "Only use it when absolutely necessary," in which case the loan was to be paid off as soon as possible.

The Elders proved an industrious pair. And after the fiasco Florina had witnessed at the A&P, she would do no less. She made her purchases then established a schedule for Nathan, the young man the Elders employed, to deliver various staple items to the house.

"And don't feel like you need to come in just for a pint of milk or a dozen eggs," said Macon's father, Franklin.

"Nathan is always out making deliveries," Irene Elder said. "He can always squeeze you in either comin' or goin'. And your food won't be sour or spoiled."

"I really appreciate that," Florina said.

Back at home Florina's frustration with Agnes grew. The Elders were her in-laws. *Family.* The food and staples the Elders sold in their store were of equal quality to those of the A&P, their service superior. She shook her head while cleaning the chicken and setting it the oven to bake. Her ire mounted as she washed the broccoli then poured the rice into the water to boil. *Did Agnes not love Macon?*

Steam rose from the platter of chicken fresh out of the oven, delivering memories of the disparaging comments Florina's aunts, Gavin Major's sisters, routinely leveled at Florina's mother, Helen. Florina set the platter upon the kitchen table and grew more infuriated.

45

"She's so angry," Major's sister, Regina, had said on one occasion.

"That's how they are," Loretta had chimed.

"Dark and forever angry," Christa, the youngest had concluded.

The three had been in the kitchen of Regina's home preparing Thanksgiving dinner. As always, the subject of Helen, Florina's mother arose.

Outside the doorway and leaning against the wall of the dining room, Florina had stood listening.

Now Florina placed the bowls of broccoli and rice on either side of the platter and joined Redmond who blessed the food.

On saying, "Amen," she relayed the incident at the A&P. "Mickey, the cashier, called Jonah 'a *nigger,*' with me and Agnes standing right there. And Agnes acted as if nothing was said. I don't know who I'm angrier with, the cashier or Agnes. She just stood there like ... nothing was happening. Like ... like ..."

"The white woman in line ahead of you." Redmond finished her sentence. He did not lift his eyes from the crossword puzzle of the Sunday edition of *The Poinsettia Times* lying open between him and Florina.

Florina recalled how Jonah had shown no anger, only hurt tucked in a quiet despair and sense of defeat. "But Agnes says that all white people are racist."

"Uhm." Redmond cut into his broccoli and chicken and ate some.

"I can't understand why Agnes doesn't shop at her in-laws' market. Except for a few items, they have everything I need," said Florina. She had gone to the Elders' market after Mr. Phillips had installed the new locks.

Redmond resumed studying the crossword puzzle.

"They seem like fine people," she said of Macon's parents. She sprinkled salt and pepper on her chicken. *"Why would he marry a women like that?"* Florina wondered of Macon Elder whom she had yet to meet.

46

"People do strange things," Redmond murmured. He lifted his pencil as he continued studying the puzzle.

"It's very strange." Florina jabbed her fork into a spear of broccoli, as she observed Redmond writing letters into the remaining empty boxes.

"Did Mr. Phillips come by?" He folded the paper, tucked the pencil within the fold, and placed the newspaper at the far end of the table.

"She spoke harshly of him too," Florina said of Agnes. She told how Phillips had been sitting upon the steps when she returned from the A&P with Agnes and Leena. "Said I needed to watch him."

"If you haven't already figured it out, Agnes Macon is not a happy person." Redmond went to the refrigerator and lifted out a soda, but not before Florina glimpsed his eyes retreating into a faraway look.

Florina regarded the word, "*happy*," how Redmond had promised, *I'll work hard to make you happy*, when he asked to marry her.

"You don't like her either," Florina said on Redmond's return to the table.

"Agnes is not from here," said Redmond.

"Place has nothing to do with common courtesy and human respect," Florina said. "Mama's from New York City and she never acted this way."

"Agnes is from Baltimore."

"How did Macon meet her?"

"He attended her father's church," Redmond said.

"Her father's a minister?"

"The Right Reverend Julius Kensington of St. Peter's African Methodist Episcopal in Richmond Circle, Baltimore," Redmond said. Again his eyes momentarily retreated. Florina struggled to reconcile the faraway look that overtook Redmond when speaking of Agnes and Reverend Kensington.

"How long have you known Agnes?"

Redmond cut into his chicken. "Like I said, she and Macon married last spring, April 4th."

47

•.•..•.•..•.•..•.•..•

Chapter 5

•.•..•.•..•.•..•.•..•

Redmond had left to see patients and Florina had been washing dishes when Agnes arrived the following morning. Still angry and bothered about Agnes' behavior the previous day, Florina refused to answer the door. Persistent, Agnes knocked several times, and remained at the front door long beyond five minutes. She eventually left.

Careful to remain hidden by the dining room window, Florina observed Agnes walk back to her house next door. She was wearing dark brown heels and a bright yellow dress with white sweater. Florina felt sorry for having left her neighbor in the cold. The same soft white pearls hung about her neck with matching earrings adorning her small ears.

The breakfast dishes washed, Florina dried and returned them to cabinet, a task that landed her among memories of her father's sisters and the disdain Florina's aunts held for Helen.

Florina carefully recalled the sting their words delivered during Thanksgiving 1955. She had been eleven, her aunts were in the kitchen, preparing to lay out holiday dinner.

Major Gavin's eldest sister, Regina, had hosted the holiday meal. As always, Florina stood outside the kitchen door, careful to remain hidden, and listening as Regina, Loretta and Christa, the youngest, conversed on the long-discussed topic of Helen Gavin.

Christa had added butter to the mashed potatoes and resumed stirring, when Regina, speaking of Helen, said, "She hasn't given him another child. Every man wants a son."

"Boys aren't everything," said Christa.

"Certainly not if there's a possibility they'll be as dark as her," said Loretta.

Florina cringed at her Aunt Loretta's biting statement.

Arrival through the back door of Major Gavin's third eldest sister, Mona, brought with it the truth of their hearts. She set a cake on the kitchen table, shed her coat and said, "I don't know why Major ever married her."

"He says he loves her," Christa replied.

"Well you know what they say," said Loretta. She repeated the oft spoken comment, "*The darker the berry, the sweeter the juice.*" Regina, Loretta and Mona broke into laughter.

Again Florina cringed, grew more sad and hurt when her Aunt Regina proclaimed,
"Helen got lucky with Florina. Florina looks like her father."

Christa said, "I wondered during her pregnancy what the child might look like."

"You mean you worried," Loretta said.

"I was certain it would be beautiful, boy or girl," said Christa.

"Florina is beautiful," Mona said. "She looks like her father."

"I'll never understand how that happened," Loretta said.

"Helen Lattimore is not who she presents herself to be," Regina said.

"What do you mean?" Christa asked Regina.

"Her hair's too straight. She may be dark. But don't be fooled. She's smart."

"Come on, Regina," Christa chided. "You can't believe all that nonsense about dark skinned people being stupid."

"Have you been on any college campuses? How many dark Negroes do you see?" Mona asked.

"I saw a lot when I was there. None of you even tried. Gavin and I went and look how that turned out," said Christa. Her words delivered a cloud of silence. Gavin had completed two years at Helen and Ava's alma mater, Christa one year.

Loretta finally spoke. "Major's running of the farm has taken care of us better than any college degree."

"Education is fine. But ownership is king," said Mona. "How many darkies with Ph.D.'s do you see walking around with no job? They're a dime dozen."

"And look who Helen, with all her education, married?" Loretta said. "She didn't seem to mind marryin' a man who hadn't finished college."

"A college degree means something," argued Christa. "Maybe Helen's education is what drew Major to her."

"It certainly wasn't her looks," Loretta said. Again she laughed.

"I'm no fan of Helen's," said Christa. "But she's not a dumb woman." Gavin's youngest sister was perturbed. "With all this talk of women's liberation I worry that I'm being left behi--"

"Maybe you should write the college and ask them to let you back in," Regina said.
"In fact go speak to Helen and her friend, Ava Reynolds. They're always going on about being alumni this and alumni that. They should know someone who can help."

"It wouldn't be such a bad thing," said Christa. Regina's words held sarcasm and derision as she challenged Christa to seek an opportunity that offered benefit.

"More the reason you need to go to Helen and Ava Reynolds," said Loretta. Her words furthered Regina's derision. "They should know someone to help you get back into college."

"It's not that easy," Christa mumbled. Frustrated with poor grades her freshman year, she had returned home the following summer and married.

After some moments of silence Regina returned to her initial concern. Florina's eldest aunt said. "A daughter who looks like her father cannot replace or make up for a son. Major wants a son. And I want him to have one."

"If he had married Jane Hadley that might have happened," Loretta said.

"It still can, if Major realizes his unhappiness."

Florina now grew afraid. Though not yet a teenager, she knew the intent behind her Aunt Regina's words.

Some hours after the family had eaten Thanksgiving dinner, Mona and Christa return to the kitchen for an extra helping of apple pie, one that Helen had baked. Florina followed them and again stood outside the kitchen doorway.

"This pie is really good," Christa said as she cut a slice and delivered it to her plate.

"Helen baked it," said Mona.

"It's still good," Christa said. "Herman says I can't cook no better than a doorknob."

"What you give him is worth more than any meal you cook."

"I want to be valued for more than my looks."

"Herman loves you," said Mona.

"He likes the color of my skin."

"You mean the lack of it."

Christa asked, "Why is it that we Negroes hate white people, but take on so many of their ways?" In Mona's lack of response, she said, "I want to go back to college, try my hand at it one more time."

"You should go."

"You say it like gettin' back in is easy," Christa said. "I had my chance and I gave it up. Now I've got a husband wantin' a baby. Never mind my grades. They were nothing like what I've heard Gavin say about Helen's," she lamented.

"More the reason you need to get her and Ava Reynolds to help you. And why wouldn't they let you in?" said Mona. "You've got somethin' neither one of them has. And I can't imagine that once the college professors see you, they'd be happy to have you back."

"It's not all about looks," Christa said. "Helena and Ava Reynolds are pretty in their own right--both in body and brains. And their husbands love them."

"You sayin' Herman don't love you?"

"I don't want to be measured by my beauty," Christa said. "I want to be respected for my mind, my thoughts and my ideas."

"Now you're soundin' like those crazy white folks talkin' 'bout how havin' an abortion ain't a crime, and that women should be able to have sex without being married just like men," Mona said.

"We should."

"I hope you haven't told any of this foolishness to Herman," said Mona. "I can't believe you want to lower women to the level of men."

"Women can do the same things as men and they shouldn't be allowed to stop us."

"Who wants to do a man's job when we have the home? Women rule the world right here. Lose this and we ain't got nothin'."

"I want more to be more than just a wife and mother. I'm smarter than that."

"And when did we reach the point where any ole' dumb woman could be a wife and mother?" Mona snapped. Florina imagined her leaning forward, her black velvety brows arched like arrows. "These same white folks you're listenin' to are the ones believin' they're better than us."

"Are we any better sitting around and talking about dark skinned Negroes like we're some high and might white folks?" Christa asked.

"You sound like that crazy Malcolm X," said Mona. "All this you're talkin' about is just another way for the white folks in America to split us up. Tear down the Negro home. It's slavery all over again, takin' away our husbands, beatin' em' down and leavin' us with nothin' just like a hundred and fifty years ago."

"Malcolm X's right on a lot of things. You sound more like him that I do."

53

"I do not," said Mona. " And if Brother Malcolm, I think that's what he calls himself, knows what's best for him and his family, he'll be quiet, or else he'll end up like that Till boy down in Mississippi a couple of years ago."

Mona's last words sent a chill through Florina.

Upon returning home that night Florina rummaged through the stack of old newspapers and magazines Helen saved, those containing articles and important news about Negroes and the quest for Civil Rights. An article from a newspaper dated two months earlier, September 1955, bore a picture of Emmett Till at age 13. Barely eight months later white men had executed the adolescent for allegedly whistling at a white woman.

Florina tucked the paper back into the pile as if to keep safe Emmett's memory and went to her father.

"He was a young boy about four years older than you," Major Gavin explained when Florina asked why he died. "Negroes down in Mississippi and where he was from in Chicago say white men killed him for looking at a white woman."

Florina grew cold. "Are the men who did it in jail?"

"Negroes *said* the white men killed him," Major clarified. "It's not been proven. And in the courts our words don't count for much."

"Is anyone working to show that they did?

"Yes. But I doubt they'll have much luck." Major appeared dismayed.

"It's because the men white."

"That and other things." In Florina's silence her father explained. "When these sort of things happen there are usually some of our people who know something. But getting them to speak up is generally hard."

"Why?"

"I'm not saying that's true in this case, but if it is, those who know something are scared they might get killed or someone in their family will get hurt if they speak out."

"But if they don't speak out how will we be able to find who did it and stop it?" Florina asked.

"You make a good point. But people do strange things-- even those who are oppressed." Major gave a crooked half-smile. "As for stopping something like this--like with young, Emmett Till--from happening ... " He took Florina into his arms. "This is why your Mama and I want you to go to college and get an education." Major pulled her close.

"And how will that protect me, or keep me from being killed like him?"

"An education is your ticket out of here and to a better life," said Major.

"I like living here with you and Mama."

Major smiled. "I'm glad you feel safe here in Laurel. But one day you're going to need to go out into the world. You'll want to get married. And a good husband wants a smart wife."

"You mean like Mama?"

"Yes." Florina's father grinned again.

"Is that why you love her so? Because she's not only pretty, but smart and educated?"

"It certainly helps. But your mother's also a good person. That's all I ever wanted in a wife." Major Gavin spoke as if he had heard the conversation between his four sisters. "Looks go only skin deep. And as we age those looks go away." He brushed his finger along the curve of Florina's cheek. The back of his hand was as pale as his palm. His face, like Florina's, approached the color of the inside of a freshly cut white peach.

"Why don't I look like Mama?" Florina asked.

"Because God made you to look the way you do."

"Like you," said Florina.

Major smiled.

She then said, "Auntie Regina and Loretta said they don't understand how Mama could have had me with her being so dar--"

Major placed his forefinger to her lips stilling them. He lifted his gaze. Florina turned to see her mother standing in the doorway of the living room where Florina had been in conversation with Major. Guilt and shame rose in Florina.

"Seems like you learned a lot while helping your Aunt Regina prepare Thanksgiving dinner," said Helen.

"I was standing outside the kitchen while she and Aunt Loretta were cooking. I stayed outside and just listened," Florina pleaded. "Even after Aunt Christa," Florina's favorite of the four, " ... and Mona came."

Helen's grim stare deepened, hurt fueling its intensification. Florina's truth could not assuage her mother's hurt.

Across the hallway her parents argued deep into the night.

"When are you going to speak to them?" Helen asked Major, concerning his sisters and their history of disparaging comments. "Now they're filling Florina's head with all this mess about skin color."

"It's all lies. And you know it."

"You should tell them that," shouted Helen.

Florina got out of bed and walked to the door of her room.

"My sisters are jealous of you," Major Gavin said. "They wish they had your education, and your friendship with Ava Reynolds threatens them."

"They only reason Ava pays me any attention is because she's brown skin. If she were fair like the wives of most Negro doctors she'd have little to do with me."

"Don't say that," Major's voice was soothing.

"It's true and you know it."

"Ava Reynolds is a true friend. She liked you from the moment you presented yourself before the school board," Major said.

56

"A school board on which you are the president, you, who has the lightest skin of any member. It's common knowledge that they keeping voting you in because they feel that white superintendent is more likely to meet our requests if presented by you instead of the other members whose skin is darker. Ole' Man Grimes is always joking about how you and Lark Benning could pass for brothers in July and August when he's tanned, that sometimes he's even darker than you."

"To Lark Benning I'm just another Negro."

"When Lark Benning sees you his sees a fair-skinned Negro. And that's not the same as when someone like me approaches him."

"That's because you're a woman," Major laughed. "And whether you or Lark wants to admit it, he's got a shine for you. I saw the way his eyes lit up when I introduced you as the teacher we wanted to hire. He thinks you're beautiful."

"I'm being serious, Major."

"So am I." Florina heard the joviality leave her father's voice. "Despite your lack of experience, Lark Benning felt that you were the best choice to fill the fifth grade teaching position. The purpose you gave for having studied education won over us board members. But Lark was thinking totally like a man. He knows you're smart and good at what you do, and pretty to boot."

"That's nasty."

"Why?" Major said. "Just the other day he was saying how he wished he had ten of you--five of you to teach at the Negro schools and another five to teach at the white schools. I told him that would be fine as long as the real flesh and blood Helen was here with me and Florina. He was none too happy."

"I don't like Lark Benning or any white man for that matter. Certainly not in that way. I saw too many of them in New York just sleeping with us for the pleasure. Love never entered into the picture."

"Still there are Negro women who marry them."

"I'm not one of them."

"And I'm proud to have you as my wife. Feel lucky that you would accept *me* as your husband. Growing crops and raising livestock is all I know." Major Gavin regretted having abandoned college to return home, unlike Lark Benning who held a masters degree in mathematics. "If I didn't have this farm I'd be where a lot of Negroes are--hustling and breaking my neck for *Mr. Charlie*." Florina knew the euphemism meant a condescending and hateful white, male employer. "And I doubt you would have been half as interested in me."

"I loved you then like I love you now," Helen spoke softly.

Some moments passed, Florina suspecting that Major's response, his efforts at consoling Helen, had taken a more sensual form. She tiptoed across the hall and stood by the door to her parents' bedroom.

"You've got to tell her," Helen said in a lowered voice.

"Florina is *our* daughter," whispered Major.

Through the crack in the door Florina saw her father wearing only his shorts and tee shirt. Helen's gown of cotton and white bestowed a luminescence to her skin, soft and dark as night. Major's hands caressed her shoulders as if holding onto a celestial being who granted meaning and purpose to his life.

"Florina looks like you," Helen said.

"Florina has the best of both worlds. She may be fair, but her mind works like yours. She knows that all us Negroes are bound to each another."

"Do you really believe that?" asked Helen.

"I know it." Major's gray eyes took on the heavy seriousness matching Helen's. "I need you."

"You need my education."

"I need your heart and your love. Without it I'm lost."

"And what will Florina need from her husband?"

"Same as what you give me and I give you," Major Gavin said.

"Men will see her differently. They'll expect other things from her than they did from me. I witnessed that at college," said Helen. "She's light like you."

"She's a person."

"Try telling your kind that. And I don't mean just your sisters."

"So we men are on the same level as my ignorant sisters?"

"You certainly think like them."

"I don't."

"You're different," Helen said.

"Then that's what I want for Florina. Our daughter. Someone like me."

Fury rooted in hurt flamed across Helen's eyes. "Someone like you. Fair-skinned. And where will that leave me?"

"As the grandmother. What else?" Major knitted his brows.

Helen lifted his arm and placed the back of her hand beside it. "The black grandmother." Helen's gaze intensified once more. "People can't even see a resemblance between me and Florina."

"Everything doesn't begin and end with the color of a person's skin. I was talking about my heart, what I think and believe," said Major.

"Me and my kind don't have that option."

"I'm one more *nigger* those white men wouldn't think twice about killin'." Major pointed his finger. "Should I get too *uppity*. Any Negro, particularly a man, who forgets that is bound for trouble."

Helen lowered her head.

Tears popped from Florina's eyes, slid down her cheeks and fell to her feet planted upon the cold, wooden floor of the hall outside her parents' room.

Major lifted Helen's chin, drew close and placed his lips upon hers.

"It hurts so much," Helen whispered between sobs. "It's one thing for white people to look down on us, think we're nothing. But when our own people, family member--"

Major kissed her again then lifted her in his arms and walked to bed. The light went out and Florina quietly returned to her room.

Chapter 6

Florina smiled at her father-in-law, Hammond Austin. Amid singing the refrain to *Hark the Herald Angels Sing* she made note of the *Austin* name etched in black upon the stained glass window across from the end of the pew. December 31st, 1967, it was Florina's first time as part of the St. Andrews A. M.E. Zion parish family.

Florina recalled the many Sundays during Advent that she had attended Laurel A.M.E. Zion with her parents. Redmond lifted her hand. She felt warm inside. The congregation entered the last stanza of the Christmas carol.

Reverend Mitchell gave the sermon. Prior to offering benediction he summoned Florina and Redmond to the altar. Redmond grasped Florina's hand and exited the space between the pews. Draped in his black robe, the minister descended from the pulpit. The newlyweds met him at the front of the sanctuary.

Mitchell addressed the congregation. "Brothers and sisters, I am pleased on this New Year's Eve, to have not only Dr. Redmond Austin who, having returned to Poinsettia, has been with his father these last six months practicing medicine, surgery, no less, but now also his new wife, Florina." The

61

minister turned to them. "Redmond and Florina Austin, we welcome you." He began clapping. The congregation of two hundred or more stood and joined in.

Florina had witnessed her Reverend Adams do the same for other newly married couples in the Laurel congregation. Yet it felt different.

St. Andrews' was not Florina's home parish. And for the first time she was not offering the welcome, but was instead receiving it.

Florina's church community never met Ennis, never even knew he existed or that Florina had married him. She wondered whether a similar scenario could have taken place had Ennis survived the war, and she had graduated college. Could she have had the strength to defy her mother and announce what she had done to Reverend Adams? And would he have looked at her the same. Ennis never had a proper burial. Though he was confirmed dead his body was never recovered.

Reverend Mitchell touched Florina's and Redmond's shoulders. They turned from the congregation to him. Sunlight streaming through the stained glass windows highlighted the red scarf against the minister's black robe.

"Let us offer them our blessings," Mitchell said. He lifted his arms, revealing the billowing sleeves of his black robe and placed his hands above their heads.

Florina imagined the congregants behind them extending their arms, palms open as were Mitchell's, and like she had done in the past and Laurel A.M.E. Zion.

Redmond grasped her left hand. Florina closed her eyes.

"Heavenly Father, grant Redmond and Florina your most precious blessings: love, mercy and protection. Bind their hearts and braid their souls as man and wife, brother and sister, father and mother, lover and beloved. Empower them to overcome the worries of our minds fueled by the troubles and wars of this world. Teach them how to pray. Strengthen them in prayer. Help them to develop the gifts of patience, grace, and forgiveness, and to come to know that that greatest act of love is giving our life so that another, the one we love most, might live and thrive.

And when all is done, this life over, grant them and us, we ask, life in eternity with you."

Reverend Mitchell's last words served as benediction.

Redmond and Florina stood at the front door with Reverend Mitchell and received further greetings from parishioners as they exited the sanctuary.

A demure lady, barely five feet tall, and with cotton white hair like Lyla's, shook Florina's hand and said, "So you're Redmond's new wife. Heard a lotta' good things about you." She said to Redmond, "You were always my nicest student, and smart too.". The woman's hair sat under a pill box hat, the color of her navy suit. She winked at Florina then brought her gloved hand to Redmond's brown cheek. "I'm glad he's found someone. Come by my house any time and we'll have tea." She walked away, aided by a cane with interesting carvings.

A tall, smartly dressed couple took her place. The man shook Redmond's hand and his wife Florina's. "We're the Cartwrights," the man said. "John and Jeanne."

"Pleased to meet you," said Florina.

"I'm the town dentist," said John Cartwright. He turned to Redmond. "I assume we'll see you at watch meeting services this evening," he said to Redmond.

"That's up to Florina." Redmond touched the small of Florina's back.

"I've always gone with my parents," Florina said.

"And what denomination are they?" Jeanne asked.

"Zion Methodist--like us," Redmond spoke.

Jeanne gave a faint smile. Three sleek and furry minks, their eyes bright and staring, lay draped over the neck of her coat. Her face appeared almost garish against the black of her coat. She could pass for white on a winter day with no sun.

"We'd better be going," Jeanne said. "Oh, and Cynthia's home from New York."

"Really?" Redmond's smooth, mahogany face lit up. "How long is she here for?"

"Just the weekend. Seems she has a class to teach in the new semester," John explained.

Redmond turned to Florina. "Their daughter, Cynthia and I went to school together."

"She's a doctor. Just like Redmond," said Jeanne. She flashed an attenuated smile. "And what is it that you say you do?" she set forth to interrogate Florina.

"As I said, we'd better be going." John ushered Jeanne away.

The Cartwrights gone, a host of other St. Andrew's congregants descended upon Florina and Redmond. Several other couples, having spoken with Pastor Mitchell, introduced themselves and gave the newlyweds congratulatory handshakes.

"Hello. And how are you?"

"You're both so lovely."

"So nice to meet you."

Hammond and Carolyn Austin diverted other individuals and couples into conversation so as not to overwhelm Florina. Still others arrived and offered congratulations and comments.

"We wish you all the best."

"I'm sure you'll make Redmond a wonderful wife."

"I know it's early, but can we entice you to join the altar committee?"

"And there's always the children's Sunday School," said another lady. "That way when you have children you'll already know the lessons."

The greetings were as varied as the twenty or more women--all reminiscent of those at Laurel A. M. E. Zion and every middle-to-upper-middle-class Negro congregation across America.

Not until Florina and Redmond had started on their way did Agnes approach.

"Isn't it impossible?" said Agnes. "Those people." She flicked open her lighter and brought it to the cigarette between her fingers then inhaled. "As for Mitchell, I never really listen to anything he has to say."

She let out a ring of smoke, flicked the lighter closed and turned to the tall man beside her, and said, "Florina, this is my husband, Macon. Macon, this is our new neighbor and Redmond's new wife, Florina." Agnes flashed a grin.

Florina wondered whether Agnes had stood and extended her hand when Reverend Mitchell said a prayer for Florina and Redmond.

"Pleased to meet you," Macon said to Florina and shook her hand.

Agnes removed the cigarette from her lips and again blew out rings of smoke.   Macon joined to Redmond and the two entered conversation under the maple tree some feet from Florina and Agnes.

"I didn't even bother getting into that horrid line," Agnes said of those who had greeted Florina and Redmond.

Florina frowned at the cigarette. "Don't you think you should put that out?"

"We're not in your house. Or mine," Agnes said. She brought the cigarette to her lips and inhaled once more.

Florina waved away the smoke with her gloved hand, and covered her nose.

"We should meet here, on the *church yard,* instead of at your house," Agnes said with a laugh. "This is the most excited I've seen you. Which reminds me I came by your house the other day. No one answered." Agnes arched her nicely trimmed brows. "I could have sworn you were there, felt someone staring out at me as I walked back home."

Florina tensed.

Agnes drew close. "We are the wives of the only two Negro physicians in Poinsettia. And by the laws of supply and demand, that's worth more than all the white ones put together." Agnes' eyes widened. ""We really should become friends," she whispered,

Florina eyed the cigarette emitting smoke from the fiery ring around the edge of gray ashes about to fall. "You should put that out," she repeated. "These are church grounds."

"Is that what they taught you back in Laurel?" Agnes held her cigarette up as if for everyone to see.

"How'd you know I was from there?"

"People talk." Agnes said and smiled. Florina remained un-amused. "Macon told me."

"Is that why you were sitting on my porch on Thursday morning?"

"Redmond and Macon grew up together. Don't you think Redmond would announce to Macon if he was getting married, tell him about his new wife?"

"Is that what Macon did when you agreed to marry him," said Florina. "Tell Redmond all about you?"

"Well that would have been a little difficult." Agnes leaned in towards Florina. "Redmond knew me before Macon entered the picture." Agnes shot a glance at Redmond and Macon still conversing under the maple tree. "In fact Redmond and I--"

Redmond called out to Florina. "Macon and Agnes are having a few friends over to celebrate the New Year. They'd like us to come."

"It'll be fun. You'll get to meet the other side of Poinsettia," Agnes said.

"What about watch meeting services?" Florina said.

"The party won't start until after Mitchell's benediction," Macon added.

"Well, I hope it won't go on as long as it did last year," Agnes proffered.

Macon and Redmond joined their wives.

"You were here last December?" Florina said surprised. Redmond had told her that Macon and Agnes had married last spring April.

"Don't worry, *Miss Inappropriate*," Agnes retorted with a grin. "My parents accompanied me down. Macon and I had just been engaged. Believe me, Reverend Julius wouldn't have allowed—"

"I think we'd better go." Macon lifted the cigarette from Agnes' fingers, dropped it upon the ground and mashed it in the dirt with the toe of his shoe. "We'll see you back at the house after watch meeting services." Macon said to Florina. He turned to Redmond and said, "There's something else I wanted to mention to you." He and Redmond started away from the maple tree, and towards the church. Their heads drew close.

"You're not as slow as you appear." Agnes gave a wary smile.

Dread that Florina could not decipher slid underneath her skin.

"Let's have lunch tomorrow, my house, at noon." Agnes said as she glanced out at Redmond and Macon conversing. They slowed their pace towards a gathering of people by the sanctuary.

Agnes left Florina and started towards Redmond and Macon. Some distance away she turned around, and began pacing backwards, calling out to Florina, "Since you have yet to hire a maid, I'll have some names when you come for lunch." She continued pacing backwards. "We'll see you at church tonight, and then back at the house." Agnes turned around, rushed towards Macon and Redmond, and reaching them, slid between the two.

As if someone had caught his attention, Macon left Redmond and went to Hammond Austin standing amid a group of men on the church steps. On reaching him Agnes cupped her gloved palm to Redmond's cheek. He gazed down upon her for a long moment.

Hope and vibrancy slipped from Florina observing in the distance.

As quickly as she had whipped around from speaking to Florina, Agnes left Redmond and went to Hammond Austin, and interwove her arm about Macon's.

———————————

Chapter 7

Florina left St. Andrew's and walked until she stood before a headstone. She knelt and slid her fingers across the name etched into the smooth face of the granite marker.

Sgt. Hallowell Burton May
May 5, 1920—July 17th, 1944

A voice spoke from behind. "He died in the Port Chicago explosion. His family didn't learn that until months later."

Florina wiped her face of tears and turned around.

The young man in a blue suit and tie helped her stand. "I'm Reverend Mason, the minister here at Poinsettia Primitive Baptist." He pointed to the white wood church some yards from the cemetery.

"I'm Florina Austin."

"You must be Redmond's new wife," said Reverend Mason. His face lit up. "We attended the same high school. Redmond was two years older." He extended his palm. "Please call me Fitzhugh."

"Pleased to meet you." Florina shook the young minister's hand.

"You're quite a ways from St. Andrew's," said Mason.

"Does everyone know everything about every person in this town? Are there no secrets?"

"Poinsettia is a small community. As for secrets," explained Fitzhugh, "--I'm sure there are many, but people work to keep them hidden."

Florina turned back to the headstone.

"Hallowell Burton was my mother's eldest brother. I never met him," said the young minister. "My mother never got over his death. 'Thick as thieves' my grandmother described them, 'loved each other better than Peter loved Christ,' she said."

"Your grandmother sounds like a country woman."

"Her and my grandfather's farm is about twenty miles outside of Poinsettia." Though younger, by at least four decades, Fitzhugh Mason reminded Florina of Reverend Adams back in Laurel.

Fitzhugh looked beyond Florina to the headstone bearing his uncle's name, and said, "'All wars are civil because all men are brothers,' said Francois Fenelon. The greatest battles we fight with ourselves."

"What brought you back here?" Florina asked. She assumed from his manner and speech he had graduated college.

"I wanted some authenticity."

"You think people in Poinsettia are honest and real," Florina quipped. "I thought I knew city living, but--"

"Poinsettia is a town," said Fitzhugh. "Quite different from Atlanta and Washington, D.C. But I would imagine Redmond is wondering where you are. Let me walk you home."

Florina had no idea where she was, except that she was in Poinsettia. "Redmond would never forgive me for doing anything less," said Fitzhugh.

"We're living in Grandma Austin's old home," Florina said.

"That would be this way," Fitzhugh said. The two exited the yard of Poinsettia Primitive Baptist and started down the sidewalk in an easterly direction. "I graduated Morehouse," said Fitzhugh on reaching the end of the street. They crossed over and turned right. "And even Atlanta is different from Washington, D.C."

"Varying levels of authenticity," said Florina. She recalled that Redmond had said Agnes was from Baltimore.

"With anonymity and privacy. I don't think you'll get much in either place. This is the south."

Now several blocks from the cemetery, Florina could no longer see the spire of Poinsettia Primitive Baptist. "I grew up on a farm ten miles from Laurel, the nearest town," she said.

"Hence your familiarity with my grandmother's words," he smiled.

"Why would Redmond marry someone like me after spending the last fifteen years in Washington, D.C.?"

"Perhaps he wanted more authenticity in his life."

Florina turned to Fitzhugh. "He wants to leave Poinsettia," she said. The image of Agnes caressing Redmond's cheek with her gloved hand returned. Florina asked, "Why would he come back to Poinsettia marry me and then leave?"

"Perhaps he wants to take some authenticity with him wherever he goes."

"Then why not take someone he's known longer?"

"Maybe you have something they don't."

"That is unless he's running from something," Florina said.

Fitzhugh pocketed his hands.

"Duty to family and community is a responsibility that we don't always carry with ease," said Fitzhugh. "We're all trying to escape something--fears, loves, secrets. "But everywhere we go, there we are." The young minister resumed walking. "I'm sure you're aware of Redmond's attributes," he said. "Last Easter during dinner the pain my mother had been experiencing in her stomach became unbearable. I called Dr. Hammond. Fortunately Redmond was with them. He asked me a few questions. I answered as best I could. He told me to get my mother to Charlotte Negro Hospital as soon as possible, that he would meet me there. My mother went unconscious during the

71

thirty minute drive to Charlotte." Fitzhugh frowned. His face went blank.

"After the surgery Redmond told us that my mother's appendix had ruptured. She could have died. We passed by Poinsettia General on the way to Charlotte Negro Hospital. Since that time Dr. Hammond has been working to secure Redmond admitting privileges to admit Negro patients to Poinsettia General," he continued. He looked in the direction of Poinsettia General. "Our taxes pay for that hospital. And yet we gain no benefits from its presence in our backyard."

Fitzhugh's story made real the importance of Hammond's desire for Redmond to remain in Poinsettia. He added, "But I'm sure your decision to marry Redmond has less to do with his accomplishments and more to do with the man you've come to know."

"I haven't known him that long. We met in July."

"Love at first sight," Fitzhugh said.

"Do you really believe it happens that way?" Florina asked.

"I believe love comes when it comes. And that time can never be predicted." His bright and hopeful smile, almost naive, reminded her of her first encounter with Ennis.

"Are you married?" Florina asked.

"Yes."

"Did you love your wife when you married her?"

"You say that as if I love her now?" said Fitzhugh. He flashed another boyish grin behind the quick-witted questions which Florina sensed rose from intense ponderings.
"On marrying my wife I learned I had no idea what love truly is."

"What if I told you I married while still mourning the death of another person, someone I loved?"

"Many people have done worse," said Fitzhugh. "What was your intention in marrying this time?"

"To grow to love him-- Redmond. I wanted to be the best wife possible."

"Redmond is a lucky man."

Florina's cheeks warmed. She felt herself blushing. She

realized she had used the past tense. The image of Agnes caressing Redmond's cheek gripped her body. Florina had enjoyed her and Redmond's lovemaking. *Serves me right for betraying Ennis.* They had yet to find his body.

Fitzhugh Mason said, "So many of us marry holding high expectations of our wife or husband. You, on the other hand, entered union with Redmond, aware of your short-comings, and with an intent on doing the best you could."

"I should have told Redmond."

"Of your intentions or loving another?" asked Fitzhugh.

"That he was my second husband." Florina feared Agnes served as punishment for not having told Redmond of her past.

"Oftentimes we reveal secrets not so much to inform the other person, but to free ourselves from guilt that in many cases is self-inflicted."

"His name was Ennis McCreary. He died April 12, 1966. He left for basic training two days after we wed. I was a wife for seven months, a widow for thirteen. The truth of her words breathed through Florina dispensing a reality she had yet absorbed. Hot tears burst onto her cheeks. "I should have waited for Ennis."

"He's not coming back," said Mason.

"I thought that if I waited, mustered enough patience, the Army would say they had made a mistake." More tears came. Through sobs Florina explained how she had met Ennis, began to love him. "He liked my writing, my poems." She recalled how Ennis had liked her poems. His comments had encouraged her to write more. Ennis' face, fair and nearly white, like Agnes' and Florina's aunts loomed before her.

Dank feelings of guilt rose higher. Florina said, "My father's sisters have always hated my mother." The heat of embarrassment swept across Florina's face. Of her mother Florina added, "She doesn't look like me."

"She's dark," said Fitzhugh.

Florina nodded and lowered her gaze. "Ennis' father never acknowledged him. Ennis' mother, Melinda, is Cherokee and Negro. I was the only Negro girl at college who ever gave Ennis any attention. He was everything I could have asked for."

Florina explained about never having told her parents or her godparents, the Reynolds, of Ennis-- nor of marrying him. "They wanted so much more for me. Neither would have been happy learning I had married Ennis. I'm sure of it. At least not without him having served in the Army."

"But you don't really know," said Fitzhugh. "Surviving Vietnam would have legitimized him."

"And by then I would have graduated college. We could have lived on our own," said Florina. "Only Ennis' mother knows. She witnessed our marriage."

"Do you keep in contact with her?"

"I used to write her every month. I couldn't write her after Redmond began coming to Laurel. I felt too guilty. And then when he asked me to marry him ... My last letter was in September," Florina said. Farther down the street Florina spied the roof of her house.

Fitzhugh said, "The Port Chicago explosion killed over three hundred men, all Negroes. Nearly four hundred others were injured. A month later when Negro navy men refused to load anymore ammunition for fear of another disaster, the Navy convicted them of mutiny and sentenced them to military jail."

Florina winced at the unfairness of racial prejudice in America, the pain it had caused so many, the toll of lives exacted.

"As minister at Poinsettia Primitive Baptist I've conducted ten funerals, all young boys, some barely twenty years old, if that, all members of our church. Some I remember from school; they were grades below me; others I graduated with."

Warm tears again streamed onto Florina's damp cheeks.

The minister said, "What matters now are the things that drew you to Redmond, how you've come to feel about him, the promises you made to yourself and to love him as your present husband."

Florina recalled the heaviness of the two crates of strawberries, her struggle to lift them from the back of the blue 65' Chevrolet Impala, the wood scraping against her fingers, her fear of dropping them as the crates edged towards freedom from

74

her hands. "I had almost given up. And suddenly there was Redmond." She recalled the touch of his hands underneath hers. "Let me help you with those," he had said on rushing to her.

Florina stopped walking. She said, "It was like he came out of nowhere. I was about to let go. Give up. But he interrupted my pain, distracted me from the memories, gave me a reason to hope. But then ... "

Florina recalled how Agnes had brought her palm to Redmond's cheek, the longing with which he had gazed upon Agnes. It held a yearning Florina knew all too well.

"Remain focused on that," said Fitzhugh. "How he took you from your pain."

Florina looked to Agnes and Macon's house and then to the home, steps away, that she now shared with Redmond.

The young minister said, "Whatever has risen between you and Redmond since you married last week don't let it obscure what you've come to experience and know of him. We all have pasts and histories that if viewed out of context, render us in a poor light."

Florina took in young Fitzhugh Mason's words. "Life. War. Death," said Fitzhugh. His lips betrayed a broken smile. "They all have a way of muddying the waters. Things are not always, if ever, what they seem. Just like in marrying Redmond you gave yourself a second chance--allow him another opportunity, more time, to show himself, all that he's made of, all the various pieces that comprise the puzzle of his life. Sometimes it's not until we meet that right person, the one God sends for us, and us towards that we realize how broken we are, have always been, that there's even a puzzle that needs putting together."

Chapter 8

Redmond was sitting on Florina's side of the bed, when she entered the doorway of their bedroom. His back was to her, his head bowed as if in prayer.

She stepped into the room. He stood and turned around. "Where were you?" He was holding a paper.

"I wanted to take a walk," Florina said. She noticed her journal on the bed, open and beside where he had been sitting.

"You just left." Confusion spilled onto Redmond's face. "I had no idea where you were."

Florina looked to the paper in his hand.

A shower of guilt washed over the confusion drying upon Redmond's cheeks.

"My poems." She walked to the bed and lifted the leather journal.

"I didn't mean to pry," Redmond said. "I didn't know where you went." He handed her the paper.

She scanned the words.

> "... The broad cloth of death extends far into the jars
> of heart and memory,
>   digs deep into the bowls of honey and soup on our tables.

The fabric connecting the meat and potatoes of our lives, it is
the eggs and bacon of mourning and grief, the fine tableware
we bring out only for special guests—
those we love and the ones we despise. ... "

"It's a nice poem," said Redmond.

Florina strained to remember when she had begun this recent journal, whether her entries contained anything about Ennis. So much had become muddled in since agreeing to marry Redmond ... the last week, and ... then this afternoon ... following church. She recalled Agnes caressing his cheek. She closed the journal and looked to Redmond, asked, "What else did you read?"

"I was only trying to figure out where you might have gone. Where you were."

"Would you care?"

"What kind of question is that?" Redmond frowned. "You're my wife. I love you."

"Why did you marry me?"

Redmond fell still. His eyes widened as if he had been punched, forcing the wind out of him.

Florina pulled opened the drawer to her night table and placed the journal and paper inside. "I'd appreciate you not rifling through my things. It doesn't have a lock like the front door." She pushed the drawer shut. Despite her mother's curiosity, Florina had never worried Helen might search her belongings. Her face grew hot, warm tears slid onto her cheeks then seething with anger.

"I'm sorry," Redmond whispered.

"I am too." Florina walked past him and went to the kitchen where she set about preparing dinner.

———————————

The congregants had entered a full chorus of *Joy to the World* when Florina and Redmond arrived at St. Andrews that night around ten. Redmond stopped at the third pew from the back, but Florina proceeded to the family pew seven rows

78

ahead, where they had sat that morning, and where Hammond and Carolyn now sat. Hammond stood and hugged Florina when she reached them. Father and son shook hands.

Florina scanned the crowd nearly as large as the one that had gathered for the morning sermon and saw neither Agnes nor Macon.

While singing the final chorus of the carol, and then seated beside her father-in-law, Florina wondered of the accounts Hammond had established in her name at the various stores. She considered his stated concerns for her happiness. *"You make my son happy,"* Hammond had said. *"Not every woman can accomplish that. Carolyn and I are grateful."* *Does Hammond know about Agnes, what she means to Redmond--whatever that may be?* Florina had concluded that Redmond and Agnes had been in love at one time. It all made sense. *That's why she was sitting on the steps when I arrived at the house. Redmond wanted her. Still does. But she's married.* And Redmond had lied--by omission. How long have you know her? Florina had asked Redmond. "She and Macon married in April." Redmond's words had offered no clear answer, rather they said, *Agnes is my business. I don't want to talk about her, my past.*

She recalled Redmond's words on how he had met Agnes before she met Macon. *"We dated,"* Redmond had said. But Agnes had married Macon last April. Redmond loved Agnes and he still wanted her. The longing in Redmond's eyes had been so apparent, so clear, when Agnes had caressed his cheek.

Memories of it now quaked inside Florina. She would never forget it.

What have I done? She ached for Ennis.

─────────────────────────────

Redmond seemed unaffected when at ten forty-five Reverend Mitchell dove into a full-blown sermon, his second for the day, and spoke of the injustices in the world and America.

Her parents would be at Laurel A. M. E. Zion sitting with the Ava and Bill Reynolds, the four of them among the congregation listening to Reverend Adams deliver this last sermon of 1967. Reverend Adams would offer the benediction by eleven, as many families, like Florina's, who lived outside of Laurel and would have braved inclement weather to attend watch-meeting services. The old year would recede into the past, the New Year overtaking its place during the ride from Laurel back to their homes in the countryside.

The earth of her father's three-hundred acre farm, hardened by winter, would lie silent and still. Inside and sitting before the fire, during those early moments of the New Year, Helen and Major Gavin-- as always--would light a candle, and offer a silent prayer, then hugged each other. They had in years past kissed Florina's cheek. Now she touched her cheek and wished for their love to warm it.

The most recent New Year's had held strain. All the while worried what the answer might reveal, Florina's mother, Helen had been determined to uncover why Florina had abandoned college with one year remaining. A year passing with Florina having produced no child served only to increase Helen's anxieties. Helen's concern had turned in to a despair Florina had never witnessed in her mother even with her aunts at their most cruel.

Florina had hurt Helen by not returning to college. The guilt that caused in Florina, combined with the loss of Ennis had, at times during the last eighteen months, become almost unbearable. Marriage to Redmond had offered the possibility of redemption where Helen was concerned. Florina had married well despite lacking a college degree. But in leaving secret widowhood, and silent mourning she felt she had betrayed Ennis. And now Florina had encountered Agnes.

The clock over the doorway of St. Andrews read eleven-twenty when Reverend Mitchell retreated from his second sermon of the day, and entered a discussion of Vietnam.

"There's a war going on," he said. "Our boys are dying over there in Vietnam, some of them never knowing why they

80

died, why they were even drafted other than the color of their skin." By *our*-- he meant Negro soldiers.

What had Ennis thought when he died? Florina wondered. He had enlisted. She turned to Redmond beside her, still and silent as if meditating upon thoughts too heavy to utter.

Had Ennis when shot, been aware of life slipping from his grasp? Or had his moment of transition been quick, and as some say, 'easy'?

Ernest Mitchell ended his sermon by urging everyone to consider their blessings over the last year, and on giving thanks, to, "... *think of your doubts—what you fear most.*"

The minister of St. Andrews then launched into a treatise that caught Florina's attention. "Dr. King is planning a march--Poor People's March. It's to take place this coming spring. I plan to be there. I ask you to join me." The sanctuary went deathly quiet, the breathing of the congregants barely audible.

Agnes. Florina thought. *Could Mitchell be the person her informing her of Dr. King's plans?* But he was older, appeared to be in his late forty's, early fifty's. Neither could imagine Mitchell having been an aspiring Malcolm X.

Florina had read some of Dr. King's articles expounding on white America's love/hate relationship with him, and also of the ambivalence that middle class Negroes held towards his recent and unyielding stance against the war.

Mitchell said, "God commanded us to, ' ...*feed my people...* '" The minister touched his chest. "God's people are our people. *We* are God's people." His words resounded across the sanctuary. "I know this may not sit right with some of you, my participating in this march. I've met with Dr. King and his organizers. It's time to take a stand."

Parishioners throughout the congregation released gasps.

"This march is going to be more powerful than, and unlike anything we witnessed in Washington five years ago," said Mitchell.

Florina recalled Reverend Agnes' words, similar to Reverend Mitchell's statement. "For those of you who attended that momentous time, you need to prepare to come back."

Negroes stood united on the issues connected to achieving Civil Rights. Matters of poverty that affected all Americans, Negro and white, drew division of belief and opinions. Regarding the war, Negroes were hesitant to criticize President Johnson who had recently appointed Thurgood Marshall to the Supreme Court, the first Negro to occupy one of the nine positions.

Mitchell shed his robe and revealed his white shirt, tie and black trousers. He extended his arms. "For those who didn't make it to Washington in sixty-three, I invite you to join me, Dr. King, and all the others who know this is the right thing to do. This war in Vietnam is tearing us apart. It's breaking this country and leaving too many people hungry and needing what no person should ever want for." He surveyed the congregation. "All of us who call ourselves people of God, God's soldiers, His servants. We need to be there and stand by Dr. King. Give God your fears," Mitchell exhorted. "Let Him deal with the battles we can't fight. But don't abandon the war. God will protect us. We have to do our part. Do what's right. Not what looks good, or what appears safe."

Mitchell rounded to his conclusion, and Florina wondered would the vows she had made to Redmond and her marriage survive the weeds of doubt sown by what she had witnessed between Redmond and Agnes. Again the image of Agnes' hand to Redmond's cheek, the yearning that overtook him, subsumed and consumed Florina.

Like the manner in which many perceived the war raging in Vietnam, a tumultuous international conflict absorbing countless lives of Negro and white American boys, Florina felt sucked within the undertow of forces beyond her understanding. The circumstances of her personal battles felt small in comparison to the injustices plaguing so many in the nation. And then there was the unfairness of her own actions towards both Ennis and Redmond, the secrets she held and that now burned within and threatened the flesh of her own conscience. She saw no end to her dilemma or graceful way to exit.

Her chest tightened, she was barely able to breathe. And then a strange thought entered her mind as Mitchell spoke of the roots of injustices sustaining the war, imperialism, and greed, attached and related to atrocities both in America and half way around the world. *How much of Redmond's desire to enlist and work as an Army surgeon rested upon his inability to have and be with Agnes?*

The idea nearly crushed Florina within, threatened to destroy all hope or possibility of surviving Ennis' death, and holding safe to her vows to Redmond. She closed her eyes.

A canvas of despair overtook Florina. She recalled Redmond speaking as she prepared dinner that afternoon. *"Because I love you."* His words had rung clear and simple, in explanation of his worry and why he had looked into her diary. *How much had he read of her journal?* Florina now worried. *Does he know of Ennis. What have I written?* Her entries, sparse and less frequent had became a blur during the months since meeting Redmond in July, barely none, by October when she had accepted his proposal.

What have I done? The question of regret echoed within.

Mitchell offered a prayer as when he had concluded morning services then invited the congregation to stand. Redmond grasped Florina's hand as they rose. He turned to her and she recalled what had prompted Redmond to say, *"Because, I love you."*

"W*hy would you care?"*

Florina had asked Redmond that question. She looked to his hand now grasping hers and wondered the same again.

Chapter 9

Florina noted the string of cars lining both sides of the street as Redmond brought their car to a halt.

"Looks like the crowd is hopping," said Redmond. A large gathering of people, various individuals speaking with one another, others in groups, each holding a goblet of wine or champagne, stood in the living room.

"We should head over," said Florina. She opened her door.

"Are you sure you want to go?" Redmond didn't seem as excited as Florina had anticipated.

"Macon's your friend. He and Agnes are our neighbors. We promised to attend."

"I'd just as soon spend my New Year's Eve with you," Redmond said.

Florina thought of her parents, felt time ticking towards something she had yet to grasp. "I want to call my parents. I'll join you in a few minutes."

Redmond appeared hurt, disappointed.

"It won't take long," Florina said. The impasse from this afternoon had claimed its place between them.

Redmond leaned forward, kissed her forehead, "Come as soon as you finish."

Florina left the car and went inside their house.

The countdown was descending, "Nine, eight, seven, six ..." when Florina entered Agnes and Macon's home.

Redmond pushed from within the crowd and presented her one of two goblets of champagne. "Happy New Year," he kissed her cheek amid the others hugging and toasting.

"No one answered," Florina later explained of her quick journey home to dial her parents. She was with Redmond in the kitchen.

"You seem worried," Redmond said. He cut a slice of pound cake and brought a piece to his mouth. Florina began crying. He placed his arm about her shoulder. "How long have your parents been married?"

"Nearly twenty-six years."

He wiped her face, lifted Florina's chin with his forefinger. "I'm sorry about this afternoon," Redmond apologized again.

"It's all right," Florina said, and shook her head and considered Ennis. *If only Redmond knew.* "I shouldn't have been so harsh."

Redmond smiled, slipped a piece of cake through her lips then pulled her into his chest. She felt comforted.

The door leading from the living room swung open and Agnes entered. "So there you are. Our two little love birds."

Agnes strutted towards them and Florina left Redmond's embrace.

"Macon's looking for you," Agnes said. She touched Redmond's shoulder. "He's over by the fireplace with Bill and the others."

With his hand to the small of her back, Redmond pulled Florina close once again, kissed her forehead and left.

Agnes observed him leave through the swinging door then turned to Florina and asked, "How was church tonight?"

"A lot of people attended, more than we ever had at Laurel."

"I can imagine," said Agnes. "Are you saying that St. Andrews has a much larger congregation than your church in Laurel?"

"Yes, it does."

Agnes offered to refill Florina's goblet but she waved it away. No cigarette lay between her fingers. Her first time in Agnes' home, Florina felt as if having entered the lion's den, the belly of the whale.

"It's only cider," said Agnes. She pointed to five empty bottles of champagne "We can only afford one round of the good stuff. Besides, I don't drink." She wiggled her sharply sculpted nose then said, "I guess you don't know what do with me when I'm without a cigarette."

Florina sat her empty goblet on the counter.

"I want you to meet somebody," said Agnes. She grasped Florina's hand, led her out into the front room filled with people. Through the window across the room Florina saw the house she and Redmond now shared.

Agnes made the introductions on reaching the sofa against the window. "Florina, this is Cynthia Cartwright. I believe you met Cynthia's parents, John and Jeanne, this morning after church."

Florina extended her hand to a tall slender woman wearing a simple black dress, and said, "Nice to meet you."

"And you're Redmond's new bride," said Cynthia. "He told me much about you in the few moments since I learned you two just married."

Despite her light mocha complexion and straight hair, Cynthia's black irises ringed in blue spoke of a woman who had moved far beyond her mother, Jeanne, in both body and spirit. Cynthia shook her palm in a soft way that reminded Florina of her own mother, Helen. In contrast to Helen, Cynthia was confident. Cynthia's nose looked to have been sculpted by Rembrandt, resembled the intricately cut diamond studs gracing her ears. Her fingers molded and articulate, echoed the carefully maintained ends of hair brushing her shoulders. She nodded towards Redmond by the fireplace across the room and in conversation with Macon. "You married barely two five days ago," said Cynthia. Her eyes sparkled in the dim light.

"December twenty-sixth," Florina replied with a mix of pride and disappointment.

"Actual newlyweds," said Cynthia. She lowered herself onto the sofa. Florina assumed the space beside Cynthia and Agnes perched herself upon the sofa's plush arm.

"See, I told you," said Agnes.

"Did any of the members at St. Andrews attend the wedding service?" Cynthia asked.

"It was small," Florina said. "At my home in Laurel. I grew up on a farm."

"Isn't that quaint?" said Agnes. She grinned. "Almost like eloping, but with all the benefits of having a large church wedding. I hear Carolyn Hammond is still receiving gifts from those who couldn't attend or you didn't invite."

"Redmond wanted a quiet ceremony. So did I," said Florina. "We met in July."

"She's very simple," Agnes spoke of Florina to Cynthia. She said to Florina, "I don't mean that in a bad way. *Understatement* is always the key, what I've come to see is Florina Hammond's middle name."

"Our farm is just outside of Laurel, a small town down east," said Florina, unsure how to respond to Agnes' comments. "It's nothing like here."

With goblet of champagne in hand, Cynthia said, "Don't do yourself any injustice." She turned and looked to Redmond across the room and in conversation with Macon and two other men.

"Redmond seems happier than I've witnessed in a long time. It's the marriage that counts, not the wedding," Cynthia said to Florina. The tone with which she spoke held a sense of inner knowing gained through experience.

The forty-five recording Macon had slipped onto the stereo turntable resounded with *I Heard It Through the Grapevine* sung by Gladys Knight and the Pips, and everyone took to the floor. Moments later, the song, *My Girl*, echoed.

Despair slid over Florina as she danced with Redmond.

Florina's mind went to Ennis on the day after they had married. She'd been crying. The following afternoon he would board a bus taking him to Fort Riley, Kansas and from there a flight to Vietnam.

"I'll be back." He'd brushed her head, and his hazel eyes had sparkled.

Florina closed her eyes as if to will the memory dead. But her heart longed for its resurrection, all she hoped to experience with Ennis to be made real.

Redmond touched her cheek.

She opened her eyes and against the music Redmond said, "You should call your parents when we get home."

Disappointed in not having reached her parents, Florina had not been thinking of them. She had married Ennis in October 1965, the fall semester, of her junior year at college. He had deployed two days later. May, six months later, Ennis' mother delivered news of his death.

My Girl, by the Temptations had topped the music charts in January 1965. That had been their song; Ennis proud to claim Florina, and she joyous to assume the role. Married barely three months, they had entered 1966, their first and only new year's with Ennis alive, as husband and wife, but not together. Ennis having just completed basic training at Fort Riley, Kansas, and on this way to Vietnam, Florina had gone home as usual. Five months later Melinda would tell her Ennis had been killed in battle.

Now nearly two and half years later she stood dancing with Redmond, the man who had proposed and she had agreed to marry three months earlier, October 1967, the second anniversary of her marriage to Ennis. Not until this moment, the song, *My Girl*, half-way through its round of playing, did Florina realize what she had done.

89

"I need some water," Florina said. She broke away from Redmond against the Temptations refrain of " ... *my girl* ..." Florina and made her way to the sofa by the window. Cynthia joined her.

"Are you alright?" Cynthia asked. "You look flushed.

"I'm fine." Florina said. "It's just a little stuffy in here.

"Would you like some cider?"

"Redmond's gone to get me some water."

Redmond arrived and handed her the glass of water. "I put some ice in it," he said. "I hope it's not too cold."

"No, it's fine." Florina nodded as she spoke. She drank the water.

"I hope you're not coming down with something," Redmond said.

The concern furrowing his brow startled Florina. "Please, don't worry. I'm fine," she said. "Go back to your friends." She looked beyond Redmond to Macon on the other side of the room.

"Watch her for me," Redmond said to Cynthia, to which she nodded.

Moments later, and Florina feeling better, Cynthia surveyed the room, dark and full of bodies swaying with the music, and said, "So what do you think?"

With temperatures rising and guests ready to dance once more, Macon put on a stack of forty-fives, brought out a bottle of rum, and began filling the cups of male guests.

"It's a nice party," Florina said.

"And of Poinsettia? You can be honest with me." Cynthia brought her forefinger to her lips to hide her mirth. "It's a lot of pretense. Then again, you have to give them credit. They're proud of this little town."

"Aren't you?" Florina asked.

"Pride's never been my thing."

Florina's surprise at this statement shone upon Cynthia's face.

"This is my first New Year's Eve party," Florina said.

"They're all the same." Cynthia drank more of her apple cider. A dim glow hovered about those dancing. "Everyone hoping for a year that will hold better times than the previous."

"Is that what you want?"

Cynthia gazed into the lap of her black dress.

Florina wanted to ask Cynthia what she wished for. Cynthia intrigued her. "So Redmond tells me you live in New York City," Florina said.

"Yes, with my husband and son."

"How long have you been married?" Florina asked.

"Ten years."

"That means you got married at …"

"Nineteen." Cynthia was the same age as Redmond. "I was a junior at NYU."

Florina was now truly interested. She had met Ennis during the spring semester of her freshman year, and like Cynthia, she had married as a junior in college.

Florina surveyed the room. "Where's your husband?"

"With his family," Cynthia replied tight and curt, but lacking anger. "He's Jewish."

"Oh," Florina answered then catching wind of her words, "forgive me."

"Don't worry. It's common."

"My response?"

"Or the noticeable lack of it," Cynthia nodded.

At that moment Agnes approached. "Let's dance. She lifted Florina's hands and tried pulling her to stand.

"I don't think so." Florina remained firmly planted on the couch.

"Tell her she needs to loosen up," Agnes smiled at Cynthia.

"She may need a break from what I was telling her." Cynthia sipped more of her cider.

"Oh, about Jack?" Agnes asked.

"That's my husband's name," Cynthia explained.

"And did you tell her that you actually had the nerve to have a child by him?" Agnes said.

Cynthia nodded.

91

All this amazed Florina. Until six months earlier, June 1967, interracial marriage was outlawed, considered a felony in most states. She did not want to offend anyone, least of all, Cynthia. Redmond had spoken highly of her. The three women continued their conversation with Agnes listening to what she already knew and making sure Cynthia dispensed pertinent details of the path towards her eventual marriage.

"I met Jack my first day at college," Cynthia explained. "Actually hated him. Not in the formal sense of the word. I just felt he was so full of himself, too self-assured. On the inside I liked it. Then again, he *was* white. At least that's how he appeared to me." Cynthia's eyes twinkled. She paused as if breathing in the memories.

"You said, ' ... was ... ' " Florina noted. "Is he no longer white?"

"Jack has never seen himself as white," said Cynthia.

"But isn't that what Jews are--white people?" asked Florina.

"Not exactly," Agnes said, exchanged a knowing glance with Cynthia.

"Jews are white. And then they're not," Agnes said. "They may look white. But they're certainly not WASPS," Agnes said.

"Jack would agree with Agnes," Cynthia chimed.

Florina understood what term WASP meant--white Anglo-Saxon Protestant, but as for the other axiom Agnes extolled ... "I'm sorry."

"Don't be." Cynthia comforted once more. "I was confused, same as you, when I met Jack. Over the years I've grown not to see his color. He's just Jack." Cynthia's gaze retreated once more

"Well go on." Agnes waved her hand still free of a cigarette. "Tell what happened when he asked you out and you put your foot in your mouth like our little Florina."

"He asked me if he could take me on a date, and I said, 'No.' When he pushed as to why, I said, ' ... *because my family wouldn't approve of me dating someone I would never marry.*'

'Why is that?' he asked. 'Your inability to marry me. 'You're white,' I said. 'And the last time I checked interracial marriage is still a crime in several states. Marrying you would constitute a felony.'

"'That's not the case in New York,' Jack said. 'My father's an attorney and he would know.'"

"'Don't be so certain,' I said, 'Prior to the Civil War, New York held a fugitive slave law.' An American History major in his junior year, Jack debated that I was incorrect," Cynthia said.

"So how did you get to the point of marrying?" Florina asked.

"First tell how he got you out on a date," prompted Agnes. She was animated.

"Jack was flabbergasted and embarrassed that I had been right about New York having been a state with fugitive slave laws," said Cynthia.

"And..." Agnes prodded.

"He apologized. *On bended knee.* Promised never to correct me again, without first checking his facts."

"Can you imagine any Negro man saying such a thing?" Agnes exclaimed.

"We married the end of my sophomore year," said Cynthia. "Or should I say we became felons. Jack had just graduated."

Florina shivered at the thought that in most of the fifty states, officials could have easily sentenced and jailed Cynthia and her husband, despite the fact Agnes added, "He's now a Civil Rights attorney, like his father. Thank God for Mildred and Richard Loving," Agnes exhaled.

Florina had been curious of Ennis' heritage from the moment they met. Despite his stated Cherokee heritage, she had felt he had inherited genes from a people of which he was not terribly proud. A kinship lay between Florina and Ennis, one rooted in that of looking like *the other*, if not one of them, not fully of one race, neither a complete genetic member of the other.

Eighteen months later, on the Saturday they married Florina grew suspicious of the man who had stood by Ennis' mother and witnessed Florina and Ennis marry. On completion of the ceremony and shaking the man's hand, Florina looked into the man's deep blue eyes, and recognized the source from which Ennis had inherited the hints of blue in his blue-gray eyes.

Florina grew even more intrigued as the man affixed his signature to her and Ennis' marriage certificate. She asked Ennis, "Is he your father?"

"He loves my mother, but they can never marry," Ennis had said then explained.

The man who was his father had also served as mayor of their small town in the Blue Ridge Mountains of North Carolina.

"And so you tell everyone that you are Cherokee," Florina had said. "Like your mother." Ennis' mother, Melinda, was half Cherokee, her father, Negro.

Ennis had lowered his head.

"I don't care that your father is white," Florina said. Like him, she knew what it was to feel ashamed of the color of your skin. Not because it was dark. But for what it's lack of color, its paleness, indicated.

Florina left her memory of Ennis and returned to Cynthia in the middle of explaining her parents, John and Jeanne Cartwright's, reactions to her choice of husband. "They were mortified."

"Infuriated is more like it," said Agnes.

"Momma had been adamant that this would damage my career as a doctor." Cynthia spoke with a detached dryness as she repeated her mother's words. "'You mean you're going to marry one of them--the enemy?' Daddy on the other hand had been—" she tilted her head as if trying to distill the answer.

"*Conciliatory John*," Agnes proffered one up. "Always middle of the road."

"It's presented some challenges," Cynthia said. "But Jack and I have helped our parents ease into the merger." Cynthia straightened her shoulders. "I come home for Christmas, and bring little Jack in the spring for Easter."

94

"Your parents only get to see you twice a year?" Florina asked.

"They only get to see my son once."

The gravity of the divide hit Florina hard.

"It hurt my mother that her only grandchild was being taught Hebrew and the Jewish form of worship. She refuses to come to New York. And I won't ask Dad to come without her."

"You don't take your son to church?" Florina asked. "Of course, but he also goes to Temple on Saturdays. In my parents' eyes that means he's Jewish, though for the Jewish community he's not--"

"That's right," Agnes interjected. "You're not Jewish." She explained to Florina, "Hebrew lineage is passed through the mother."

Cynthia said, "My parent's main concern is that their grandson and only child is not being taught to love Christ, or to believe in a Judgment Day when you have to give an account of your actions."

The great day of execution," Agnes said. She frowned and her lips curled as if a bitter taste overtook her tongue.

Florina sensed Agnes and Cynthia had discussed this topic many times, implying a relationship that pre-dated Agnes' marriage to Macon last spring.

"On the other hand, my father is thrilled that Jack has joined his father's commitment to Civil Rights," Cynthia said. "His work in this life trumps the fact that Jack's religion does not acknowledge the existence of an afterlife."

"And Jack doesn't work for just *any* of our people," Agnes added. "He and his father provide legal counsel for the movement, Dr. Martin Luther King and his inner circle."

"More like the outer circle," Cynthia said. "Jack nor his father, Hiram Edelstein, work directly with Dr. King. They provide additional counsel after they've consulted Dr. King and lawyers working directly with the movement. Jack and his father offer what you might consider second opinions. And since they almost always agree with the advice offered by the primary attorneys--"

"She's being modest," Agnes interjected. "Jack and his father were the first ones to suggest Dr. King speak at Riverside Church last April."

"I'd say they work pretty close," Florina smiled.

Cynthia returned the favor, a bit of pride flowing through. "It was important to my father that Jack understand what he was doing in marrying a Negro woman, that we have a history and a culture of immense suffering, suffering that's made us stronger. But has wrought many wounds." A warmth resonated in Cynthia's voice.

While she did not advocate Jeanne Cartwright's behavior or perspective, Florina understood her fear. The thought of marrying a man of another race, particularly white, or Jewish, frightened Florina. *Could that man care for her as a Negro man would? Would he want to?*

Perhaps Helen had felt the same or held similar fears when she had said, "I think Florina will be happiest with someone who looks like me or whose coloring is between yours and mine."

"But what if she marries someone white?" Major Gavin had asked.

"That won't happen. It can't."

"Two of your girlfriends in New York have white husbands," Major had commented.

Florina regarded Cynthia. She recalled how her mother, Helen, had replied with a sigh, "And they lived to regret it. When they were pregnant everyone was holding his breath wondering how the baby would look--light or dark. White people are the same as Negroes."

"Where do you think we got it from?"

Florina's parents, Helen and Major, had fallen silent.

Florina admired Cynthia's ability to follow her heart and marry the person she loved more than her diamond earrings. Had Florina done the same she would have insisted Ennis marry her when she had accepted his proposal. But marrying Ennis McCreary would have crushed Helen's heart and manifested her deepest fears.

Ennis was fairer than Major Gavin. His father was white. No problem would have existed had the color of Ennis' skin been darker, and not reflecting his European ancestry. Florina could have said his father had died, or like Ennis had told fellow students at college, *"His father is Cherokee."*

The sting his death had injected into her life caused her to accept Redmond's proposal after knowing him barely three months. Loss and death brought living into perspective. She had grown greatly depressed after receiving the tragic news. *You never think people will die, even when they go to war.*

Florina contemplated her decision not to return to college in the wake of Ennis' death juxtaposed to Cynthia's many accomplishments in the face of her own adversity. *How could I have been so weak?* Florina chided herself. Life could not have been easy for Cynthia. At times it seemed race and ethnicity were all Americans could consider-- the color of a person's skin the determining factor in their destiny, the essential element of who they could or would become, or dared to wish. Yet Cynthia had endured, persevered and thrived.

And Agnes. Florina observed Agnes' excitement concerning Cynthia's life. Agnes definitely understood people, how to get them to reveal the heart of their story. *But what was her story? What role did Agnes play in the narrative of Redmond's life?*

Florina grew anxious with regret in not having told her parents about Ennis, loving him and their marriage. *But would that have saved him, kept him from being shot and killed in Vietnam?*

Florina observed Agnes chatting with Cynthia and considered her father's sisters, Florina's aunts, Mona and her twin, Christa.

She said to Cynthia, "Despite your mother's concerns, it seems you have a wonderful husband, one who has come to understand us for more than the color of our skin."

"More so than some of us," Agnes said. She frowned. Bitterness spread across her buttermilk-colored face.

"You're going to have to forgive Macon at some point," Cynthia chided Agnes.

Agnes folded her arms, said, "Macon Elder chose to marry me on the one day I could have heard Dr. King announce his stance against the war to get married. I could have met him."

Cynthia explained, "Jack invited Agnes to join us in hearing Dr. King speak at Riverside Church in New York. It was his first speech against the war, April 4th, 1967."

"Dr. Macon Elder had to have his way," Agnes interjected. She rocked her head side to side. Gone was her animated smile and glee.

"I always thought the bride chose the wedding date," Florina said.

"Not when you're the daughter of the Reverend *Right* and *Righteous* Julius Kensington."

"Macon insisted April 4th was the only day his parents could close the store and travel to Baltimore for the wedding," Agnes said.

"But they didn't come," said Cynthia.

"The whole thing was a lie, the reason he wanted us to marry on April 4th, why his parents didn't come, " Agnes said. "Macon wanted to please my father. And my father hates Dr. King."

Cynthia explained. "Like a lot of Negroes, even my mother, they have concerns about where the movement is going."

"It's going where it needs to go," Agnes retorted. "To help the poor and change things for the better."

Advocating and marching for Civil Rights is fine," Cynthia explained. But speaking out against the war, now that's troublesome."

"It's hypocritical," Agnes said. "Dr. King is at the same place Malcolm X found himself months before he died."

"Not that I want to agree with you," Cynthia said, "Jack's father saw Dr. King last month. He said Dr. King was depressed. Some who were his strongest supporters are questioning the purpose of the Poor People's March."

"Well, I'm going," Agnes said.

Florina recalled the morning she had spied Agnes
perched on the steps of the verandah of Florina and Redmond's
home.

"Things are unfair," Agnes said. "Our economic system
is rigged against the poor and in favor of the rich."

Florina stared at Agnes and recalled the incident in the
A&P.

"You know I'm right," Agnes said to Florina. "I'm going
with Reverend Mitchell for Dr. King's sit-in on the White
House lawn. I'll be there for as long as it takes."

"Are you sure you want to do that?" Florina asked.

"I'm committed to Dr. King's mission. As much as my
father thinks Dr. King's a heretic," Agnes said. She excused
herself and went to the kitchen.

Shocked at the passion with which Agnes spoke, Florina
looked to Cynthia, said, "I think she's had a little too much to
drink."

"I doubt it," Cynthia said. "Agnes rarely drinks. She's
Islamic."

Florina stared at her again. "She converted after
Malcolm X was killed."

"But she ... " Florina looked towards the swinging
kitchen door, behind which Agnes had gone.

"She's more herself this evening than I've seen in a
while," said Cynthia. "She's also not smoking."

Florina again considered Agnes' gloved palm against
Redmond's cheek earlier that afternoon following morning
services.

"It's not lady-like." she said. "And Redmond hates those
things."

Cynthia too looked towards the kitchen door. "Macon's
been urging Agnes to stop," she said. "He wants a children."
Cynthia turned to Florina. "But some people say it's an
addiction. That people smoke to calm their nerves."

Florina could not imagine Agnes nervous or worried
about anything. Agnes seemed like a person who knew what she
wanted and was accustomed to life granting it. She asked
Cynthia, "Which Agnes is committed to participating in the

99

Poor People's March, the anxious one, or the one that appears calm?"

"Perhaps it's the real Agnes, the one whose both worried and who can also appear confident," said Cynthia.

Florina found it hard to believe such disparate parts of a person could reside so closely within the same person. She had never considered herself as harboring such a conflict. And yet she did. She loved Ennis, but Florina had grown to love Redmond, a realization that hit heady when she observed the longing in Redmond's eyes, Agnes' hand to his cheek. He wasn't simply her husband. Florina loved Redmond.

Cynthia said, "Whatever Agnes does with Dr. King will achieve the same ends as her going to the Audubon Ballroom."

"Agnes asked where I was when Malcolm X was shot," Florina said. "Told me she saw him shot."

"Agnes was definitely there," Cynthia said. "But her father wasn't going to have her back on the psychiatric ward so that's why he had her marry on April 4th."
Florina frowned. "Agnes is impressionable," Cynthia continued. "Jack's and his father's work with Dr. King has taught me many things--one is that there are few people who join the movement with a real commitment to bringing about change. Most come fighting an inner war--what Malcolm said he learned was the *jihad*."

Florina recalled Fitzhugh Mason's words. *"Every war is civil, the family of man fighting with his brothers and within himself."*

"I suppose you're right," Florina mused.

"Don't be fooled, " said Cynthia. "Agnes is everything *but* what she appears. She's fighting for her life. That's the only thing she had in common with Malcolm X and now Martin Luther King." Cynthia sipped the last of her cider. "Trust me, Agnes is ahead of her time. When true change arrives in America, we'll all be running, afraid of who we might meet on the other side of our secrets and facing the person they've made us."

Florina shuddered at the prophecy and insight of Cynthia's statement.

100

Agnes returned with three goblets of cider. Their discussion of race and politics segued onto personal matters rooted in family and home.

Cynthia said, "When it comes to economics, my mother can be pretty conservative. To hear her speak you might think she's a down home segregationist."

"And definitely on a cold, winter day when there's no sun you might assume so," Agnes added. She had returned and was smoking a cigarette. Jeanne Cartwright was extremely pale, could at times, pass for white. "But at least you've got your father to hold her in line."

"My mother is no match for Father. Obeys him like a servant. She's from the old school," said Cynthia.

"It's a wife's job to obey her husband," Florina spoke.

"See all of us aren't dead." Agnes said, then inhaled from her cigarette.

Agnes arched her brows and blew several out rings of smoke. "And who told you that?" she questioned Florina.

"It's what we do," said Florina.

"And you believe that lie from the Bible?" Agnes' thin brows remained arched. The frown upon her face cast the demeanor of a witch betrayed.

"The Bible is not a lie. I don't agree with everything in it, but it's what we Negroes here in America live by," Florina said.

"You mean what our slave masters fed us to kill our anger." A cold stare overtook Agnes' blue-gray eyes. She held up her cigarette as if to draw attention to it despite other around the room smoking. "All that noise about forgiveness. I always thought '*an eye for an eye*' works quite well."

Macon approached and said to Agnes, perched once again on the plush sidearm of the sofa, "Put that out. Your parents are on the phone."

Agnes inhaled and brought the cigarette to her lips. "I'm busy," she said then turned back and resumed her conversation with Florina and Cynthia.

"Your father wants to wish you a happy New Year." Macon touched her shoulder.

"Tell the Right Reverend Julius Kensington I'm busy seeing to our guests." Agnes never looked back to Macon, but remained focused upon her conversation.

Macon lifted the cigarette from between Agnes' fingers. "I want you to speak with your parents," said Macon.

Agnes' eyes grew cold as blue ice. "I'm no child, Macon Elder."

"It's New Years Agnes, and I'm just saying—"

"Well let me say something." Agnes whipped around. "I want all of this alcohol out of my house!" She threw her arm as if to encompass the room.

Those dancing slowed to a halt and turned towards the four. With forefinger to her lips, Cynthia lowered her head.

Goosebumps spread across Florina's back in imagining the shame Macon must have felt. His pride and excitement of hosting the gathering had been obvious.

"We have guests," Macon said.

"Then let me see to them. I've told you I don't want to talk to my father, nor his sidekick, my mother."

After enduring several seconds of what Florina felt certain was excruciating embarrassment, Macon Elder, the go-between for something larger than words could explain, turned and left.

The party went on without further incident. But the argument between Agnes and Macon left an impression upon Florina.

How could Macon tolerate Agnes' behavior? She ruminated later that night, the wee hours of the next morning, as she and Redmond prepared for bed.

She lay down and Redmond crawled in beside her. "I didn't know Cynthia's husband was white," Florina said. Agnes' behavior had made Florina think of Cynthia's semi-estrangement from her parents, the Cartwrights.

"How were you supposed to? You just met her."

"You could have at least told me Cynthia's married name was *Edelstein,* tipped me off.

"Quite frankly, I didn't think about it. Didn't think it mattered," Redmond said. "She's always been, and still is, Cynthia Cartwright to me. Jack rarely, if ever accompanies her when she visits."

Florina drew the covers to her neck. "It's against the law, their marriage. At least it was until this past June."

"Well, Florina Austin." He rolled onto his stomach and smiled. "I believe you are a segregationist."

"I'm no Jeanne Cartwright. If that's what you mean."

"You're coming to understand our little community quicker than I imagined," Redmond said. His smile widened.

"I don't make a practice of putting my foot in my mouth, saying things that can be misconstrued ... " Florina bolstered her pillow. "I'm just saying--"

"*Why didn't I tell you*?" Redmond finished her sentence. "After Agnes' outburst I don't think anyone cared."

"Is she always to rude to her parents and Macon? How can he permit her to speak to him that way?"

"Agnes and Macon's marriage is unique to say the least."

"You say that like they have different rules," Florina said. She sat up. "Would you like it if I spoke that way to you?"

"You still have yet to tell me why you left the church yard without saying a word." Redmond stared at her. His smile was gone.

Florina lay back down. "It's my first New Year's away from home. I was missing my parents." She refused to meet Redmond's gaze still upon her. He turned over and flicked off the light.

After some moments Florina spoke into the darkness. "Agnes doesn't like her father."

"The Right Reverend Julius Kensington." Redmond spoke the name with familiarity of the personality it represented.

"They're a lot alike, Agnes and her father." Redmond appeared caught by a memory. "I suppose you could say each mirrors the other."

103

"Why didn't Agnes just tell Macon that she'd call her parents back? She was so rude. It was like she was angry."

"Probably because Reverend Julius wouldn't have accepted that."

"But why take it out on her husband?"

"Probably for the same reason Macon kept pushing Agnes to speak with her parents."

Reverend Julius. Florina considered how Redmond had spoken his name, with the same inflection as Agnes. Macon seemed to have been operating as a go-between for Agnes and her father. "Agnes didn't choose her wedding day. Macon wanted them to marry on April 4th."

"Who told you?" Redmond asked.

"Agnes."

The image of Agnes caressing Redmond's cheek loomed within Florina's memory. She turned away from Redmond and towards the window opening onto Agnes and Macon's house.

"Cynthia said Agnes had a breakdown after Malcolm X was killed and she was admitted to the psychiatric ward."

"Agnes was there. She saw everything," Redmond spoke somberly, as if he, too, had been present.

"Did you visit her in the hospital?"

"Yes," I admitted her.

"So you've known her for a while," Florina said.

"Yes. We dated. Before she married Macon."

Tears formed behind Florina's eyes. She lowered her eyelids and tried to imagine Ennis, warm and alive, touching her cheek.

Chapter 10

Florina's mother called the next morning, New Year's Day, and explained that following watch meeting services they had driven to the Reynolds' home for a small gathering.

"It was nice," Helen said from Laurel, the distance of a four-hour drive. "What did you and Redmond do?"

"We went to church and then to our neighbors for a party."

"Oooo. That sounds exciting," said Helen Gavin. "Did you meet anyone interesting?"

"One of Redmond's childhood friends attended." Florina thought of Cynthia Cartwright, her accomplishments and life in New York City. "She's a doctor," Florina said. "Her husband's a Civil Rights Lawyer. They've met Dr. King."

"Imagine that. A lady doctor whose husband works with Dr. King."

Amazed at how people's hopes embellished their perspectives of others, Florina said nothing of Cynthia's husband offering second opinions to direct legal counsel to movement insiders, nor of his being Jewish. Cynthia's semi-estrangement from her parents invaded Florina's thoughts. "I miss you," she said to her mother.

"We miss you too. But don't worry about us. You have a new and wonderful life with Redmond." Helen spoke in a nurturing tone as she had throughout Florina's childhood. Florina wished she had been able to tell her mother of Ennis to have heard that supportive tone in the wake of Ennis' death. Maybe if she had had the strength to introduce him to her parents Ennis would not have felt the need to enter the military and prove himself.

"How's Redmond doing? Working hard?" Enthusiasm and pride imbued Helen's every word. "Does he have many patients?"

"He went to visit his parents." Redmond had walked down to his parents' for an after breakfast chat with his grandmother, Lyla. "He's really close to Grandmother Lyla," Florina said. "She's a very nice woman. I like her."

"That's good. Becoming close with your husband's elders is always helpful."

Florina recalled her conversation with Redmond's father. *Carolyn and I can see that you're good for Redmond,* Hammond Austin had said. *And as Redmond's father my job is to ensure your happiness.*

Helen's voice came through the phone. "I'm sure Redmond's parents and grandmother are so pleased and excited to have him following in his father's and grandfather's footsteps," said Helen. "The whole town of Poinsettia must be amazed and delighte-- "

"I've met someone," Florina interrupted. "She lives here in Poinsettia. The wife of the couple next door. They hosted the party we attended last night. Her husband is a doctor too."

"Well, this is wonderful. Seems like you're fitting right in. Who is she?" asked Helen.

"Her name is Agnes Elder. She's from Baltimore," said Florina.

"I would think she's very refined." A new strain of excitement encapsulated Helen's voice. Florina thought her mother's assumptions of Agnes ironic. Agnes was fairer than Florina's aunts--Regina, Mona, Loretta and Christa--who so disparaged Helen. And yet Helen appeared to contrive that

Florina and Agnes would become close friends, near sisters, like Helen and Ava Reynolds.

"You can learn a lot from her," Helen spoke with heightened anticipation. "Tell me all about her. What does she look like?"

"She's about my height, has black hair like Mrs. Reynolds." Florina said nothing of Agnes' fair complexion, nor of her smoking. "Her husband is the other Negro doctor in Poinsettia."

"How does she dress? What's she like? Does she have much to say about what's going on in the country? Being that she's from Baltimore, so close to Washington D.C., I would imagine." Again, Helen's inquisitiveness rose to an overwhelming level.

"She is very interested in Civil Rights," said Florina. Beyond the need for Negroes to get an education, Florina's mother had never expressed political interests during her childhood. That had been her father's domain. "But we've only just met. She's offered to help me find a housekeeper. But I don't know—"

"Why not?"

A chill ran through Florina. Helen had never had domestic help. "I don't see why we need anyone. There's only me and Redmond."

"But it's what Redmond's accustomed to. His parents have Mrs. Brooks. Redmond has spoken very fondly of her." Helen's statement edged towards a reprimand, her tone echoing Agnes'. "His father is a doctor. And Redmond's grandfather, Jonas, was a doctor like the husband of your new friend, Agnes."

Florina recalled the Austin pew at St. Andrews, how she had sat between Redmond, namesake of his grandfather, Jonas Redmond Austin, and Redmond's father, Hammond, with Carolyn next to him, and Mother Austin to the other side of Carolyn.

"You've entered a new life," Helen Gavin instructed. "One that we feel very fortunate to have you participate in." *We* meant Florina's father, and Ava and Bill Reynolds. "With

107

everything good comes responsibilities," Helen continued. "More the reason you need to return to school and get your degree," she further directed. "A housekeeper will allow you to do that, let you take care of Redmond, like a good wife. *An educated wife.*"

Anger, under which lay hurt, burned upon Florina's tongue. Her mother's words expressed everything she feared. The question of what to do with her life had hovered like a heavy noose over Florina's head, and landing upon her shoulders would tighten around her neck. *I should have told my parents about Ennis.* Florina wished for Cynthia's strength. Cynthia had told the Cartwrights about Jack who was Jewish and white.

Florina began to construe how she could have lived openly as Ennis's widow.
Ennis could have listed me as his wife and beneficiary. I would have received the lump payment of his pension when he died ... instead of his mother, Melinda, whom he had listed as his only relative. I would have had money. If I had told my parents of marrying Ennis maybe he'd be alive.

Helen would have still urged Florina to return to school even if she had received Ennis' death benefit, *But at least she and Daddy would have known the source of my sadness, that they had done nothing wrong. I wouldn't have been dependent on them. There would have been no need to marry Redmond-- Redmond who was in love with Agnes.*

Florina considered Redmond's admission that he had dated Agnes prior to her marrying Macon. He had lied about having known Agnes longer than her marriage to Macon. Though newly married, Redmond, Agnes and Macon, had long histories, with Florina the newcomer having to play catch-up.

Florina closed her eyes, ashamed of her inability to follow her heart and marry the person she loved. She now wafted between frustration with her mother and guilt for having married a man who did not know of her previous marriage.

Perhaps Agnes is my punishment for having lied. Florina thought. *Serves me right.* Both Florina and Redmond had omitted telling each other of the sensitive and intricate parts of their pasts. Regret overtook Florina.

"Redmond is a nice young man," Helen Gavin began again. "He loves you."

Are you sure? Florina wanted to say. Helen's words echoed those of the demure eldress who had greeted Florina and Redmond the previous morning after church services at St. Andrews.

Florina grew tense, her shoulders and neck tightening. Helen's words momentarily faded into the image of Redmond gazing down upon Agnes with her gloved palm to his cheek.

"So many of our young men are dying in this unjust war," Helen said. "Give Redmond something to live for." Florina's mother echoed Hammond's counsel to Redmond regarding the reasons against enlisting, albeit as an Army surgeon. "You've just married. What are you trying to do, son--make your wife a widow? You've just married. You don't even have a child, someone to carry on your name."

"You mean like I'm carrying on yours?" Redmond had questioned. The tacit response surfaced into Florina's memory.

"*We've discussed this before, son,*" Hammond had said.

Florina now wondered about Redmond's statement. On first hearing their argument she had assumed it related to Hammond's efforts to keep Redmond from enlisting in the military. The memory now stood in a different light, against the image of Agnes touching Redmond's cheek, one that illuminated Florina's need to identify what lay between the two..

What bound them? Florina sensed a tightly knotted link. *Agnes and Macon had been married barely nine months.* But this would not explain Agnes' condescending tone with Macon. *She didn't love him.* Florina's thoughts picked up steam.

Florina recalled her conversation with Cynthia last evening at the New Year's Eve party. "Agnes is fighting for her life," Cynthia had said. And then, "She's ahead of her time. When true change arrives in America, we'll all be running, afraid of who we might meet on the other side of our secrets. *The people we really are.*"

Helen's voice through the phone grabbed Florina's attention, pulled her from the downward spiral into the waters of despair in which Florina now found herself treading. "Give Redmond his due. There's too much death around us." Helen admonished Florina. "Attend to your husband. Become the woman he needs. Johnson C. Smith College is in Charlotte, not more than thirty minutes from Poinsettia." For Helen Gavin, the schoolteacher, education served as a prerequisite to becoming a good and useful wife. "Redmond will love you more for earning your degree. You'll feel better about yourself, have more confidence. I love you, and so does your father." Florina heard Helen's longing to understand Florina's unexplained departure from college, the ensuing depression still a mystery.

Florina's chest ached. Her mother had spoken words that held truth.

It was as if Helen had sensed Ennis' presence throughout the conversation, perhaps even before Florina had met Redmond. *Something to live for--* the words rang within Florina's mind like a church bell calling congregants to worship. *How could she know?* Florina wondered about Helen's words as she hung up the phone.

Florina felt, at times, she had nothing to exist for. She had dwelled in the lake of sadness long before meeting Ennis. Florina had always felt her mother had eyes in the back of her head, for that matter, far-reaching eyes that traveled wherever Florina went. Perhaps this was her conscience. Whatever the case, it hurt not feeling she had ever measured up, or could ever attain the goals her mother had laid out

I'm too much like Daddy's sisters. Florina considered her Aunt Christa who had attended North Carolina College for only one semester. *Daddy at least finished out the year.* She then reminded herself, "*You only have one more year.*" Two semesters of courses remained for Florina to receive her degree.

Graduating college had been her main priority until Ennis' death offered the key to freedom and the confidence to release her secret. She had planned to tell her parents of having married Ennis on graduation day, after the ceremony. It mattered not whether Ennis could have been present.

So happy that Ennis had married a person who loved him and whom he also loved, Melinda had not criticized Florina's decision to not tell her parents. *"They're your parents and you know what they can and cannot accept,"* Melinda had said. *"I respect your decision to keep silent."*

Florina found it painfully ironic that Melinda, the mother of a son whose father refused to openly acknowledge him because she was half Cherokee and Negro, had so easily accepted Florina's decision to hide her marriage to Ennis. Melinda had instead remained focused on maintaining Florina's respectability and virtue.

"I won't have Ennis laying with you as anything but your husband."
Melinda's requirement of her son had touched Florina's heart, catalyzed her determination to complete college.

She would invite Melinda to her graduation and introduce her to her parents along with Ava and Bill Reynolds who were certain to attend. After all, Melinda had given her blessings, witnessed them taking their vows, and excitedly accepted Florina as her daughter-in-law. Florina would make clear her need for them to accept Ennis and Melinda. Florina could do no less, but she had needed her degree to stand her ground, to feel confident and sure. Helen knew her daughter well.. Florina's parents and the Reynolds valued education, as did most Negroes, even those who lacked it.

The history of plantation owners having so vigorously denied Negro slaves the opportunity to learn to read and write, and killing them should they attempt it, made education all the more desired and crucial in obtaining freedom. Slaves who were literate presented a constant threat of escape. They could write their own walking papers. And so it continued after Emancipation. Education beyond high school became a right of passage, offering the Holy Grail of acceptance into the upper

111

echelons of Negro society. It delivered a stamp of approval, indicated commitment and perseverance, the ability to delay gratification of folly and fun in favor of the responsibilities of life. As well, education not only offered the opportunity to improve one's economic status, it fed the soul. The ability to read the words of those who had lived prior dispensed wisdom from the ages.

One more year. Florina lamented then chided, *I only had two semesters left.*

Florina's parents had held high aspirations for her. *"We have hopes for you,"* Helen had always said. Ava Reynolds would add, *"You're going to go very far. I can see that. We all can."*

Along with that stood the last of Helen's commands. *"Marry well."*

"With a college degree you will," Ava always assured.

Florina waxed and waned between aggravation with her mother's demands and shame for having failed at living up to her standards and achievements as well as Ava's.

And yet while lacking a college degree Florina had married Redmond, a surgeon.

So much for having a college degree. Florina considered her mother. *Daddy was the reason the board hired her instead of those teachers with experience.* Her thoughts drifted to Ava who had operated as the lynch pin introducing her parents and then two decades later Florina to Redmond. *I owe her more.* Florina concluded.

Guilt for having married Ennis threatened once more to overwhelm Florina in the midst of her failure. An image of Agnes, cigarette in hand burst onto Florina's consciousness. The ever-present memory of that same hand, absent the cigarette, caressing Redmond's cheek followed in the wake of its passing.

She recalled Redmond's words from last evening, his arms around her, the two of them lying in bed. *"I dated Agnes."*

Florina had returned the washed and dried plates to the cupboard when a knock resounded at the front door. She went to the living room and opened the door to Agnes whose face momentarily became her mother, Helen's. The contrast of the light and dark hues of their faces mesmerizing Florina. For a brief moment Florina imagined her mother standing before her, Helen having transported herself to Poinsettia in the hour since she had ended the telephone conversation.

The cigarette between Agnes' fingers brought Florina back to the present.

"Aren't you going to say, '*Hello,*' or tell me how great the party was last night?" She stepped inside, removed her coat and handed it to Florina. On surveying the room Agnes turned to Florina not yet settled into the present, and hit her with a questioning look.

No ashtrays. Florina thought. Redmond had forbid her to buy them. "*I won't have Agnes or anyone smoking in our home,*" he had said.

"Aren't you going to make me put it out?" Agnes asked. She extended her hand with the cigarette.

"Let's take it back to the sink." Florina walked to the kitchen, Agnes following. Upon reaching the sink Florina turned on the faucet and indicated for Agnes to place the cigarette under the stream. She turned off the faucet. "You can put it over there." Florina pointed to the trashcan across by the doorway.

Drenched, its life extinguished by the water, Agnes dropped the cigarette into the waste can. "So what do we have on the agenda today?" She strutted to the table and sat.

"There's no need for me to go to the A&P. I have all I need to prepare dinner," Florina said.

Agnes pursed her lips, destroyed the smile with which she had arrived. "I hear you're having your groceries delivered from the Elders' store."

"Macon's parents."

"You've met them?" Agnes asked.

"They're good people."

"Simple." Agnes said. "And that store is dingy."

113

"I supposed that's why they didn't attend your wedding."

Agnes gave a hot stare.

"Your dislike of them."

"You're a judgmental one," Agnes said. "Then again with the Austins as your in-laws you can afford to--"

"The Elders are no different from Mother and Father Austin."

"Oh, stop with the pretense. You and I both know that there's as much difference between Carolyn and Hammond Austin and the Elders as a thoroughbred and a donkey."

"Why are you so mean?" Florina said. Her ears and cheeks warmed to a burn.

"I'm truthful and honest and not willing to lie."

"If you equate being nice to lying then perhaps you shouldn't have married."

"You're right," said Agnes. "Then again, every woman can't be the wife of Redmond Austin."

"Redmond said he knew you before you met Macon."

"And he knew her not till she had brought forth her firstborn son: ... His name was called Jesu--" Agnes quoted Matthew 1:25.

"I love Redmond," Florina spoke.

Again Agnes flashed a stare.

"I also have a list of things to do. And I'm sure you need to see to Leena."

"That sop of a girl," Agnes said. "She's not coming today."

"Is it because she took the day off, or you can't afford to pay her?" Florina asked.

Agnes' stare returned this time with an angry hardness. That Macon had not paid his bill at the A&P had not gone unnoticed. "You're a quick study," Agnes said and pointed her finger. "I'd better watch you." She plastered a smile then stood.

Florina saw Agnes to the front room, presented her coat and opened the door.

She closed the door on Agnes' exit, Redmond's words playing through her mind. *"No one could accuse you of being like Agnes Macon."*

Memories of Florina's first afternoon in Poinsettia arose. She recalled the touch of Redmond's hand, his passion entering her body and lifting her heart above the river of sadness and loss filling her chest. Florina's breasts grew warm as the memory of falling asleep in Redmond's arms enveloped her.

116

Chapter 11

Carolyn Austin immediately spoke of a friend when Florina stated her wish to return to college. "He teaches literature at Johnson C. Smith over in Charlotte," Carolyn said. It was the second day of the new year, 1968, and they had been having lunch in the front room at Carolyn's the next afternoon. "Your idea is wonderful. And with Willa Mae to help with the house you'll be finished in no time," Carolyn spoke as Agnes had predicted. Florina grew tense.

"Redmond will be overjoyed." Carolyn continued. "And Willa Mae, has been wanting to stop working the local plant." Willa Mae was Mrs. Brooks' daughter. "Willa Mae working for you and Redmond is the perfect solution now that she's three-months pregnant with her and David's second child."

Cautious of the idea of having someone working in her home, Florina recalled
Agnes' warning. "*You want to choose someone with discretion. Carolyn and Hammond are nice people but Redmond is their only child, and Carolyn without meaning to be is quite possessive. I wouldn't want their domestic working in my home--were I their daughter-in-law.*"

117

Florina grew concerned at the idea of Mrs. Brooks'
daughter working for her and Redmond. She said of Willa Mae.
"But can she, should she, work while carrying a child?" The
idea of a hiring a pregnant woman to clean her house seemed
unfair to both mother and child. And while pregnancy was not a
communicable disease, Florina could not help but wonder if
Carolyn held ulterior motives in suggesting Willa Mae.

"Willa Mae needs the job," Carolyn said. "The money
she receives from David in Vietnam barely covers the rent."

Florina's heart warmed after she caught her breath. "It
must be difficult with her being pregnant and him half a world
away and fighti--"

"They're taking all our boys who don't have an
education." Carolyn lamented the military draft that had called
David. "He was only twenty when they called him up. It's so
unfair." She shook her head. "The way they treat us like sub-
humans--beasts to which they assign less value than their pets.
But when the war becomes too much for them to handle, they
demand *our* sons and father, brothers and uncles give their
lives."

Florina knew her mother-in-law to be speaking of white
Americans, and the United States government.

"This country is despicable."

Carolyn's words fell hard upon Florina, sank to her
stomach like a heavy rock. She surveyed the room, noted the
French provincial furniture of mahogany carefully set about,
observed the blue silk draperies gracing the windows,
commissioned and hand made by a local seamstress. In contrast
she imagined Ennis wounded and bleeding, fearing death as it
overtook him.

"It must be a trying time for Willa Mae," Florina
repeated. "You're right."

"Willa Mae will be so grateful for the job," Carolyn
repeated excitedly.

"It would be my pleasure to hire her," Florina said.

"You responded just like Redmond said you would, once
I had explained," Carolyn beamed. "But first I have to introduce

you to Robert." Carolyn lifted her forefinger, a sign that she had more plans underway.

"You spoke with him?" Florina asked of Redmond.

"Hammond had suggested that Redmond hire a housekeeper. We've had Mrs. Brooks since Hammond and I married. Grandmother Austin would have it no other way." Carolyn's cheeks softened. "But this is a new day. You young people like to make your own choices. Redmond said you might not feel comfortable. We do so want you to be happy here."

Florina's anxiety faded. The sincerity on Carolyn's face made clear the truth of Hammond's words, *"Carolyn and I see that you have made Redmond very happy. You're a good person. And we want you satisfied here in Poinsettia."* If only they knew about Redmond.

Would Hammond had said the same, Carolyn feel the same if they knew of Florina's previous marriage, that she had not told her parents, nor her godparents, Ava and Bill Reynolds?

On a worse note, perhaps they did know of Redmond's relationship with Agnes. Perhaps this fueled their desire to keep Florina happy and in Poinsettia married to Redmond. Tension rose in Florina once more.

"As for Robert, we'll need to take him some of your poems. As well as summon your transcripts from Durham." Carolyn resumed the topic of Florina re-entering college.

"Robert?" Florina said. Her heart was fast sinking, about to surrender to the undertow of self-recrimination, guilt and confusion.

"Robert MacIntosh. Forgive me," Carolyn explained. "He's a professor over at Johnson C. Smith in Charlotte. Once I speak with him, you'll have no problems returning to college and completing this last year."

"You'll absolutely love him, as I'm certain he will you and your poems," said Carolyn, " ... as much as Hammond and I do." Her brown eyes twinkled.

"But first I must introduce you to Robert. He's a wonderful poet. As Redmond says of you."

119

Florina's anxiety increased with a bound. *He showed them my poems.* <u>She thought.</u> *How much of my journal has he read?* She felt invaded. Again she worried, *Does he know Ennis judged life unfair to women? He keeps his secrets. Why must he pry into mine?*

Florina's heart was fast sinking, about to surrender to the undertow of self-recrimination, a mix of emotions, when Carolyn said, "You've brought Redmond so much joy. We haven't seen him this happy in a long time. Just this morning he was saying how much fun he's having with you, how at peace he feels. He loves you. And it shows."

Florina warmed with gratitude and hope despite her worries. And yet her mother-in-law's words had left her ever more confused.

How does Agnes fit into this? Florina silently questioned. *Do I even want to know?*

Helen's voice rose within Florina as Carolyn spoke. None of that matters. Go back to college. Complete your last year. Make Redmond happy.

Carolyn poured tea in the cups on the tray sitting upon the table. Florina accepted the saucer from her mother-in-law, brought the cup to her lips and allowed the warm tea to bathe her throat.

Chapter 12

The following week Robert MacIntosh hosted Carolyn and Florina at his home by the campus of Johnson C. Smith. A professor of English Literature and Poetry, Robert had attended Howard University with Carolyn Austin. Towards dessert Florina recognized that more than a simple friendship existed between alumna and alumnus.

"Robert is an incredible lover of poetry. Langston Hughes is his favorite. But he's been known to quote a little bit of Byron. And Eliot." Carolyn lifted the cup from her saucer and sipped more of her coffee.

"Carolyn is too kind, "Robert said. He exchanged glances with Redmond's mother, his eyes betraying a sense of familiarity. He turned to Florina. "Besides, we're here to talk about you. I received your transcripts from North Carolina Central. You achieved stellar work there. Dr. Drayton expressed high praise for your commitment to analyzing the written word, both in prose and poetry. He also spoke extensively of your talent in the latter."

Florina felt relieved that perhaps Redmond had not shown her poems to Robert MacIntosh. She straightened the lap of her dress in an effort to absorb the professor's compliment.

"As you have said of Mrs. Austin, I think Dr. Drayton too is extremely kind," said Florina.

"Walter Drayton's an exceptional literary critic," said Robert MacIntosh. "He does not bestow praise where it is not warranted, least of all upon students."

Where MacIntosh's walnut-colored skin contrasted the hearty mahogany of the Redmond's angular cheeks, his brown eyes demonstrated matching intensity. MacIntosh asked Florina, "Why did you not return for your senior year of college?"

"A friend of mine died." The words slipped from Florina's tongue.

"That must have been difficult," Carolyn said. She shifted her attention to Florina.

Why did I say that? Florina chided herself. That she had never spoken of Ennis to her parents allowed Florina to create a poetry to her own fiction that fit the truthful lie of her life. "They died in Vietnam." As when speaking of the ubiquitous and omnipotent 'One,' Florina's use of the almighty '*They*,' cast an illusion of distance between that for which she felt shame and wished to affect a sense of estrangement--Ennis, and her marriage to him.

"Death can do that to us. Open up clogged places," the professor of literature continued. "Blast through passages that have long blocked our creativity." The intense gaze of his brown eyes returned reflective of a deeper sense of knowing. "And ourselves."

Robert had eloquently described Florina's experience of moving to Poinsettia, most particularly the effects of her interactions with Agnes. Beyond that it felt as if an unknown piece of underclothing or lingerie was showing. She felt exposed, yet not quite sure what his words had uncovered.

"I'm ready to return to my writing, crafting poetry," Florina said. "My friend is not coming back. The only way I can live and honor them, what he gave me, is to start writing again. For that I need to return to college, get my degree."

"Then it's set." Robert brought his palms together Minutes later he left the table and returned with a form that would allow her to register for classes. "School began a week ago, but we're still in the middle of add/drop." Shocked and thrilled, Florina examined the form. "Having evaluated your transcript and after speaking with Dr. Drayton, I took the liberty of enrolling you in my Comparative Poetry class." Florina looked to Robert. "It seemed the right thing to do especially since Carolyn asked me to watch over you." The professor offered the slightest of smiles.

"I'll be driving in each day," Florina said.

Robert looked to her, his gaze intense. "Carolyn tells me that you and Redmond being newly married have hired Mrs. Brooks' daughter, Willa Mae, to help with the house."

"Yes." Florina spoke calmly, her cheeks warming in shock.

"Forgive me for our forthrightness," MacIntosh said. "But Poinsettia is a small town and even though I'm here in Charlotte--"

"Laurel, where I'm from, is even smaller," Florina interrupted. Still she wondered what had provoked Carolyn to tell Robert MacIntosh, the man who would be Florina's English professor, of Willa Mae work for her and Redmond.

"I'm available to discuss your poetry, help you with editing," said Robert. His tone was light, as if not to betray the depth of hope to work with Florina.

"But you don't know me." As with his and Dr. Drayton's compliments, the offer awed Florina. "I'm truly grateful. It's just that--"

Helen Gavin's words returned. *"Figuring out what motivates people. That's the key to understanding them, and getting what you want."*

"Oh, but I do know you," Robert spoke. "I've read your papers, your poems. Walter Drayton mailed me some that you wrote in his class. With the understanding that I would return them to you." He handed Florina the manila envelope. She met his gaze. "Thank you," sincerity having softened his irises. "For deciding to return to doing what feeds your soul. And those who read your words."

123

Across the table, the eyes of her mother-in-law held warmth and caring, what seemed a kind of reverence, unlike what Florina feared.

"Thank you," Florina spoke to Carolyn across the table.

"Not at all. You love my son."

A peaceful truth of acceptance flowed in being both wife to Redmond and daughter-in-law to Carolyn--a realization she could no longer deny.

••••••••••••••

Chapter 13

••••••••••••••

The ticking of the grandfather clock in the foyer punctuated the solitude encasing Robert MacIntosh's library. Shelves lined with books stretching from floor to ceiling filled the walls and provided an excellent abode for solitude and reflection.

"This is an wonderful place for writing," said Florina. She sipped her tea.

"Into the noise of our hearts we gallantly gallop to do justice, and render mercy that our souls might bathe in the light of surrender and death," said MacIntosh.

"It's beautiful." Awed by his words Florina looked to MacIntosh, her heart and imagination mesmerized. "Who wrote it?"

"A young man during World War II," said MacIntosh. "Eight days shy of two months following the Normandy Invasion." His gaze retreated as if summoned by a memory.

"That would be somewhere around the end of July 1944, say the 29th," Florina said. She lowered her cup onto the saucer.

"You know your history."

"It's the basis for all poetry and stories."

"You're quite right." The English professor with a love of poetry shook his head. "Most particularly regarding *your* poetry." Vibrancy energized his voice. He opened the satchel beside his chair, lifted out a paper then slipping on his glasses, he began reading.

"The fields of my father's farm are barren. It is autumn.
The rice paddies surrounding Saigon are alive with the stench of
human bodies
laid waste in a war that divides our country
And separates our hearts from its Soul.
The ghost of a lover wanders the empty fields of my father's
farm,
where corn grows in summer,
Corn that nourishes the livestock, and feeds us.
Who feeds the people of Saigon?
Who fills the breasts of mothers made empty by the loss of men
husbands and sons, grandsons, and nephews, brothers and
uncles?
The stench of their rotting corpses renders us drunk with guilt ...
... res ipsa loquitur..."

MacIntosh stopped reading. "Now where did that word come from?" he asked, removing his glasses. The poem was Florina's.

"Redmond used the word one night when describing our neighbor. He said it meant the words are self-evident."

"And who might this neighbor be?"

"Agnes Elder." Florina felt uncomfortable answering.

"So Redmond's using a legal phrase to describe Agnes Kensington, the daughter of the Reverend Julius Kensington. She casts a wide and arduous shadow."

"You know her?"

126

"We were introduced and spoke briefly, once. I've mainly observed her from a distance," he responded.

"What did you come to think of Agnes while observing her during that *brief* introduction?" Florina asked. MacIntosh's way with words had left an impression upon Florina. He saw more than most, and appeared to say less than all he discovered.

"I'd be shocked to find that she writes poetry." The English professor arched his eyebrows, the right slightly more than they left. "And certainly not stanzas bearing as much depth as yours." His comment mirrored oblique aspects of Redmond's responses to Florina's questions about Agnes, as did the glow of recognition in his eyes.

Florina eagerly accepted MacIntosh's offer to stroll through the garden behind his house during which time their discussion returned to the topic of Florina's poem, *Transubstantiation*.

"I suggest you unite the narrator of the poem with, " said MacIntosh, quoting from her poem, "... '*the ghost of a lover... who. ...wanders the empty fields*' ... searching for <u>her</u> ...'*Beloved ...laid to rest in the fields of Vietnam.*'"

"I revised the ending," Florina said. "This morning before I left for school."

"I'd like to read that when we return to the house." They continued down a path hard from winter and lined with trees bare of leaves. Moments later and farther down onward MacIntosh said, "I always take a walk after my time of writing and revising, even when it's cold--get back to nature."

"I like walking," Florina agreed.

"It's important that we writers stay close with nature, the earth. The soul needs grounding after it's has taken flight in the words our heart serves up."

"Is that what it's like for you? When you write."

"Somewhat," said MacIntosh. His piercing brown eyes ran sharper than she had witnessed. "What is it like for *you*?"

Florina dug her hands deeper into her coat pockets. "I forget about everything, lose grip with time and space. Even myself."

"And when absent yourself, what is that like?"

Florina lifted her head to the sun-filled sky. The January cold invigorated her senses.

"I feel free, forget about how I look, or who I am," Florina said. "It's not like I can't remember. Only the words count," she clarified. "And how I feel. Even my thoughts stop. Or perhaps they merge with my feelings. I have a sense of peace, feel that I am at one with the world." Expressing the truth of her experience, the cornerstone of her process for writing poetry, allowed acceptance of the person she was.

They had reached the deepest part of the garden when she took in MacIntosh's face, chestnut brown, and softened by what Florina sensed lay rooted in a deep loss, the latent effects which he revealed only in his writing. She marveled at how much he resembled Redmond in both serious demeanor and refined movement.

MacIntosh and Florina wound their way through a line of sycamores. The vines between them lay bare like their branches. "You miss your father's farm," MacIntosh said.

"How can you tell?"

"Your poem emphasizes the land. I'm interested to see if there's more of the land in your revision."

Florina warmed within, grew hopeful that the words she strung together might blossom into something meaningful, and touched the hearts of others like they had for Ennis. How good it felt to converse with someone committed to his writing and who also took her words seriously. The hard earth supporting her feet, she said, "As a child I used to spend hours, entire days running across the fields, roaming the woods."

"I hope not in fall and *winter*." Again MacIntosh turned. "And that if you did, you wore an orange jacket."

"Hunting season," said Florina. "My father and his father before him never allowed hunting on the farm." Again MacIntosh had impressed her with the broad spectrum of his interests. "I had the five-hundred acres of my father's farm all to myself."

"Still there are trespassers. Could you trust the white men not to come hunting?"

"That's why he put up an electrified, barbed wire fence."

128

"Your father sounds like a determined man."

"Not as determined as Redmond," said Florina." While making the bed that morning, Florina had discovered underneath Redmond's pillow a packet, beside his newspaper crossword puzzle, detailing information about a hospital in Los Angeles Redmond wants to leave Poinsettia despite Father Hammond's plans for Redmond to stay."

"And carry on the name," MacIntosh said. "Redmond wants to go to California."

Florina turned to him.

"Carolyn's mentioned his desire to leave." They had started back towards the house. "She, too, wants Redmond to remain in Poinsettia."

"What would you like to see him do?" Florina asked. She had this uncanny feeling that Robert MacIntosh's desires for Redmond mattered heavily.

"I'm more curious to hear what you want?"

"I love my home. But I want Redmond to be happy. And if that means leaving Poinsettia ... " Florina's voice trailed off. She stared at the ground beneath her feet.

They had nearly reached the house when MacIntosh asked, "How much do you know about Poinsettia?"

"It's a nice little town."

MacIntosh laughed. "You say that having come from a farm?"

Again Florina pushed her hands farther into the pockets of the coat she was wearing, Redmond's coat. He'd given it to her to wear her first day of classes at Johnson C. Smith. "For good luck," he had said. "And to feel my arms around you."

"Doesn't sound like your words. Now had you said, ... *it was quaint*... I might--"

"It's how Agnes describes it."

"Your neighbor," MacIntosh said. "And how is that going? You living next door to her and Macon."

"Redmond says they have an interesting and unique relationship."

"What do *you* say?" asked MacIntosh.

129

Redmond's words, "We dated," came trampling back. The image of Agnes caressing Redmond's cheek pushed to the forefront of Florina's thoughts. The two incidents had during recent days taken a back seat to the practicalities of Florina and Redmond setting up house and settling into their marriage.

Florina said of Agnes, "She's not like anyone I've met."

The English professor flashed Florina a glimpse of deeper knowing concerning the person about whom they were speaking.

Student and teacher remained silent during the walk back to the house.

Back inside the study Florina opened her notebook containing the revision of her poem, *Transubstantiation*, and handed it to MacIntosh. The professor studied the page, reciting in a whisper. *"The rice paddies surrounding Saigon are alive with the stench of human bodies."* He handed Florina her notebook. "I want you to read it."

She grew still. Softly, the words came forth.

Transubstantiation

The rice paddies surrounding Saigon are alive with regret and
anger. Bodies laid waste in a war that divides our country
Separate our hearts from its Soul.
The spirits of men line the countryside.
The ghost of a lover wanders the empty fields of her father's
farm,
Fields that in summer yield corn,
Corn that in autumn and winter nourishes livestock.
Livestock, the meat carcasses whose meat feed the lover and her
family.
Who feeds the people of Saigon?
Who comforts the breasts of mothers made empty by the loss of
men--
--breasts mourning for sons and grandsons
husbands and brothers, nephews, and uncles.

130

The stench of their rotting corpses stretches across the seas and
turns us ill.
Res ipsa loquitur...
My Beloved lives in the rice fields,
his soul laid to rest with mercy and grace,
his body eaten in service of his duty,
by those who hunger in Saigon.

Over coffee and cherry pie, Robert MacIntosh pointed out the places where the lines of Florina's poems diverged from the path established in the opening lines.

"As with fiction, and particularly short stories, the first lines of a poem tell the reader what to expect in both form and substance, structure and content. We lose the reader's attention when we veer away from the pattern establish in those opening lines." The intensity with which he had offered previous suggestions had returned. He handed her several papers.

"You'll see what I mean in notes I wrote in the margins."

Red marks lined the pages on which Florina had written several poems. "Do you examine the poems of all your students with such detail?" Florina asked as she flipped through the pages containing *Transubstantiation*, its revision, and other poems she had written.

"Not all of my students display as much talent and depth. Nor do they write poems that grip and hold my attention like yours have."

"*It takes a breadth of soul ... and a heart that's been broken to write poetry,*" said the English professor whose class Florina now attended Tuesday and Thursday mornings and with whom she met for lunch afterwards. "Life has shattered the hearts of many. Yet very few of us will write poetry. And of those who do, even fewer will put words on paper that lend hope, and resurrect our dreams."

Florina clutched the papers on which she had written her poems. Her heart pounded, tears knocking at its door.

Chapter 14

Almost three weeks into attending Johnson C. Smith in Charlotte, Florina sat at the dining room table, textbooks on 17th Century British poetry and Greek mythology spread before her.

The ironing board in front of her, Willa Mae spread out one of Redmond's shirts and lifted the iron. She said, "Dr. Redmond's offer couldn't have come at a better time."

"The timing was good for both of us," Florina agreed.

"Ole' Mr. Johnson at the factory been lettin' go of people," Willa Mae said as she moved the hot iron across the shirt, wrinkles disappearing into the steam. "What he don't lay off, he makes to work part-time. I don't like the man no way. But I need the money." She hung the first of Redmond's ironed shirts, attached the metal hanger to the top edge of the door and placed another shirt on the ironing board.

Barely months older than Florina, Willa Mae patted her stomach, just beginning to bulge. "Dr. Elder say the baby should come in late May, early June."

Willa Mae went onto add, "Mama and I are already planning for how she'll take over here when I have the baby."

"Don't worry about that," Florina said. "Redmond and I will manage just fine."

"Dr. Redmond says you'll be returning to college for your last semester and graduation. He's so excited about you going back and getting your degree."

"I'm lucky to have the college nearby, more than a little shocked they accepted me so quickly," said Florina. The decision had come fast. Meeting Robert MacIntosh had renewed Florina's faith and infused her with enthusiasm about life. MacIntosh's presence and verve for poetry catalyzed her creativity and imagination. She now carried a notebook with her at all times, and would fall asleep, after making love to Redmond, thinking of how to reword and modify the structures of stanzas in her poems. His passion released during their intimacies stimulated her imagination and desire to write, something Florina had not experienced since Ennis died.

The image of Agnes caressing Redmond's cheek along with memories of Ennis and regret lost steam, as always, in the presence of Redmond's passion and the wake of their intimacies.

Willa Mae again looked to the small bulge of her stomach, spoke of her husband, a private in the Army. "I was so happy to see him." Willa Mae surmised she had conceived her second child during her husband, Thomas' ten days at home from Vietnam.

What seemed regret for having conceived a second child underscored the lilting sweetness in her voice. "Thomas' pay from the Army is good, but with another mouth to feed."

Florina turned to Willa Mae, same age as Florina. "Don't worry. I have no intention of hiring someone in your place.

"Thank you, ma'am. I like working for you and Dr. Redmond," said Willa Mae

"And you've been a lifesaver," Florina said. Thrilled that she had returned to college, and to Redmond pleasure, Florina, taken with Willa Mae's soft demeanor, had engaged her to come every day.

Willa Mae placed another of Redmond's shirts she had ironed on a hanger. Holding her stomach, the young woman bent over and lifted a pillowcase from the basket of freshly washed laundry that had dried on the line out back. "My mother says if it's a boy...I should name him *Redmond*. I like the name too. Then again I wouldn't want to disrespect Dr. Redmond. I'm not sure that any child of ours will ever grow up to be as successful a person as Dr. Redmond or his father, Dr. Hammond."

"Your son or daughter can become anything he or she sets their mind to," said Florina. "And should your baby be a boy, both Redmond and I would be honored to have him child bear Redmond's name."

"I think it's a horrible idea." The words rose from the front room, followed by the sound of heels. Agnes appeared in the doorway of the dining room.

"When did ... How did you ... get in?" Florina stood. Willa Mae ceased ironing.

"Don't stop on account of me." Agnes waved her hand at Willa Mae. "Everyone knows you have a penchant for shirking your duties. That's probably the reason Mr. Johnson let you go."

Willa Mae lowered her head, was about to let the white shirt burn. On seeing a gust of steam rise, Willa Mae lifted the iron. "Oh, no." The young, pregnant woman sat the iron down, and lifted the shirt, revealing a scorch mark.

"Don't worry about it." Florina's sadness for Willa Mae's hurt and concern turned to anger. She instructed Agnes. "Come with me to the kitchen." Once there, she closed the door. "You can't speak to Willa Mae that way."

"I just did."

"Don't do it again. I don't like it. And neither will Redmond."

"My, my." Agnes flashed a sly grin. "Returning to college has given you a bit of grit."

"No more than I already had."

Agnes set her hands upon her hips and strutted past Florina towards the sink. "So how are classes going?" She filled the kettle with water, set it on the range, struck a match and lit the fire bringing it to boil.

"They're going well."

Agnes opened the cupboard above the faucet, and lifted out two cups and saucers.   Florina grew perturbed with Agnes overtaking the kitchen, and appearing more interested in preparing tea than hearing Florina's response about school. It was as if Agnes knew the layout, had previously lived in the space Florina now occupied.

The effects of Redmond's passion drained away.

"I laud you for going back. It must be hard, excruciating." Agnes lowered the two cups and saucers upon the table. "How many years has it been since you quit?"

"It's good to be back. And I didn't quit."

Agnes whipped around. "Two years is a long time to stay out of school and have no direction."

Florina walked to the stove, turned the knob and killed the flame. "I have to finish studying." She turned to Agnes. *How did she get in?* Florina wondered. *Redmond had Mr. Phillips change the locks.*

How did she know Florina had been out of school for nearly two years. Or was it just a guess?

"You'll want to watch that Willa Mae," said Agnes. "Don't say I didn't warn you." She started for the doorway leading from the kitchen.

"You may disrespect your father and mother, even your husband, but I don't allow such talk in my home."

"She's a maid, a domestic." Agnes whipped around. "Or as the whites like to call them, *the help*."

"I'm not white. And neither are you."

Agnes knit her eyebrows, "But we sure could pass," hit Florina with a hard stare.

"Perhaps *you* would do such a thing. But, I have no intention," said Florina.

"But you could." Agnes drew close. "Come on. Don't tell me the idea hasn't crossed your mind just once, probably more than once. There has to be at least one white person who's assumed you one of them. Keep your mouth shut, and no one's the wiser."

"Except when they see me with my parents."

136

"Which one?" As if a white person herself, Agnes inspected the back of Florina's hand.

"Both."

Agnes' eyes registered shock.

"My mother," said Florina.

"What does she look like?"

"Redmond."

"Your mother is as dark as Redmond?"

"Don't use that word. I don't like it." Florina grew angry. "And don't feign surprise. We Negroes come in all colors and hues."

"Which word is it you don't like 'dark' or 'Redmond?'"

Florina's eyes burned as she took in Agnes' stare.

Florina returned to the dining room where Willa Mae was still ironing. After assuring her that Redmond would hold no grudges, nor fire her for having scorched his shirt, she attempted studying. Yet images of Agnes' face contorted in anger would not fade.

What does she want? Florina blurted within. She seemed so ubiquitous and all-knowing. *Agnes.* Realizing she had broken her pencil she excused herself from Willa Mae, went to the bedroom, and closed the door. Florina opened the drawer to her bedside table, lifted out and opened her journal. She sat upon the bed and began to write.

My love is alive; a secret threatens it.
My love is alive; a lie it enfolds.
My love is alive; my truth has no hold.
My love is alive; its roots form a pit.
Each day sadness brings; my love is alive.
Each day I greet arrives like an age
Time eternal moving slowly, I its hostage.
My love is alive. How will I survive?

My secret lives. As does another lie.
My love holds a secret. I want to know.
I want to break it open, land it a blow.
My love is keeping secrets from me. Why?
Is it for this love that lives and grows so ...
Or its secret that I live, or will Die?

Memories of Ennis returned along with questions and concerns of Redmond's gaze filled with yearning.

Florina laid her pen upon the table. *What keeps Agnes coming back to this house, my and Redmond's home? What lives between her and Redmond?*

She closed the journal, placed it in the drawer and pushed the drawer closed.

Chapter 15

During dinner that night Florina said nothing to Redmond of Agnes' visit. When Redmond approached in bed hours later she surrendered herself despite the nagging questions about his and Agnes' relationship, or at least the illusion of one if none really existed.

Florina longed for the anesthesia of Redmond's passion. It numbed her to worried about Agnes, dulled the sharp pain of recalling times with Ennis. Florina had never doubted his love, or commitment. But Redmond had a way with his hands. During the ensuing days Florina concluded one existed, or at the very least had lived, and perhaps thrived. The lingering aroma remained much too pungent.

Agnes and Macon were absent from services at St. Andrew's the following Sunday. Bursting with curiosity, Florina heard no congregants mention, or question their whereabouts. During the drive home she asked Redmond, "Did anyone happen to say where Agnes and Macon were?"

"No." Redmond turned to her. "I thought you might know."

"I haven't seen Agnes in days."

"Oh?" Redmond appeared dumbfounded. "She said nothing of them going away?"

Florina shook her head, recoiled within from memories of Agnes unleashing her anger days earlier. "Has Macon not been in his office seeing patients?"

"I don't know." Redmond shook his head. "Now that you mention it, Father said he saw him Friday over at Charlotte Negro Hospital."

"Maybe they went away for the weekend."

That would be nice. Florina commented within. *Agnes giving attention to her husband.*

"I doubt that," Redmond said. He has five patients in the hospital. If Macon and Agnes have gone away, Macon would have asked me or my Father to look in on his patients."

The two continued home, Redmond driving, and Florina's mind digging further on possibly reasons for their neighbors' absence.

It was Wednesday afternoon, three days later that Florina was signing for groceries from his parents', the Elder's, store that Macon left the sidewalk and joined her and the deliveryman.

"Hello, Horace," Macon shook hands with the deliveryman. "How's that new son of yours?"

"Growing fat and raising hell at night." Horace smiled. "Other than that I can't complain."

"A screaming baby is usually a healthy one," Macon said. "But still you might want to have the doctor look at him."

Florina looked on with interest.

"Well, Dr. Hammond said he was fine. Just a little fussy." Horace's eyes brightened. "He even had Dr. Redmond to look at him. He's a surgeon, you know. Like his daddy, he said Jonah was fine."

"I'm sure if Dr. Redmond gave his seal of approval your son is fine." Macon appeared somewhat disappointed though his words held energy.

Florina extended Horace the signed receipt. "Thank you, Horace."

"You're quite welcome, Miss Florina."

And here's my list for next week." Florina handed him a second slip of paper. "Same time next Wednesday."

"Yes, ma'am." Horace tipped his cap, walked past Macon and headed down the steps.

"My parents appreciate your business," Macon said. "As do I."

"They sell quality products at a competitive price," Florina said. "Never mind the service." She looked into the direction of Horace heading down the street in his truck.

"Agnes wouldn't disagree with yo--" Macon halted.

"So what brings you by?" Florina forced herself to look at Macon. Curiosity lingered about Macon and Agnes' absence from church but she hadn't considered a visit from Macon might deliver an answer.

"When was the last time you spoke with Agnes?" Macon asked.

"Last Wednesday. Is she okay?"

Confusion and frustration spread across Macon's clean-shaven, and maple-colored face. ""I wouldn't know since I haven't seen her since last Wednesday morning when had breakfast and ..."

Florina gasped despite herself. "Please come inside." She walked through the doorway and led Macon back to the kitchen where she offered him tea.

He lowered himself onto a chair at the table.

When the water was hot Florina poured two cups and joined him. "Do you have any idea where she could be?"

Macon shook his head as he sipped his tea. He lowered the cup onto the table. "Has Redmond said anything?"

"No."

"I don't mean to be rude, but they are friends."

"Have been for quite some time," Macon said.

Florina returned to the sink.

"What kind of friends?" She spoke back to Macon.

141

"They met each other when Redmond was a first year intern at Howard Hospital. I was in my third year of residency," Macon said. "I'm surprised Redmond didn't tell you."

"Why should he?" Florina gripped the edge of the porcelain sink.

"I told Agnes all my secrets, at least the ones I was aware of, before we married."

"How can you not be aware of secrets?" Florina turned around.

"Sometimes we don't want to believe things about ourselves. I'm convinced it's those things we keep hidden not just from others, but from ourselves that cause the most damage."

"So you think Redmond doesn't want to believe something about him and Agnes?" Florina retorted.

"Agnes dated Redmond before she met me." Macon spoke what Redmond had said.

Florina considered Ennis and her marriage to him, which she had kept secret from her parents. And Redmond.

"How did she come to marry *you* Agnes?" Florina asked.

"I fell in love with her. The same I as suppose you fell in love with Redmond."

"You speak as if you know me," Florina said.

"I think we have a similar course and cause."

"I love Redmond."

"As I do Agnes."

"Redmond is my husband." Florina said.

Memories came alive. Her body grew warm in recalling the intense undulations that shook her body when Redmond made love to her.

"As Agnes is *my* wife," Macon said. He looked towards the window.

"And yet sometimes one would be hard pressed to see that when they look at ... " The front door opened and closed. Footsteps trailed back to the kitchen, Redmond arriving at the kitchen doorway. Macon stood. "Florina invited me for tea." Macon's pinky finger trembled.

Redmond walked to Florina and touching the top of her head, kissed her cheek.

"Dinner's almost ready," Florina removed the chicken from the oven.

"We missed you and Agnes at church on Sunday," Redmond said to Macon.

"She's gone." Macon said. "Agnes left sometime left Wednesday. After we had breakfast. I came home that night. The lights were off. I thought she might have been over here with you two. Then I looked through my window and saw the both of you eating."

"Why didn't you come over and say something?" Redmond said with what seemed restraint amid concern.

Macon stood and pocketed his hands, ambled towards the doorway.

Florina placed the platter of chicken on the table.

Redmond stood. "Have you called Reverend Julius?" Restraint in Redmond's voice gave way to obvious anxiety.

Macon turned back. "You'll let me know if she contacts you." He aimed his words at Redmond.

"Of course," Redmond assured.

"I'll call you if we hear anything," Florina added, approaching Macon to say good night.

Macon's tan eyes softened as did his words. "I'll see myself out."

_____

During dinner Florina asked Redmond, "How long have you known Agnes?"

"Why do you ask?" He returned his glass of iced tea to its spot on the table by his plate.

"Macon said you two dated."

A mist of disappointment clouded Redmond's face. He looked past Florina to the refrigerator then eyes retreating he regained his focus. "I told you that."

"Why didn't you marry her?"

143

"I married you."

"But you knew her before me."

"Why are we talking about this?" Redmond flashed a stern gaze. "So that's what his having tea with you was all about?" Redmond grasped the back of his chair. "Macon illuminating you on my life before meeting you."

"Macon arrived when Horace was delivering groceries. When he said Agnes was gone. I invited him in."

"What for? She's his wife, not yours?"

Florina frowned.

"I'm sorry. I didn't mean it like that."

"Like what?" Confusion mounted in Florina.

Redmond rubbed his forehead. "Macon and Agnes don't have the easiest of marriages." He twisted his face as if the words pained him. "Poinsettia is nothing like Baltimore, not to speak of Washington, D.C."

"That's where you met Agnes?" Florina interjected. "Washington. When you were an intern."

Again Redmond's gaze took on a cold hardness as he sat. "I was an intern, my first year of residency and on my way inside to work. Agnes was outside in front of the hospital, Howard University Hospital, handing out fliers for a civil rights rally. "He leaned back, Once again his eyes retreated. "Agnes has always been involved in one kind of protest or the other. Always fighting ... for this cause or that cause." He sighed. " First it was equality for Negroes. Then she wanted to end the war in Vietnam. I suppose with a father like Reverend Julius, who wouldn't protest?" Redmond's description mirrored, substantiated, what Cynthia Cartwright Edelstein had said.

And yet Florina fought to reconcile these aspects of Agnes with the person Florina had come to know, the person who held judgments about Redmond having married Florina who had not graduated college, and who had criticized and berated Florina for now returning to complete her last year.

Florina considered how vehemently Agnes had refused to speak to her father on New Year's Eve. That Agnes' father was a minister drew even more curiosity. "What's he like, her father?" Florina asked, then "Cynthia said he's pretty strict."

144

"The Right Reverend Julius Kensington of St. Peter's A.M. E. Church, Richmond Circle, Baltimore, Maryland." Redmond again pronounced the name with *gravitas*. His gaze retreated. He leaned against the back of his chair and crossed his legs. "I don't think I've seen a more obstinate man, or person, for that matter." He gave a bittersweet laugh. His eyes ran sad. "I suppose God asks different people to carry His word. I just never understood how Julius Kensington's words were supposed to draw anyone to God."

"How does he maintain a congregation?" Florina asked. "Or is the church dying?"

"Quite the opposite." Redmond's eyes twinkled with remembrance. "But people don't join St. Peter's congregation for comfort. You're invited only if current members deem you qualified."

"So he doesn't extend membership to congregants after each service?" Florina was mortified, disgusted.

"Gaining membership is not the challenge. Getting inside the church--now that's another matter," Redmond explained. "If you don't accompany a current member or you are unrecognizable, the ushers will stare you down, their eyes demanding, 'Why are you here? Who are you?' And if you persist in going inside, few congregants, if any, will greet and welcome you."

"But that's ungodly, not Christ-like."

"It is."

Silence passed between Florina and her new husband, she mulling over all that he had shared. "Do you love her?" she asked Redmond of Agnes.

He sat upright. Fierce determination filled his eyes. "You're the person I want to spend the rest of my life with. I love you."

Redmond's words exuded a truth and comfort Florina could not deny. And yet if given the opportunity to resume her life with Ennis, should life revive him from the dead, Florina realized she could not say the same to Redmond. Intimacies she had shared with Redmond outstripped anything she had experienced with Ennis. And she knew his words to be true and

145

right. Yet the presence of Agnes in their lives cast a shadow, one that in the midst of rendering Redmond in a disingenuous light, forced Florina to confront her own dishonesty.

The question hung in her mind, "*How much did the secret concerning her previous marriage to Ennis predispose her to suspicions about Redmond?*"

Chapter 16

Florina was gathering her books the following day when Robert MacIntosh approached her at the close of his poetry class. "Our department chair has cancelled this week's faculty meeting. I'm free for two hours. Would you like to discuss some of your work?"

Shocked on hearing his voice, so submerged in thoughts about her discussion with Redmond the previous evening, Florina turned around, and lifted her head to hear her professor. Lean and tall, like Redmond, MacIntosh towered over her, even when she stood.

"I hope I didn't frighten you," he said. His eyes glistened. "We poets tend to live in our heads."

Florina considered the poem she had written last week following Agnes' surprise entry.

My love is alive; a secret threatens it. ...

MacIntosh said, "You shared little in class today."

"I was tired."

"Life for newlyweds can be that way." He nodded.

Florina and Redmond had been married exactly one month that day. "I should be going. I need to prepare dinner."

147

"Are you all right? Everything okay with you and Redmond?"

"We're fine." Florina spoke with a sense of forced belief.

"I hope to see you next week. Don't forget our weekly meeting next Tuesday after class."

"I'll have something for you then," Florina promised as she turned to leave for home.

The weekend came and went with no sign of Agnes.

Florina entered St. Stephen's sanctuary on Sunday morning to find Macon sitting alone on the second pew from the front. The vulnerability that sat upon his shoulders, enshrouded him, tore at Florina's heart. Tears dropped from her eyes during the communal prayer following the sermon.

On Reverend Mitchell pronouncing the benediction, Redmond grasped her hand and said, "Let's go." Offering a wave to his father then speaking with two of the church trustees, Redmond gave his mother and grandmother quick kisses on the cheek. As they did Redmond announced, "We have to get home. Florina has to study."

Carolyn patted Florina on the back as she followed Redmond down the aisle to the side door where they exited as others stood in line to exchange greetings with Reverend Mitchell at the front.

Florina and Redmond ate dinner that night in relative silence as they had the previous evening, speaking only of trivialities such as the weather and various patients he had and was attending. They said nothing of Agnes nor Macon.

Though having expressed to Macon concern for Agnes' absence, Redmond had maintained a cool distance. Florina had come to wonder whether her reprimanding Agnes had contributed to her leaving.

Come Tuesday, Florina grew anxious as Robert MacIntosh brought class to a close. Having written nothing else, she had only the poem written two weeks earlier in the heat of anger following her last encounter with Agnes.

Florina and MacIntosh began their usual trek across the main yard towards his house on the east side of campus.

"I've prepared cheese cake for dessert today," MacIntosh said.

The bounce in his step drew Florina's attention. "You look forward to our meetings," she said.

"At least as much as I would hope you do."

"I do," Florina said. And yet she knew not what to make of his interest in her work.

On reaching his house MacIntosh pushed open the door and Florina entered.

After eating their soup and salads, both of which he had prepared, he sat the cheese cake before her and offered her a knife. "I'm going to let you cut this."

Florina turned to him in surprise.

"This is my mother-in-law's recipe. My wife valued it over all the others she received."

Florina felt both sad and honored. Carefully she pulled the knife down through the dessert, placed one slice on the small plate, then a second slice on the other.

"How did she die?"

"Cancer. We don't know where it started. By the time the doctor diagnosed her she had only months to live."

"Were you living here in Charlotte?"

MacIntosh nodded. "She was a patient at Charlotte Negro Hospital. Carolyn and Hammond were very supportive. So was Redmond. He was in his last year of surgical training, translated what Ingrid's doctor said, explained everything that was going on. I was a mess." MacIntosh shook his head and lowered his plate onto the coffee table in front of them. "It's been nice having someone to share your poetry with me, and I can offer what little knowledge I've gained."

"You know a lot," Florina said.

"About poetry or life?"

"Both."

MacIntosh slipped on his wire-rimmed glasses. "On that note," he said, "How about showing me what you've written?"

Amid waning anxiety Florina removed the journal from her purse, opened it and began to read.

My love is alive; a secret threatens it.
My love is alive; a lie it enfolds.
My love is alive; my truth has no hold.
My love is alive; its roots form a pit.
Each day sadness brings; my love is alive.
Each day that I greet; arrives like an age
Time eternal that moves slowly, I its hostage.
My love is alive. How will I survive?
My secret lives. As does another lie.
My love holds a secret. I want to know.
I want to open it, land it a blow.
My love is secreting a truth. Why?
Does he hold love for another also?
Will this secret make me live, or Die?

MacIntosh leaned back upon the sofa, and looked to the window across the room.

Worry flaring back, Florina placed her journal upon the coffee table and stood. "I'll take these back to the kitchen."

"Please sit down." MacIntosh patted the sofa cushion.

Florina lowered herself back onto the seat.

"This poem reveals the brutality of despair," MacIntosh said. He glanced down at her purse and then turning to the

150

coffee table, he said of her journal, "It has become your constant companion."

Florina lowered her gaze.

"Nothing to be ashamed of," MacIntosh said. "It's what we do--voice the soul's utterances not yet spoken--longings, fears, *regrets*. As for secrets," he continued, "They bind the soul in ways that not even Christ can liberate us."

Florina blanched.

"You disagree?" asked MacIntosh.

"I don't like secrets. But sharing certain things would hurt the ones you love, even destroy them."

"Only the unwillingness to let go of dogmatic beliefs-- blind faith in that which has never existed except in the illusion of our mind--can destroy," said MacIntosh. "And it is not us, or our bodies that it kills, rather our self-deception, the lies we have told ourselves."

Florina's face grew hot. She wanted to run and hide.

MacIntosh lifted her journal from the coffee table and read aloud.

Each day that I greet; arrives like an age, an epoch

Time eternal that moves slowly, I its hostage.
He paused, then ...
My love is alive. How will I survive?
My secret lives. As does another lie.

Again, he paused. Florina absorbed the stark truth of her words.

My love holds a secret. I want to know.
I want to open it, land it a blow.
...
My love is secreting a truth. Why?
Does he hold love for another also?
Will this secret cause me to live, or Die?

151

"The narrator's not questioning the secret as much as doubting the fidelity of the person she loves."

Florina cleared away the dessert dishes in silence, MacIntosh helping her. On their return to the living room she said, "You said you met Agnes Macon briefly. When?"

"I first saw her about three years ago. When she accompanied Redmond and Macon home for Easter," MacIntosh revealed having seen Agnes more than once. He said, "Redmond and Macon were still training in Washington."

"Which one was she dating?"

"I don't know that she was dating either one at the time," said MacIntosh. He sat his cup of tea and saucer on the coffee table. "Is she giving you problems?"

"What kind of problems might she give me?"

"The usual kind. *Jealousy, envy, mischief, anger stifled-- misdirected.*"

"You speak as if you came to know her very well during these *brief* occasions," Florina said.

"As a writer you develop the ability to assess character very quickly. He clasped his hands, interwove his fingers. "Poems, like stories, contain plot. And plot flows out of character."

Florina gazed upon her journal lying open upon the coffee table. "How did you come to know Carolyn?"

"Nineteen thirty-six," MacIntosh said unfazed. He lifted the pot and refilled their cups with tea. As if he had been expecting the question, almost welcoming it, he said, "Carolyn's father, Dr. Whitworth, was chairman of the English Department at Howard. I entered the university two units shy of being a sophomore. Dr. Whitworth liked my writing, took a special interest in me. He's the reason I remained there and earned my Ph.D. in Comparative Literature."

Florina was amazed. "Carolyn's never said anything about her father, nor has Redmond about his grandfather."

"Redmond bears his paternal grandfather's Christian name and his maternal grandfather's surname. That along with his father having graduated Howard Medical School, made

Redmond well-received at both the university and the medical school."

"*Redmond Whitworth Austin,*" Florina recited her husband's full name.

"He keeps Dr. Whitworth's memory alive."

"When did Dr. Whitworth die?"

"In 1944, just after I received my Ph. D.,"' MacIntosh said.

"I'm surprised he didn't invite you to remain there and teach."

"He did. I chose instead to join the Navy," MacIntosh spoke in a regretful tone. "My way of avoiding the draft and being shipped off to Europe."

"Most Negro men were excited at the possibility of going to Europe," Florina said.

"And with my interest in poetry it would have made sense. Enlistment sent me back home to Oakland in California. I was station at Port Chicago in Richmond."

"Where you saw war of another kind. What brought you to Howard?"

"I came on a lark. During my last year of junior college. *Esquire Magazine* had just published Langston Hughes' poem, "*Let America Be America Again.*" I heard that Hughes was to read at Howard," said MacIntosh. "I rescheduled my finals and left as soon as could for Washington. Seeing Langston Hughes speak, hearing him read that poem ... it let me know it was okay for me to be a writer, a poet. I wasn't crazy, or less than a man."

The professor explained. "Dr. Whitmore hosted a reception at his house for Hughes afterwards and I went hoping to speak with him."

"Did you?"

"I stayed up all night talking with Langston Hughes. He told me how he came to write the poem, how he came to writing. His mother's mother, Langston's maternal grandmother was his inspiration."

MacIntosh recited the first line with gravitas.

Let America be America again.

Let it be the dream it used to be.
Let it be the pioneer on the plain
Seeking a home where he himself is free.
(America never was America to me.)

MacIntosh gaze retreated. He nodded. "He was wonderful. Langston left around midnight. I was heading out when Dr. Whitmore introduced himself, asked where I was from. We kept talking. By dawn he'd persuaded me to enroll at Howard."

"Carolyn was already married to Hammond then in medical school."

Florina sipped more tea as MacIntosh continued. "I began the fall semester with Dr. Whitmore having me over for dinner nearly every night, first to discuss what classes I should take, and then he mentoring my writing. He was a widower," MacIntosh explained of Redmond's maternal grandfather. "Carolyn's mother had died in childbirth. Dr. Whitmore's younger sister raised Carolyn. When Carolyn entered college her aunt married and moved to New York. With Hammond in medical school and studying at the library Carolyn was often over at Dr. Whitmore's. She was close with her father. And he valued her opinion"

"Did you and Carolyn ever take any classes together?" Florina asked.

"We were both sophomores. And English majors."

Florina thought of her and Ennis, how she had met him in her sophomore English class.

MacIntosh said, "With Carolyn's father's help I was able to graduate the spring of '38 with her."

Florina's thoughts returned to Agnes as she drank more of her tea and considered all MacIntosh had shared. "Redmond told me that Agnes' father is the minister at a church in Baltimore."

"St. Peter's African Methodist Episcopal in Richmond Circle," MacIntosh chimed.

"You know of it?"

"Carolyn and I accompanied Macon to his and Agnes' wedding back in April," said MacIntosh.

"The fourth of April."

"Agnes was less than happy." MacIntosh confirmed what Agnes had said during the New Year's Eve party. "She had been invited to hear Dr. King speak at Riverside Church in New York."

"But the bride chooses her wedding day."

"Reverend Julius chose Agnes'," MacIntosh said. "He also performed the ceremony. Carolyn and I stood in for Macon's parents who could not attend."

"Carolyn said the Elders couldn't find anyone to mind the store."

"They weren't invited," MacIntosh said. "Compliments of Reverend Julius."

"How could a minister do that? And why would Macon want to be a part of Agnes' family with them acting that way?"

"We humans do a lot to fit in, hold a lot of secrets to gain membership into the *right* groups," said MacIntosh.

Florina absorbed the English professor's words. "Was Redmond there?"

"He was to serve as best man, but was held up at the hospital. I took Redmond's place."

Florina looked towards the window across the room. *Could Redmond have been jealous of Macon marrying Agnes? But why did Agnes not marry Redmond? She clearly held him in high regard and carried deep feelings for him. And how could Reverend Julius not approve of him?*

MacIntosh had drunk the last of the tea when she asked, "When did you move here to Charlotte?"

"Nineteen fifty-four, nine years following Germany and Japan's surrender."

"And a decade following the Port Chicago explosion," added Florina.

MacIntosh's gaze retreated as he focused on Florina. A knowing passed between them. "Redmond was sixteen. I hadn't seen him since he was christened." He drank more of his tea. "As godfather to Redmond, I am partial. Agnes Kensington

155

Macon can be very difficult. Redmond is a good person. He's not perfect. He tries to do the right thing. He's the best son any man could ever wish for. *Or have.*"

•.•.•.•.•.•.•.•.•.•

<u>Chapter 17</u>

•.•.•.•.•.•.•.•.•.•

Florina did not know what to make of her conversation with Robert MacIntosh. It had been good to learn of how he came to love and teach poetry and the roots of his incentive to mentor her. Yet learning that Carolyn had been the daughter of Robert MacIntosh's mentor, whom MacIntosh clearly held in awe, incited many queries concerning the familiar way between them. For that matter, MacIntosh, not unlike Agnes, saw Redmond as a person with integrity of intent, if not actions.

Florina found it difficult to see how anyone could consider loving or coveting another man's wife as right.

"*He's not perfect,*" MacIntosh has aid of Redmond. His deeming Redmond the ideal son, in light of Redmond's grandfather having mentored MacIntosh stirred questions on another level regarding how MacIntosh truly felt towards Redmond's mother, Carolyn.

That night at dinner Florina broke the thread of suffocating silence separating and binding her and Redmond since Agnes' disappearance. Redmond had been cutting into his trout when she joined him at the dinner table and said, "I had no idea that your mother and Robert MacIntosh graduated Howard the same year."

Redmond ate a slice of trout then lifted the bowl of Brussels sprouts and scooped some onto his plate.

"He tells me that your mother's father, your grandfather, Dr. Whitmore was his mentor."

"I suppose as MacIntosh is mentoring you." Redmond again cut off a slice of trout.

Florina ate some of her Brussels sprouts, then said, "I'd like to read some of your grandfather's poetry. Professor MacIntosh says that your grandfather was a well-respected professor of English at Howard, chairman of the department, that you bear his name."

"I supposed he also told you that while my father was studying at the library with his friends," Redmond's words were both metered and biting, "He and my mother read poetry at my grandfather Whitmore's home."

Unwilling to pursue the tension-filled topic Florina chewed long and hard on her Brussels sprouts then said, "It was nice of your mother and Professor MacIntosh to stand in for Macon's parents when they were unable to attend Macon's wedding."

"I thought Robert MacIntosh was mentoring you in writing poetry, not giving you a backdrop of my life prior to our marriage," said Redmond.

"We were talking about Agnes and Macon."

"So now he's peering into our marriage."

"My life, what happens here with us, influences my writing," Florina said.

As if it were a scalpel, Redmond placed his fork on the edge of his plate. "Did you tell him that Agnes was missing?"

"Would it matter if I did?"

"I'm asking you," said Redmond.

Florina held a burning need to understand the nature of her mother-in-law's connection with Robert MacIntosh.

Carolyn Austin had swiftly introduced Florina to the English professor when she had announced her desire to return

158

to college. Upon their meeting, Robert MacIntosh had practically adopted Florina as his mentee.

Pursuing what lay beneath the surface of Carolyn and Robert MacIntosh's interactions had provided a map assisting Florina to decipher the elusive intricacies tying her and Redmond's marriage to Agnes and Macon's.

Redmond's anger towards MacIntosh's discussion of his life, as with Macon, opened a new door of curiosities. Uncertain of the root of his anger, Florina now felt that learning more about Carolyn and Robert MacIntosh would offer answers to questions about Redmond.

Florina placed her napkin on her lap. "Professor MacIntosh said you were supposed to serve as best man for Macon and his and Agnes' wedding. Professor MacIntosh stood in when you didn't show up."

"I was needed at the hospital for emergency surgery. I warned Macon that might happen," Redmond said.

You couldn't get time off?"

Redmond observed his fork teetering on the edge of his place. "Macon didn't want his parents to attend his wedding."

Florina recalled Robert MacIntosh's explanation, *"They weren't invited."* ached at the truth of his words. *"The lengths we go to fit in and belong."*

Redmond said, "I didn't like what Macon was doing."

"Macon's parents weren't going there to join St. Peter's," Florina said. "They would be witnessing their his wedding,"

Florina grew even more frustrated, said, "The Elders are hardworking people. They own a business, employ people like Horace and others to deliver groceries, never mind they're the only Negro-owned grocery in town."

"Don't you get it?" Redmond hit the table. *People don't just show up for services at St. Peter's. You have to be invited.* "Reverend Julius could want Macon as his son-in-law, but absent Macon's parents."

Redmond stared at Florina as if to will her to digest and comprehend what he could not say.

159

Silence ensued, Florina retreating, while cleaning up the dishes, into a reverie of thoughts attempting to untangle the intricate history binding Redmond, and Macon with Agnes as the lynchpin.

Redmond went to the bedroom where Florina assumed he lay working on the crossword puzzle from Sunday's paper.

She had placed the last dish, washed and dried, into the cupboard and was headed for bed when loud and fast rapping resounded from the front door.

Florina entered the hall and followed Redmond into the living room. He opened the front door to a woman with alabaster skin and whitish blonde hair.

"She didn't say you'd be--" the woman said and raised her gloved hand to her lips.

"She, who?" Redmond asked.

"Mrs. Kensington," said the alabaster woman. She knit her blonde brows nearly invisible against her skin. Her blue eyes receded, as if she was delving into thought. With an elongated drawl, she said, "You must have been the baby's daddy. I supposed that's why she--"

"Where is Mrs. Kensington?" Redmond demanded.

"She's in the car," the woman pointed to the sedan on the street.

Opening the door wider Redmond pushed past the woman and stepped onto the verandah. Rushing down the steps, and he ran out to the car parked in front of the house.

The woman looked to Florina. "Are you the maid?"

"Are you speaking of Agnes when you say, Mrs. Kensington?" Florina asked perplexed and all the while aware.

"Then again, you must be her sister," the alabaster woman said to Florina.

"She's my wife," Redmond said stepping onto the verandah. Agnes lay limp in his arms, limp and her face as pale and lifeless as the alabaster woman.

"What are you doing?" said the alabaster woman to Redmond as he moved past her and entered the house. Appearing even more confused and distraught she followed him to the guest room.

Florina closed the door and followed the woman, her blue eyes scrutinizing Redmond's every step.

Redmond laid Agnes upon the bed. The scant evidence of life her face possessed drained from the cheeks of the alabaster woman, and widening the contrast between it and the red of the woman's Chanel suit when Redmond rolled back Agnes' crimson-stained dress.

"I say," the woman shouted from behind Redmond. "You shouldn't be doing this. We should call a doctor."

"If that were the case then why did Agnes, or as you say, Mrs. Kensington, have you bring her here?" said Redmond.

He spread apart Agnes' legs, placed his dark hands to Agnes' pale thighs. Blood flowed from her abdomen like the River Jordan having become the Red Sea. Florina grew mesmerized by the contrast in colors, light and dark, white and black encased in red, each defining and enlivening the other.

You shouldn't be doing this!" the alabaster woman urged again.

"I *am* a doctor, *her* doctor," Redmond declared. He examined Agnes' pelvis.

Florina blanched.

Redmond called to the alabaster woman behind him. "Where did she have the abortion?" In a mad scramble to find other signs of life he lifted Agnes' arm, examined her wrist. "What time?"

"This is against the law," said the alabaster woman.

"She's Negro." Redmond whipped around and said to the alabaster woman. "What time did she have the abortion! I need to kno--"

"Two-o-clock," Agnes murmured, her eyes closed.

The alabaster woman began to shake. Her hands twitched. She clutched her arms.

Redmond said to Florina, "Get me a blanket and some towels."

"This is not right," said the alabaster woman. Her long drawl irritated Florina despite the woman's obvious worry.

161

Wrapped in confusion she brought her gloved hands to her head. "She's my friend."

"You might want to think about that," Redmond said. He stood from Agnes and turned to the woman. "Unless there's anything else you want to tell me I think you'd better leave."

Florina accompanied the woman, encased in a stupor, to the living room and opened the front door.

The alabaster woman stepped outside then turned back. "That man back there with Agnes." The woman's blue eyes, dazed by truth, looked past Florina in the direction from where they had come. "Is it true what he said?" Her focus settled back upon Florina.

"Yes, he's a doctor."

The woman absorbed the words. "But Agnes." Again, the woman's gaze retreated, she appearing to search for an honesty that could ground her amid the turmoil still roaring within her. "I've known Agnes for nearly a year, ever since she moved here. I've taken her to our club, my mother's house." The alabaster woman shook her head, her face now whiter than anything Florina thought possible.

"Until six weeks ago we saw each other every week, lunched together over in Charlotte at the club," said the alabaster woman. The woman surveyed Florina's face, observed her arm.

Then as if grasping some remnant of what she had missed the alabaster woman turned, walked down the steps, and out to her black Cadillac sedan. Like Agnes, perched upon the first step beneath the veranda the day of Florina's arrival at the house, the woman had never asked Florina her name.

Chapter 18

Macon conceded with a nod to Redmond's decision that Agnes should, for the next few days, remain in bed there and not be moved home..

"Moving her might trigger the bleeding again," Redmond said. They were standing in the front room, Agnes asleep in their guest bedroom. "She should be home by Friday," Redmond explained. "In the meantime Father will take over her care. He'll let you know how she's doing."

"Leena can come here and see to Agnes," Florina said of the young girl who worked for Agnes. "Willa Mae and I will prepare *your* meals."

"That won't be necessary," said Macon.

"You need to eat," Florina urged.

"I'll eat at my parents'."

"Are you sure you want them to know what's happened? asked Redmond.

"Agnes has been gone for two weeks," said Macon. He glanced back at the front door now closed, then to Redmond. "The neighbors saw you bring her inside."

"It was dark and late," Redmond said. The wall clock read 1 am. "I doubt if anyone was up."

"Preparing your meals is the least we can do with Agnes being here," Florina said.

"Agnes'll be home by the weekend," Redmond reiterated.

Macon observed Redmond. To Florina he said, "I appreciate everything you're trying to do," then left.

An hour later Florina slipped into her nightgown as she and Redmond prepared for bed. "Macon's upset" Florina said.

"Most men would be on learning their wife nearly bled to death from a botched abortion."

"That's not the only reason he's angry," said Florina. She walked to Redmond undressing by the closet. "She came to *you*." Florina recalled Redmond's words to the woman with alabaster skin concerning Agnes. *I'm her doctor.*

"You couldn't expect her to go to Macon after aborting his child." Redmond shut the closet door.

"You told that white woman that you're Agnes' doctor." Florina went to her side of the bed, Redmond his.

"I was putting her in her place."

Florina was still fuming that the alabaster woman had neither introduced herself nor asked Florina her name. "Why would Agnes kill her child, Macon's child?" Florina's back was to Redmond. She lowered herself onto the bed.

"Every woman doesn't want children or to be a mother."

"You're not bothered by what she did," Florina said. She whipped around. "--think having an abortion is okay?"

"As a man, I *think* it's none of my business what a woman does with *her* body or chooses to do with what's growing *inside* her body."

"So you wouldn't mind if I aborted a child I was carrying--your child?"

"I'd hope we'd have a strong enough marriage and you'd love me enough to want our baby," said Redmond.

164

"So Agnes aborted their child because she doesn't love Macon?" Florina's cheeks grew hot.

"I don't know why Agnes had the abortion. What I want is for her to get better and out of my house. The quicker she mends, the sooner she can return home to her husband." Redmond spoke clear and clean. Yet the matter over which he and Florina debated held intricate riddle entangled by more questions than their discussion offered answers.

As Florina sensed in Macon, she, too, held concerns as to why Agnes had sought medical attention from Redmond. She pursued the question across the folds of her mind.

Then again, Florina thought, *to what other doctor could Agnes have gone? Who could she have trusted to keep that kind of secret?*

Agnes, like Florina, was new to Poinsettia. It was not their home.

I would have gone home had I needed an abortion, felt that desperate.

Yet Florina had never told her parents of Ennis, that she loved and had wanted to marry him, nor that he had died in Vietnam leaving her a widow. Florina had mourned in silence even when Ennis' presence no longer presented the threat of excommunicating Florina from her mother's love.

Agnes had been away two weeks, plenty of time to have home gone to her mother in Baltimore. Instead she had gone to the nameless woman, white as alabaster. Neither Redmond nor Robert MacIntosh had said anything of Agnes' mother when speaking resolutely of Reverend Kensington, a point that asserted volumes.

Florina went out and greeted Leena the next morning on seeing the young girl that was Agnes' housekeeper step onto the verandah to Agnes and Macon's house. "Agnes has returned from her trip," Florina said. But she's fallen ill,"

Leena stared as if unaffected.

165

"She'll be staying with us while Dr. Elder is seeing to patients," Florina explained. "Over the next few days I'll need you to come to my house and care for Agnes."

"Yes ma'am," Leena said, donning a disconcerting look as she nodded. She went with Florina. Inside she removed her coat. Florina led her back to the guest room. On Florina opening the door Leena looked to Agnes, and Agnes to Florina.

"I've explained to Leena that you returned from your trip not feeling well," Florina said to Agnes, "hat the next few days she'll be coming here and seeing to you."

Absent lipstick, Agnes' lips, and face, paler than usual betrayed a vulnerability Florina resisted acknowledging. "Thank you." She spoke weakly. Grateful for Florina's discretion, Agnes seemed sad, as if disappointed, that Florina had engaged Leena to care for her.

While Willa Mae saw to her regular duties of washing, ironing and preparing dinner, Leena came and went seeing to Agnes. At Florina's request, Leena remained with Agnes until the evening.

That night when Leena was preparing to leave, Florina said, "Dr. Elder will drive you home." Florina then asked, "How much does Agnes pay you?"

"Two dollars for the day," said the young girl. She put on her coat.

Florina handed her four dollars, then said, "Tomorrow, can you stay until 11 at night? I have classes until three in the afternoon, and in the evening I have to prepare dinner and see to Dr. Austin. It would be a help if you could remain with Agnes into the evening same as today. I'll pay you double like tonight. And again, Dr. Elder will drive you home."

Leena nodded in what seemed eagerness for the extra pay.

Dutifully she arrived the next day, and saw to Agnes' needs. Around 11 pm she came to Florina then putting the dinner dishes away, stating, "Miss Agnes is asleep. I'll be going next door for Dr. Elder to drive me home," at which time Florina again, paid Leena for her services.

Upon the Florina's return home the next afternoon she set about studying at the dining room table. Willa Mae, as usual, ironed the day's wash, the two of them discussing various events during Florina's breaks.

When making ready to leave that second evening Leena said to Florina as she saw her out, "Why you pay me each night?"

"Because you earned it and that's what I said I would do," Florina said. "When did you expect me to pay you?"

Leena stared at Florina as if searching for answers. "Miss Agnes pays me once a month."

"Did she pay you in January?" Florina asked. Agnes had been gone for two weeks. "No ma'am." Leena shook her head. It was then February 16th, 1968.

"I'll have the money she owes you tomorrow."

Again, Leena inspected Florina's face. "You look like Missy Agnes. She say you her friend. But you ain't nothin' like her."

Florina touched Leena's shoulder. They young girl left.

Friday came with Florina, much like Redmond, anticipating Agnes' transition home. Over the last three days, Hammond Austin, Redmond's father had come twice daily and examined Agnes, whereupon speaking with Redmond and then bidding Florina, '*Good-night,*' he walked next door and reported Agnes' progress of healing to Macon.

Upon exiting the guest room on Friday morning, Hammond said to Florina, then putting away the breakfast dishes, "I've told Agnes she can go home this afternoon. I'll call Macon once I've reached my office and tell him to come for her when he arrives home after work." He closed his bag that was sitting on the kitchen table. "Come this tonight you and Redmond should have no more problems."

Florina shut the cabinet door and accompanied her father-in-law, who with medical bag in hand proceeded out to the living room. "This has been quite a difficult matter," Hammond said. "One that many women could have never

167

handled with the grace and discretion you've displayed. I now know why Redmond was so eager to marry you."

"Agnes needed a place to heal," Florina said. She lifted her apron.

"But it didn't have to be in your home," Hammond said. "Everyone's been watching, from the moment Agnes disappeared two weeks ago. Despite the fact that it hasn't quelled the gossip, your allowing Agnes to recuperate here was a privilege. It says volumes about your character."

Hammond planted a fatherly kiss upon Florina's cheek. "Carolyn wants to have you and Redmond for Sunday dinner. As well Grandmother Austin wants to see you."

"That would be nice," Florina said. She opened the door and as Hammond descended the steps to his car Florina saw Willa Mae and Leena approaching.

Once inside the two women set about their tasks, Leena taking Agnes breakfast and coffee.

Florina went to her bedroom, opened her journal and began writing. With three sentences written, a knock rose from the door. Florina opened it to Leena.

"Missy Agnes would like to see you, ma'am."

Concerned that Agnes was not feeling well, Florina rushed to the guest room, a tailspin nipping at her heels as she neared the door to the guest room, and she fearful of the possibility that Agnes might not be able to go home that afternoon.

Florina pushed open the door and stepped inside. Agnes was sitting up in bed, pillows bolstering her back, a breakfast tray standing over her lap. Agnes gestured for Leena to leave. Leena went to the door and closed behind her.

"You must think me an evil person for aborting my child," Agnes spoke.

"It was your husband's child too," said Florina.

Agnes clasped her hands and set them upon the tray across her lap. "You don't know how lucky you are. And I'm not talking about your being married to Redmond--despite the fact I can't smoke in this house."

168

Florina drew closer. The tailspin within Agnes picked up speed as if a twister gathering steam to fuel the vacuum expanding and thriving at its center.

"You are a good person," Agnes said to Florina. "I envy Redmond."

Agnes' words rattled Florina. She wanted desperately to understand their meaning, yet to grasp that might thrust Florina into a place of no return, one that yielded no escape. "What do you want?" she asked Agnes.

"The same as everyone--a friend, strong and loyal, who will accept me as I am, and who will love me, perhaps more than I have loved myself."

"You have Macon?" Florina said.

"Macon loves who he thinks I am, what my father has promised him I would be," Agnes said. "I can't help Macon achieve the life he wants."

"Then why did you marry him?"

Anger bubbled within Florina, threatened to overtake her. "I wanted to escape," Agnes said. "But now I've created a bigger hole. A tighter prison."

"Why did you come back?"

"My mother sent me back."

Florina's heart sank. *"So you did go to Baltimore?"* Despite Florina's instincts she got closer to Agnes sitting in bed, pillows to her back and blankets covering her.

"I don't have anywhere to go," Agnes said. " You're my only friend." She looked to Florina.

Emptiness grasped Florina's chest, filling it with a hollowness, the depths of which she knew no comfort to assuage the sorrow that followed.

Chapter 19

Florina had been studying when Macon came mid-afternoon and took Agnes home. The care with which he assisted Agnes down the stairs and to the house next door Florina found touching. He did not return to work.

She was peeling potatoes when Redmond arrived an hour later. Like Macon, he too had left work early.

Seeing the guest room empty Redmond said, "Finally. That chapter's passed." He walked to the refrigerator and as usual lifted out a Coke.

"But what of the book?" Florina said. She dumped the potato peels into the rubbish can.

"It must have been difficult for you having Agnes here all that time." He popped the cap from the glass soda bottle, and drank some of the Coke.

"She really wasn't a bother," Florina said. She had now set the potatoes on the stove to boil. "Leena took care of her."

"Thank god for that," said Redmond. He sat to the table, opened the newspaper and began working the crossword puzzle.

The fish in the oven baking, Florina took to the table two plates with forks, knives and spoons for each. "As Agnes' doctor did you know she was going to have an abortion?" She

171

set the plates on the table. "Better yet, did you perform it?" Florina trod farther onto the rock terrain of Redmond's relationship with Agnes.

Redmond lowered his pencil onto the table.

Florina met his gaze. "I want to know."

"I could lose my license for that," Redmond said.

"Did you do it?"

"No. And I would never."

"You have no problems with women having abortions, but you wouldn't perform one, even if to protect your marriage?"

Redmond knitted his brows. "Yes and no," he said.

"How do you explain being Agnes' doctor but not knowing she's pregnant? In fact why didn't you tell me that you wer--"

"I wanted that white woman to shut up," Redmond stammered. "I'm no more Agnes' doctor than I would allow Macon to tend you."

"You examined her."

"I had to stop the bleeding. You were there. Along with Agnes' so-called friend."

"I think she truly likes Agnes."

"I wouldn't be so sure of that now that she knows Agnes is Negro," Redmond said.

"Agnes must have wanted her to know, intended on telling her at some point."

Again, Redmond frowned.

"She had the woman bring her here."

"She was bleeding and afraid," Redmond said.

"Since Agnes passes for white so well, she could have let the woman take her to Poinsettia General."

"That would have been too risky. Agnes is high strung, but she's not foolish. Undergoing an abortion is a crime. Never mind the doctors would have had to call her family. With her secret out no telling what would have happened to her and Macon. Whites would have been angry as hell, the Negro community would have felt betrayed. And that's not counting the abortion."

172

"Which secret?" asked Florina, "That she's black? Or her abortion?"

Redmond then said, "You may not believe this, but Agnes came here not simply for my help. She came because of you." His words stunned Florina. "You're her friend," he said.

Did Agnes interpret Florina's grace under pressure as friendship. *Worse still, did Redmond see it as weakness?* Agnes had said, *I had nowhere to go. You're the only one that I trust.* Florina said, "I don't like what I sense between you and Agnes. There's a history. And ... "

A knock arose at the front door.

Redmond return to the kitchen on seeing it was Leena.

"I'm sorry to bother you during dinner," Leena said when Florina invited her inside. "But I wanted to give you back your money." The young girl handed Florina six twenty-dollar bills. Miss Agnes paid me this afternoon as soon as Dr. Macon brought her home. Florina observed the bills. Leena said, "She paid me for January and the extra money you gave me for staying late these three days, plus two dollars for tip."

Florina recalled Redmond's words, "You've been kind to Agnes," and Agnes' confession, *"You're the only person that'll put up with me. I trust you."*

173

Chapter 20

Florina and Redmond attended Sunday services at St. Andrews.

Prior to Reverend Mitchell offering the benediction, Macon stood quiet, as the minister offered a special prayer for Agnes' quick recovery from emergency surgery.

The cover-up of Agnes' abortion pushed Florina further into a growing anger with both Redmond and herself, concerning her own secrets. Judgments Florina had erstwhile hurled towards Agnes, she now flung at herself. With these came a paradoxical sense of betrayal by Redmond.

Florina felt a sense of kinship with Macon, standing downcast, hurt reveling in his eyes. The sadness and embarrassment of Agnes' husband was palpable when Reverend Mitchell, as he prayed, caressed the young doctor's shoulder. The minister's words, beseeching God's assistance, were as much for Macon's recovery as Agnes' process of healing.

Florina tempered her anger following church and during the ride home. On entering the house Redmond said, "Father and mother have invited us to dinner."

Thankful that she would not need to prepare dinner, Florina said, "Tell your mother and father, '*Thank you*,' but I have to study. You go instead."

Florina steeled herself against the disappointment that followed in Redmond's eyes, held out hope that some plausible explanation for Agnes and his behavior awaited discovery. For now Florina had chosen to accept that at the least, she had married a man who prior to marrying Florina, had been having an affair with a married woman. At the very worst he had perhaps continued the affair but was most definitely still in love with the married woman.

Florina gathered her books and began studying at the dining room, was doing so when three hours later, Redmond left for his parents' home where he would eat dinner.

"I'll bring you home a plate," he said on leaving. He did not attempt to kiss Florina's head as he had continued doing even during the three days when Agnes had recuperated in their home.

Florina had been at the table revising a poem when Redmond returned that night around ten and went to prepare for bed. Still unsatisfied with her poem, most particularly the inability to create a rhyming pattern for the couplets at the end of her sonnet, she closed her journal and with a sigh, decided, *Perhaps I'll think of something tomorrow morning.* Robert MacIntosh would offer inspiring prompts on their Tuesday afternoon mentoring session, but Florina wanted to work this out herself.

She had tucked away her papers, and with journal in hand, was headed to the bedroom when a knock arose at the front door. Redmond was out from the bedroom and whisking past her before she could go him. Donning his pajamas, Redmond opened the front door to Macon, still wearing the suit he had worn to church and looking very distraught. Macon's hands shook, his fingers twitched when, on Redmond's invitation, he stepped inside.

"Is Agnes all right?" Redmond asked.

The raw redness of Macon's eyes shone against the light of the front room.

Florina grew worried when, on concluding, *He's drunk,* she saw too that Macon had been crying. Before Macon could answer Redmond's question she said, "I didn't cook tonight, but if you're hungry I can make you a sandwi--"

"We ate at my parents," Redmond interrupted with a lie.

"Maybe some water. That would be nice."

She started for the kitchen as Redmond again asked Macon, "How's Agnes?"

"She's fine as you or anyone could expect in light of what was done to her."

Florina held onto those words as she hurriedly removed a glass from the cupboard and filled it with water from the tap. On returning she found Macon and Redmond locked in mutually frigid stares. Florina handed Macon a glass of water. He drank some then set the glass upon the coffee table.

"What do you want?" Redmond asked Macon. "You can get a glass of water at home."

"One would assume so," Macon said. "Then again, there's other things I have difficulty getting. And keeping."

Florina's chest tightened as she heard the slur, barely discernible, in Macon's voice.

Macon surveyed the room then set his gaze upon Florina. A momentary softness enveloped his eyes. "You forced my wife to have an abortion so you could save your marriage."

Redmond arched his brows as he had when Florina proposed the same theory. She swallowed hard.

"The baby she killed was yours," Macon said.

Oh, no. Florina thought. She lowered her eyelids.

"Believe me," Redmond started, "I'm the last person who would ... "

The front door burst open. "Macon!" Agnes shouted upon entering. She was wearing a pristine white nightgown.

177

Despite the trauma she had undergone, her incredible beauty shone through. Still she remained pale and weak.

Florina rushed to her. "You should be in bed," she said.

As if on a mission, Agnes pushed past Florina and went to Macon. "It's time to go. You shouldn't be here," she said to her husband.

"Easy for you to say." Macon slurred his speech full force. "Not too long ago you came and went from this place like it was your second home. Or was this your first home and ours the second?" Agnes slapped Macon's cheek. He grasped her wrist.

"Let her go!" Redmond reached out for Macon's hand.

Macon wrapped his arm around Agnes' neck and placed his hand into his suit pocket. "Stay away." He flicked open a knife and placed the blade to her Agnes' jugular. "Not even your steely surgical hand could repair that."

Agnes blinked once, then twice.

"Don't do anything foolish." Redmond spoke in a calm tone.

"You mean like marrying a woman who despises you and the earth you walk on?" Tears started down Agnes' cheeks.

Macon's hand to the knife, its blade to her throat, trembled.

Footsteps started up the verandah. The door front burst opened and Hammond Austin entered. "Put down the knife," he said.

Macon looked to Redmond's father. Shame overtook Macon's face.

"Take the knife away from Agnes' throat," said Redmond's father. The elder physician counseled, "Agnes is your wife. This is no way to behave. Let her go." Hammond extended his gloved hand, palm open.

Macon removed his arm from around Agnes' neck and released her.

Florina rushed towards Agnes and caught her from slumping to the floor. Redmond came around and grasped Agnes' other arm.

Macon laid the knife on Hammond's palm and left.

Chapter 21

The room reeked of cigarette smoke and stale coffee with cream. Florina had pushed open the front door and saw Agnes sitting in the middle of the floor, a hailstorm of newspapers, nine or ten ashtrays spread amid the chaos with seven or eight cups of coffee. Still wearing her white night gown, she looked pale.

Has she been sitting here all night? Florina wondered. Shadows hung under Agnes' eyes. The canvas of encircling newspapers gave the impression of her having died and gone to heaven with the sole purpose of reading them.

Florina closed the front door, and Agnes looked up. "Henry Loeb is a mean man," Agnes said. She was holding a cigarette in one hand, a crisp, white newspaper, in the left. An additional ashtray, empty unlike the others, lay among a pile of yellowing newspapers stacked in front of Agnes. Florina frowned while trying to fathom the image before her. "He hates Negroes and he's a Jew," Agnes said of Loeb, the newly inaugurated mayor of Memphis, elected for a second term. She inhaled the cigarette. "Doesn't he remember what the Nazis did to his people in Germany?"

Florina knelt down and glanced at the newspaper Agnes was holding. Agnes handed it to her. Florina began to read.

Amid citizens' demands for a resolution, Mayor Henry Loeb holds firm against Negro sanitation workers now in their second week of striking in protest of their working conditions and demanding a higher wage.

"Do you know someone in Memphis?" Florina asked.

Agnes arched her brows and a rush of color invaded her face. "*Must* I know a Memphis sanitation worker to support their cause, relate to them?"

Florina lifted another newspaper. The front cover, dated, November 22, 1963 read, *President Kennedy Dead.* Another headline--*Medgar Evers, a veteran of World War II, was buried with full military honors at Arlington National Cemetery.*

"He fought in Europe," Agnes said. "Was there on either Utah or Omaha Beach." She began to cry. "Why can't these people see that we're just like them. They're no better than us or anybody?"

Florina knew Agnes to be speaking of American whites. "Have you eaten anything?" It was nine-o-clock and the February cold resisted warming even against the bright, morning sun.

Florina found three eggs, bacon, and butter inside the refrigerator. On detecting no scent after sticking her nose to the milk carton, she prepared breakfast with toast.

"Would you like some coffee?" she asked Agnes, emerging from the bedroom having showered. The papers now gathered from the floor lay in a neat stack, towering ten inches or more upon the table.

Agnes nodded, sat to the table and buttered her bread. "I supposed you've eaten?" she said.

"Redmond likes to eat at least an hour before he leaves for work. He needs the time for his foo--"

"Food to settle," Agnes took over.

Florina stared as Agnes cut another sliver of butter and spread it upon her toast.

182

"Redmond had a standing invitation to breakfast here, but he never came. I cook breakfast late."

Florina went to the stove and loaded the pans and utensils into the sink in preparation of washing them.

"Don't be angry," Agnes called in between bites of scrambled eggs. "No matter what Macon says, Redmond loves you."

Florina turned around. "And why should I believe you?"

"Because it's true," said Agnes.

By the time Florina had finished cleaning up the kitchen, Agnes was eating her last sliver of bacon. Florina lifted her plate and fork and Agnes said, "I'd like some tea."

"Are you asking me to prepare you some tea?"

Agnes glanced at the stack of newspapers.

Chapter 22

Proud that she had driven to Redmond's office without a wrong turn, Florina locked the car door and proceeded to the sidewalk. Hammond had driven Redmond to work that morning. She was half-way up the steps when the front door flew open and Redmond rushed out.

"I've been calling you." He grasped her arm and headed toward the car.

"Macon's got an emergency. One of his patients is in labor."

They were down the road, Florina driving as Redmond explained. "The baby's breech and the mother needs a C-section, but there's no way she's going to make it to Charlotte Negro Hospital."

On reaching Macon's office, Redmond hopped out. Florina followed.

Macon's nurse, Annie, greeted them at the door.

"Where is she?" Redmond asked.

"She's out back in her husband's truck." A strange anxiety hung upon Annie's brown face as she pointed to the back door.

A heart-wrenching cry resounded as Redmond rushed

towards the beat up 1957 International pick-up truck. "Oh my God! Harrell! Somebody help me!" The tone of the scream sounded nothing like that of a Negro woman. Annie's downcast gaze said something was amiss.

A white man with stringy hair, wearing tattered overalls with dark splotches of oil, came around from the driver's side of the truck as Redmond kneeled down to the woman on the passenger's side. Blood covered the seat, and poured onto the floorboard, creating puddles around her pale feet attached to swollen ankles. Her head lolled left to right, as she writhed in pain, gripped her stomach. Redmond lifted the hem of the white woman's grimy dress and spread apart her legs. Blood gushed forth adding to the river of crimson already flooding the floor of the truck.

"The baby's breech," Redmond said. "I can already see the feet."

"You don't have to school me, nigger. I know the baby's coming out the wrong way."

"Your wife's lost a lot of blood. And it's getting worse," Redmond said to the husband whom Florina had already sized-up as a Klansman. Redmond stood, anger piercing his veneer of restraint,.

Though a four-hour drive apart, the parishes of both Laurel and St. Andrews A. M. E. Zion, consisted mainly of well-educated Negroes who maintained an insular society that buffered them against the economic assaults launched by white America, and racial epithets fired by those like the man standing before Florina and Redmond.

Redmond spoke firmly. "You need to take her to Poinsettia General."

"Ain't there nothing you can do?" the scruffy, white man's angry demeanor shifted to a plea. "When the baby's like this don't the woman need surgery or something?"

"And that needs to be done in a hospital," Redmond said.. "Which is why you need to get her to Poinsettia General as soon as possible. I suggest you leave now."

"I ain't got no money for no hospital."

"That may be," Redmond said. "But we're talking about your wife and baby's life."

"We done had three to come just like this," said the woman's husband. "Feet first. First one died. Doc Hanley took out the second one with surgery. The third we lost with the midwife." The man now spoke with penitence. "Doc Hanley ain't makin' no more house calls. Delivers all his babies at the hospital. The man at the hospital told me I can't come back less I got some money."

His blatant honesty left Florina awestruck. The woman released another wild cry.

Redmond knelt to attend the woman once more. "I'm sure they'll make an exception this one time," he said. "Perhaps you can take some money from where you'd intended it and--"

"No, you don't understand. I got no money and without something to hand them, they won't let her in the hospital. Not now, not tomorrow, and not the day after!"

Florina registered shock. The man was dirt poor, and pleading.

Laurel A. M. E. Zion community held those who consistently fought to
make ends meet. Yet even they held a modicum of standard by which they dressed and behaved. Florina had been aware of the existence of poor whites but had never witnessed them, their needs so blatant and their vulnerabilities exposed. Social integration would insure and increase encounters such as these.

"I don't know what I can do for you," Redmond said to the woman's husband standing behind him.

Annie joined Redmond in attending the woman who was still writhing in pain.

"Ain't you a doctor?" the white man said to Redmond. He turned to Macon. "You told me he was surgeon."

"He is," Macon started, "but--"

"I have no admitting privileges at Poinsettia General," Redmond said. He stood and again faced the woman's husband.

"Harrell do something!" the woman screamed once more and grasped Annie's hand. She sat up and doubled over, again gripped her swollen belly.

187

From all observations her life stood half the globe from the alabaster woman who had brought Agnes to Florina and Redmond, bleeding after the abortion. The woman trying to give birth might as well have lived in the poorest villages of Africa or towns of Europe following World War II for as much as America had done for her.

"The baby's nearly out," Annie said. The amount of blood pouring from the woman's vagina had increased two-fold. "The fetus is going to crown at any moment."

"Help me lay her down," Redmond said to Macon. He turned to Florina, "Go get our car."

Minutes later and down the highway, the woman lay stretched upon the back seat with Macon administering anesthesia and Redmond making ready to perform a caesarean. Annie, who knew the route to Poinsettia General, drove as Florina, in the front passenger seat, held surgical instruments and gauze.

Annie slowed the sedan to a stop on reaching an intersection. Florina drew in breath as Redmond, the car then still, placed the scalpel to the woman's bulging white belly and made an incision. Blood seeped forth in the wake of the scalpel's path.

"Go," Macon called to Annie at the wheel. The car pulled off and Macon wiped away the blood.

Florina gazed through the car windows and wondered, *What if a police officer or the sheriff stopped them?* On banishing that thought she grew fearful of a worse possibility.

She lifted her gaze to the back window, observed the woman's husband following behind in his pick-up truck. A rifle hung in his back window. How would the husband behave should the woman, child or both die? Astounded at the man's rapid shift in presentation, Florina, as had Redmond, became angry. One moment the man had called Redmond 'a nigger.' A second later he had described the economically poor and disempowered station he occupied. Redmond was putting his career on the line. No matter how dirty or poor this woman was,

188

she was still white. And should she or her baby die--worse still, both--Redmond, despite his hard work to save them would be seen as a nigger who had killed them.

If Redmond were to work as an Army surgeon in Vietnam, no one would blame him like this. He would have the best tools available. Perhaps we do need to leave North Carolina, Florina thought.

Beads of sweat dropped from Redmond's brown face. Against every fear that said, *"Don't interrupt him,"* Florina reached across the seat and wiped Redmond's forehead with a square of white gauze.

Redmond eased his hands into the woman's belly and instructed Annie, "Run inside and get someone when we get to Poinsettia General."

Again Macon wiped blood from the woman's stomach. Sweat entered Redmond's eyes. Florina wiped his brown once more.

Careful to avoid any bumps that Florina knew lined the road, Annie delivered them to Poinsettia General in what amounted to less than ten minutes. Florina felt she had lived three times over during the five-mile drive. Annie brought the black Riviera to a gentle halt under the canopy outside the emergency room, then hopped out and rushed inside the emergency room of Poinsettia General.

"We can take over from here," a prim white woman with dark hair spoke from behind Redmond. A second younger nurse stood beside her.

"I need another scalpel to cut the cord," Redmond said. "The first scalpel fell to the floor of the car."

"The doctor will take over," said the nurse.

"I need to cut the cord and focus on the mother. She's lost a lot of blood. At least let me save the baby's life!" Redmond said.

"And I said we have a doctor here." The nurse was firm.

The young nurse ran inside. Rushing back out, she opened the white cloth, revealing a scalpel.

The prim, gray-haired nurse looking on, Redmond lifted the instrument, severed the cord then handed the infant to the young nurse who carefully wrapped the white towel around the infant. "He appears a little lethargic. A glucose drip should perk him up," Redmond said to the young nurse.

Nodding, the young nurse scurried back inside the hospital emergency room with the infant.

Two orderlies appeared and indicating no awareness of Redmond's presence they lifted the woman onto the gurney. Observing from a distance, one might have thought Redmond an individual or good Samaritan with no training. They wheeled the woman inside when a doctor approached the nurse.

"Finally, someone from our staff," said the prim nurse. "Dr. Schaeffer, I was just telling this man that he--"

"Dr. Austin," the doctor spoke to Redmond and extended his hand, pink and clean, *unlike* those of Rose and Kenan Thornton, the parents of the infant Redmond had just delivered. "I'm the new assistant chief of staff--Stuart Schaeffer."

Redmond held up his hands redolent of blood in the sunlight of the cold afternoon.

"Please get Dr. Austin a basin of warm water and soap," Schaeffer said to the older nurse. "Yes, doctor," she said, surprise and shock registering on her pale and wrinkled face.

Schaeffer turned back to Redmond. "I know your father, Dr. Hammond Austin, very well. He may have mentioned me."

"He has," Redmond said.

The nurse arrived with a basin of warm water and held it out to Redmond, who as Schaeffer looked to Florina, washed his hands.

"And this must be the new Mrs. Austin," said Dr. Schaeffer. He extended his hand to Florina and she shook it.

"Pleased to meet you," she said.

Redmond dried his hands and the nurse left.

"I've had your father and mother out at the club several times. I and a few friends of mine are working on ascertaining membership for *your father* and *you*," Schaeffer said to Redmond. "More importantly, I hope your father's told you how much we'd like to get you on our staff."

Redmond glanced at Florina.

190

"He's also told me a Los Angeles hospital has invited you to join their staff," said Schaeffer.

Florina looked to Redmond. She knew of his interest in working in California, but he had said nothing of a job offer.

"We need more doctors like you *here* at Poinsettia General," Schaeffer said. Again he extended his hand to Redmond.

His hands now clean of Rose Thornton's blood, Redmond grasped Florina's hand, and said, "But will the trustees allow me to treat my Negro patients also?"

"We have every confidence that once you and Dr. Elder begin seeing patients here at Poinsettia General you'll be allowed to admit Negro patients within a year or so," Dr. Schaeffer said.

Redmond lifted his gaze and surveyed the pristine white building housing the seven floors of Poinsettia General Hospital. "Dr. Elder might jump at the chance to work here at Poinsettia General, but I won't give up treating patients who are a part of my community and who've known me since childhood, just to gain entrance into hospital with doctors who leave patients out in the lurch like the woman whose baby I just delivered."

Florina ached for Redmond speaking a truth larger than both men.

Schaeffer lowered his gaze.
"I appreciate the offer, but I also like sleeping at night," Redmond said. Still clasping Florina's palm, and against all lessons in Southern courtesy, Redmond helped her into the sedan. With Macon and Annie sitting in back, he entered the driver's seat and drove away.

———————————————

191

Chapter 23

It was two-o'clock when Redmond returned to his office after driving Macon and Annie back to their office.

"I rescheduled most your afternoon patients for later this week," Redmond's nurse, Clara, said when he entered his office.

"But what of Mr. Wenley and Mrs. Grice?" Redmond lifted two charts from his desk. "They're just home from surgery?"

"You did their surgeries two weeks ago. Your father instructed me to send them over to his office. With you seeing to Dr. Elder's patient I knew you'd want your father to see them."

"You should go home and rest," Florina said to Clara, thankful that Clara had rescheduled Redmond's afternoon appointments.

Florina reached for the car keys on their way down the steps from Redmond's. "I'll drive."

The trip home was quiet.

Having not cooked the previous evening Florina entered the kitchen prepared to cook a meal. She wanted Redmond to

193

eat and rest. She was quite pleased, thankful once more, on reading the note Carolyn had taped upon the refrigerator door.

Hammond let me know Redmond had gone to Macon's office. Inside you'll find a roasted chicken, okra, rice and some pound cake for afterwards.
I'm so glad you were with Redmond.
    ~~Carolyn
    P. S. Willa Mae let me in.

Dinner eaten, the dishes washed and put away, Florina and Redmond were savoring their slices of pound cake with ice cream and coffee, when Florina asked Redmond, "Does your mother know how I first met Agnes, that I found her at the house, the door unlocked?"

Redmond looked to Florina. "She knows I had the locks changed."

"But did you tell her why?"

"I'm not sure. Why do you ask?" He stood, appeared perturbed, went to the refrigerator and lifted out a bottle of soda, like he always did when seeking to evade an uncomfortable topic.

"She made a point of telling me in the note left with the food that Willa Mae had let her in," Florina said. She then added, "One time after you changed the locks Agnes came over and was inside as if she'd still had a key. Willa Mae had just started coming. I could have sworn I'd locked the door."

"Perhaps Willa Mae didn't lock it."

"I always let her in and lock the door behind her," Florina said. She then remembered. "But that morning I'd been out back, dumping the trash. Willa entered the back door with me." Florina never let Willa Mae, pregnant, dump the trash.

"The trash bag had broken and some of the trash had spilled out. I'd been picking it up. Wasn't inside to hear her at the front door. She'd walked around to the back yard." Florina

194

set her gaze upon Redmond. "You were the last person to walk out the door that morning."

A haze spread across Redmond's eyes. He set the soda bottle, yet opened back onto the refrigerator shelf and closed the door. He returned to the table, moved to sit as if about to speak when voices resounded from next door. Florina walked past him, left the kitchen and entered the bedroom where their window delivered a clear view of Agnes and Macon's house. Their curtains drawn, Florina flicked off the lamp and peeked through the curtains. Expecting to see them in the yard or front room.

The light in Agnes and Macon's bedroom was on. Despite the February cold, their window was raised, their curtains pulled back. Below the window lay a suitcase open and empty. Agnes stood by the window holding a suit on a hanger.

"What are you doing?" Macon demanded.

"I want you gone!" Agnes said.

"This is my house. I pay the rent here."

"Rent, that's right, rent. And with the way you're going, that's all we'll ever pay."

"It takes money to buy a house. And with the way you spend--"

"Maybe if you'd stop tending all that poor white trash out by the county line we'd have some money," Agnes said.

"*Those* people pay me. Their money keeps us eating those steaks you so love to purchase at that A & P. We'd have no food bill if you'd go to my parents' sto--"

"I don't shop from people who hate me," Agnes shouted. "Besides, you're a doctor, you should have money."

"My parents don't hate you. And doctors have to work just like everyone else." Macon's voice cracked.

Florina ached listening to Macon pleading for Agnes' love and respect. She lowered her eyes, certain that neighbors were hearing them just as she and Redmond did.

"Close the window," Redmond said. He moved to lower their window.

"I want to hear," Florina said.

"Agnes likes an audience." Redmond stared.

195

At that moment Agnes said, "You had no business calling Redmond to help you with that woman and her baby."

"She needed surgery," said Macon.

"You should have sent her to Poinsettia General."

"They never would have made it."

"You mean they have no money."

"I couldn't let them die, mother and child."

"They certainly haven't minded letting us die," Agnes shot back. "Never mind you and Redmond could have gotten killed. Just think of what would have happened if the woman or her baby had died. Or both of them."

"Times are changing. And Hammond would have never let that--"

"Some would say for worse. And you're not Hammond Austin, nor his son."

Agnes' statement intrigued Florina in light of how she had seen Agnes the previous day, surrounded by newspapers detailing the plight of Negroes in America. But her last words cut to the bone.

"I may not be Redmond Austin, but I am your husband."

"And a stupid one at that," Agnes said. "Don't let Hammond Austin's relationship with Stuart Schaeffer go to your head. Schaeffer's a Jew. And those white trustees don't like him anymore than they like Hammond. Or you."

"And what of Redmond?"

"Redmond's not trying to get on staff. He's content to keep treating Negro patients, that pay him, and who I might add, don't call him, 'nigger.'"

"Why is it okay for you to mingle with white people as if you're one of them, but wrong for me to attend their illnesses and them pay me?"

"Because you think they're some kind of deity. I know who they are. And I don't want to become one of them," Agnes said.

"I'm doing the best I can," Macon grasped her shoulders, attempted to caress them.

"Oh, like you did with that knife to my throat." Agnes hit his hand, and pulled away.

"I love you." Macon reached for her.

Agnes swatted Macon away. "Get your black hands away from me." Florina drew in breath. Macon slapped Agnes and she gripped her face. "Get away from me you black beast! I've never loved you! And I never will!"

As Macon staggered Florina realized he was drunk. "How is it that you can love him, a thousand times darker than me, and call me black?" Macon's speech was slurred.

"Because that's what you are, the worst kind of black person there is, a white folks' lovin' nigger," said Agnes. She was gripping her face. "And that's what you'll remain, until the day you die."

So taken with the vehement of Agnes' words, Florina did not remember lowering the window, nor if she actually did.

The shock of what she saw and heard threw her into herself, lulled her to sleep. Not until the next morning did she return-- re-entering the present reality of her life.

Florina was scrambling eggs when Redmond entered the kitchen soft and quiet as if not wanting to disturb his wife from her inner thoughts. On setting Redmond's plate of eggs and bacon on the table before him, she sat.

"You aren't going to eat?" Redmond asked, observing the empty space before her.

"I'm not hungry." She placed her elbows, folded, upon the table and left the waking nightmare of her dream. "My father's sisters hate my mother because she has dark skin." His fork mid-air above his plate, Redmond looked to her." They've always been cruel to her. All four of them," Florina explained. "Three of them barely graduated high school. My aunt Marcia, went one year then got married. It's not clear whether she married because she was pregnant, failing college, or *both*."

Redmond breathed in, lowered his fork onto the plate. "Why did you stop?"

Relieved, but also awed and frightened by the attentiveness and depth of his question, Florina resisted her desire to confess her truth. She instead crafted a fiction.

197

"A friend of mine died. It took me by surprise. We were very close, shared everything, particularly my writing, my poems. I couldn't go on."

"But you have," Redmond said. His voice was soft.

"Your mother. I'll always be thankful for her introducing me to Robert MacIntosh."

Redmond lifted his fork and touched his eggs.

Florina felt Redmond slipping away.

"He seems to have had effect on you, MacIntosh," Redmond said.

"He's a good man, and an excellent teacher."

"Anything else?" Redmond said.

"About Dr. MacIntosh?" Florina squinted. Redmond's question confused her.

"On what helped you see you could go on?" Redmond was not speaking of simply returning to college.

"You eventually see that time moves on," Florina said. She went to the sink, turned on the faucet, and set to washing the breakfast dishes. "You can either get back into life or remain left behind."

Redmond came to Florina and gently grasped her shoulders from behind. Leaning in he whispered, "I would like to think that marrying me and coming here to Poinsettia has helped in your fight to move on."

"It has," Florina whispered. She leaned her head back upon Redmond's warm chest, and closed her eyes. "I'm scared. I'm afraid."

In an even lower voice, Redmond said, "I love you. *And only you.* Never forget that." He kissed her neck, ran his fingers along her cheekbones. Florina's eyes remained closed, her heart pounding and her chest growing ever more full and warm.

———————————

Chapter 24

Willa Mae had gone for the day when Florina stepped onto the verandah and discovered the box wrapped in the paper of a grocery bag, bearing her name.

Seeing no one, and since the box bore no postage, she looked to Agnes and Macon's home. Florina assumed that Agnes had left it.

Back inside and sitting at the dining room table, Florina grew amazed. Hot tears formed behind her eyes, rolled on to her cheeks, warmed to a slow burn, as she read the words.

I will always love you, no matter what. My father may compel me to marry a man I don't love, but he cannot force the choice of my heart. It will always beat for yours. Its affections are forever wedded to you. You are my one and only god. My soul seeks to join with no other but yours.
... Agnes

"*She wrote this to Redmond,*" Florina concluded. The letter had been dated March 31st, 1967, five days before Agnes had wed Macon.

Florina grieved for the loss of hope, that what she had feared might rest in her imagination was reality. She now had physical evidence of a truth that resisted acknowledgment. Agnes had married Macon while still loving Redmond.

Florina sifted through the other fifty or more letters dated from times prior to the one she had read. On reaching the letters at the bottom of the box she chanced upon two envelopes bearing postage, and each dated *after* Florina had met Redmond in late July 1967.

Heart pounding, she slid the letter from within the envelope, stamped and dated, *October 22, 1967*, and unfolded the pages.

Redmond:

I now know why you're gone each weekend. You've met someone. Everyone at St. Andrews is talking about it, or her, I should say. And now your grandmother has confirmed it.

You can't do this to us. I love you. I'll leave Macon. But I need more time. I've ached just as you during these last six months. I need you and you need me.

... Agnes

The letter in the second of the two stamped envelopes was dated December 20th, 1967.

Redmond:

Why do you keep ignoring me? Who is this Florina? And what has she done to turn you away from me, against all we love? I will always love you. You are mine. I am, and will

200

always be yours. Everything I carry and that lives inside me is yours.

You may marry her, but I will never give up. I will own your heart and soul from now until the world ends and begin again, when the last shall be made first and the first put last. ...

———————————————

Florina struggled against blurring tears and cheeks aflame to return the letter to its envelope. Redmond had married Florina to assuage the loss and pain of Agnes who had married Macon. This was Florina's conclusion. *But why did Agnes marry Macon when she was so in love with Redmond*? And why would Redmond allow Agnes to marry Macon. Why didn't Redmond simply marry Agnes?

Florina's mind flipped back to her conversation with Hammond Austin the night after she had arrived in Poinsettia.

"I'm a fairly decent judge of character," Hammond Austin had said. *"You're a young and intelligent woman, just the wife Redmond needs."*

Redmond's father said, *"You've made Redmond very happy."* He then opened a drawer and lifted out two small leather folders containing checkbooks. *"As such I want very much to keep you happy."*

The answer onto which Florina's thoughts latched was short-lived.

Florina had returned the letters to the shoebox and placed the box on the top shelf of the closet that housed her clothes when she heard a knock at the front door.

She walked to the front room and opened the door to Macon. "I was expecting Willa Mae to answer the door," he said eyebrows raised. Surprise glimmered upon his face.

"She's not feeling well," Florina said. She wiped beneath her eyes.

Macon seemed unfazed.

Away from the February cold and inside at the kitchen table he revealed his dispassion. "How was Redmond this morning?"

"Tired, but fine." Still under the shock from the contents of the letters she had read, Florina gave curt answers. She would not confront Agnes, instead would tell Redmond about the letters she had discovered. Florina was certain Agnes had left them, despite her protestations that Redmond loved Florina.

Perhaps with a plausible explanation--Redmond finally admitting he loved Agnes, and explaining he had married Florina to please his parents-- Redmond and Florina might find a way to salvage their marriage. The letters contained only Agnes' words, her confession of love.

Macon said, "I shouldn't have called Redmond yesterday. I should have had Kenan drive Rose to Poinsettia General."

"You were doing what you thought best, trying to save the life of a mother and her child."

"The doctors at Poinsettia General would have seen Rose," Macon said. "They wouldn't have turned her away."

"But Rose's husband said he owed the hospital money."

"I've sent patients owing much more money than Kenan Thornton to Poinsettia General. The hospital delivered their babies. They just don't allow the mother and child stay overnight."

"But what about Kenan's story of Dr. Hanley?" Florina asked.

"Albert Hanley is not the only doctor who delivers babies at Poinsettia General."

Florina sat up. "Then why call Redmond and put him and yourself through all of what took place?" she asked growing anxious. *And angry.*

"I wanted to show Poinsettia General that we, Negro doctors, are just as good, if not better, than the white doctors at Poinsettia General."

"Rose Thornton or her baby, perhaps both, could have died!" Florina said. "And what if the sheriff had stopped us. You could have been killed. *We* could have been killed!"

Macon lowered his gaze. "Things are changing," he spoke. "Both around us. And in our homes. Yours and mine." He touched his chest then pointed to Florina.

202

She frowned.

"Agnes loves your Redmond," Macon said. "He's been the apple of her eye from the moment she met him."

"And what of Redmond?" Florina steadied her voice and hand.

"Redmond Austin gets whatever Redmond Austin wants."

"That's no reason to try to destroy his medical career, get him killed and perhaps yourself to boot," Florina said. *Redmond is an excellent surgeon,* Florina concluded, *despite what Agnes had written and Redmond's lying about his feelings for Agnes.*

"That was never my aim," Macon said, "Because of yesterday, and Redmond saving Rose Thornton and her baby, Poinsettia General is one step closer to allowing Negro doctors on staff. Negro citizens are one step closer to not having to travel thirty miles away to Charlotte Negro Hospital, where so many of our people have driven by Poinsettia General and died trying to get to the only hospital within a hundred miles that has Negro doctors attending to Negro patients."

Florina understood the importance of Macon's quest. While Laurel had Dr. Reynolds, the closest hospitals for Negro citizens of Laurel was fifty miles west and east. Still she was angry. "You took a big risk," said Florina. "Had it failed Redmond would have never forgiven himself."

"He would have refused had I asked him," Macon said, adding, "I respect Redmond. But with Hammond Austin as his father, Redmond's never had to stretch himself, leave his comfort zone. Redmond plays it close to his vest. Safe and careful. Some of us, most of us, don't have that luxury."

"Maybe that's what Agnes likes about him." Florina said. She recalled Agnes' slur at Macon last evening. *Get your filthy, black hands off me.* Now looking at Macon, his hazel eyes and tan skin Florina wondered what Agnes could have meant. As Macon had said, Redmond's skin was much darker than Macon's. Florina clasped her hands and settled them upon the lap of her dress.

Macon said, "The box I left on the verandah is gone."

203

Florina took in breath.

"Did you read the letters?"

Why would Macon do such a thing? Florina forced herself to breathe.

"She will never stop loving Redmond," Macon spoke.

"Those letters said nothing about him loving her," Florina shot back.

Macon's eyebrows went straight as arrows. A wet sheen glazed over of his hazel irises. A raw and primitive redness overtook the whites of his eyes. "Two days after our wedding," he started, "I came home and found Redmond in bed with Agnes. I told him to leave and never come back. He did as I asked. But--" He stopped, lowered his gaze.

"What do you want from me?" Florina spoke barely audibly. Her heart was breaking. "I don't know anything about this."

"Redmond is your husband. Take him away. He never wanted to come back here. Take him to California. And let me have Poinsettia. Agnes. *And some peace.*

Chapter 25

Florina had yet decided how to approach Redmond about the matter of Agnes' letters, and Macon's assertion that Redmond had slept with Agnes after she had married Macon. Watching Redmond toil at saving the life of Rose Thornton and her infant the previous day had exposed Florina to an entirely different side of her husband. Skillfully wielding the scalpel, his forehead releasing droplets of sweat, displayed him at once both strong and vulnerable. That he had saved the life of a woman and her child, the husband and father having called Redmond a 'nigger,' lifted Florina's respect for him beyond that which she had held for any person. Her admiration had soared. Arriving home she had wanted to embrace Redmond, offer homage to what she had never before witnessed, and had no idea was possible.

And yet Macon had accused the person and husband, Florina was growing to love--despite the seeds of doubts Agnes' behavior sowed--of having committed adultery. Florina had not known Redmond at that supposed adulterous time, and whatever had occurred between him and Agnes was in the past. Alas, the memory and image of Agnes' gloved hand, caressing

Redmond's cheek remained and had reared its head as it had when she read Agnes' letters.

Macon's visit, his confession of having delivered the box of letters, and of having partly staged the event of Redmond delivering Rose Thornton's baby, left Florina furious at his plotting. Still his belief was correct that Negro citizens should not have to travel past a hospital their taxes sustained.

Florina despised Macon and his tactics. He did not deserve peace or tranquility of any sort. She wondered how her decision to confront Redmond about the matter might play into whatever plan Macon had devised to achieve his goal of contentment. If that was truly what he wanted.

She was sitting adjacent to Redmond at dinner as always when she cut into her string beans and said, "Macon came by today."

Redmond lifted a sliver of trout onto his fork. "What did he want?"

"He asked how you were doing."

Redmond placed the slice of trout in to his mouth and chewed.

"He said that had Rose Thornton gone to Poinsettia General, the emergency room would not have turned her away."

"There wasn't time," Redmond said on swallowing.

"She had been at his office for more than forty-five minutes before he called you. Macon *wanted* you to deliver Rose's baby," Florina said. "It was his way of showing physicians and administrators at Poinsettia General that Negro doctors are just as good as white doctors."

Redmond gently lowered his fork to the side of his plate. He pushed his chair back, was on his feet and headed for the kitchen door when Florina said, "I read Agnes' letters. The ones she wrote to you before she married Macon. And before you married me."

Redmond turned around, arched his eyebrows.

"I have them in a shoe box."

Redmond walked to her. She was still sitting. "How did you get them? I gave them back to her."

206

"Macon gave them to me," Florina said. Redmond slumped into his seat, stared upon the table, his eyes reflecting the revisiting of a history with which Florina had not been acquainted. "Macon said that you slept with Agnes right after they married."

Again, Redmond stared at her, this time, his eyes widening with fear, and then shame. "What do you want to do?" he said after some minutes.

"Do you love her?"

"No."

"But she still loves you."

"Is that what Macon says?"

"It's what I see."

"You aren't looking very carefully."

"You don't deny having slept with her?" Florina shot back.

"We weren't married. I hadn't met you. We didn't even know each other."

"She was married."

"And I'm not the first person to sleep with someone else's spouse." Redmond stood.

"You don't think what you did was wrong?"

"Of course it was wrong. I'm not proud of it."

"But do you feel badly about it?"

"I certainly didn't tell you," Redmond said.

"It would have been nice knowing what I was walking into."

"And would you have married me?"

Florina thought of Ennis, whom she had been married without her parents' knowledge or permission. What would Redmond have said had she revealed that she was a widow, her husband killed in Vietnam? Would his attraction to her have been any less? Or would it have grown in light of the torch she still carried for Ennis?

"We all have secrets," she said.

Redmond's eyes flashed an interrogating demeanor. He searched her faced as if to decipher the meaning shaded by her words. "Did Macon explain how he got those letters-- Agnes' letters written to me?" Redmond's question gave words to a discomfort that had been gnawing at her. "I gave them back to her, all the letters she had written me. I did that right after I met you."

Florina's heart lurched with hope. Perhaps there was an opening, an explanation that would release her from the judgment she now held towards Redmond, along with the admiration she held for his ability to save lives, and Macon's deception for what he deemed a higher cause. Since marrying Redmond, memories of Ennis had ceased to dominate Florina's thoughts. The fight to save her infant marriage, fraught with challenges, had propelled Florina past the pain of her loss, had demonstrated she live, and do so faithfully beyond Ennis' death.

"I wanted to start fresh and clean," Redmond said.

Florina yearned to understand the nature of Redmond's love for Agnes, a love that allowed him to sleep with her after she had married Macon, but had not allowed, or rather had prevented him from marryi--"Why didn't you marry?" she said. "Did Agnes reject you?" It was a moot question in light of Agnes' way with Redmond.

"I rejected her," Redmond said.

Florina lowered her eyelids, crossed her arms and squeezed tightly. "I don't understand," she said. "The two of you clearly love each other." *Why?*

Florina flashed her lids open. "Did your parents not approve of Agnes? Is that it?" She squinted in confusion, a memory of Hammond speaking in the study that first night in Poinsettia, his promise to keep her happy, played in Florina's thoughts. "Or was it that they liked me, approved of the woman I was?"

"I don't love Agnes," Redmond said. "Not the way I love you."

"So you admit to still loving her!"

"You are my wife," Redmond pleaded. "I want to be with you, *forever*. I knew it the first time I saw you."

Florina recalled the feel of the wood scraping against her fingers--she weighed down by Ennis' death, all she had withheld from her parents and the Reynolds, and her mother's

frustrated desire to know why she had abandoned college. Florina had been losing grip, the crates slipping through her fingers, the strawberries about to spill when, Redmond rushed out from the home of Ava and Bill Reynolds and caught the crate.
to help her.

"Did Macon tell you how he got those letters? What his purpose was in giving them to you?"

"He wants peace," Florina said.

"Ha!" Redmond threw back his head. "And he hopes to gain it by destroying our marriage?"

"That doesn't make right what you did with Agnes."

"I never said it was."

"Why did you do it?"

"I didn't know you. We weren't married," Redmond pleaded.

Florina shook her head. "That's not the point."

But that is the point. Redmond knelt and grasped her shoulders, caressed them. "I hadn't met you. Don't you see? Had I known you the day Agnes married, or even before, none of this would have happened."

"You would have stopped loving her?" Florina looked to Redmond, inspected his eyes. His gaze fell. "What are you saying, Redmond? Don't tell me that your love is that fleeting," Florina said. "Otherwise, the love you claim to hold for me may disappear on meeting someone new."

"It's not like that." Redmond refused to lift his head, continued to gaze upon the floor. "Sometimes what we assume is love, *is not love*."

"You thought you loved Agnes, but when you met me you realized that you didn't?" Florina said.

"I truly thought I loved her."

"And yet you rejected her, refused to marry her and allowed her to marry Macon. Then you slept with her after she became his wife?"

Redmond lifted himself to stand, looked to Florina and said, "I love you. And I know I won't, I can't, love anyone else the way I love you."

209

Everything in Florina wanted to believe Redmond. Her heart pounded at his words. Her soul recognized a truth that her thoughts could not deny, and yet they strayed into far off regions of doubt, where questions defying answers lurked like ghosts searching for bodies to inhabit and shield their unwelcomed presences.

Chapter 26

Florina left Poinsettia on the seven am bus headed for Rocky Mount, North Carolina. Five hours later she arrived in Laurel and with suitcase in hand headed for Ava Reynolds' house. Florina was set to knock a second time when Ava opened the door. Joy filled her eyes. "Where's Redmond?" Ava asked as she looked beyond Florina.

"I came alone," Florina said. "Took the bus."

Ava ushered Florina into the house, and closed the door. "Did anyone see you walking here?" Caution enveloped Ava's words. She helped Florina out of her coat. "Then again, it's winter." Ava thought aloud. "Not too many people are out." She turned to Florina. "Have you eaten?"

Florina shook her head.

"Come." Ava motioned for Florina to follow her to the kitchen.

With Florina settled at the kitchen table and Ava preparing lunch--it was moving towards one-o-clock--Ava began the questioning Florina knew was to come.

"What time did you leave Poinsettia?"

"Seven," Florina said.

"Does Redmond know you've left?" Ava spoke while removing a plastic container from the refrigerator.

Again, Florina shook her head.

"And since you came here first, I'm to suspect neither your mother or father know you've left, that you were even coming?"

"They don't," Florina felt herself becoming a child again in answering. She had undergone a similar scrutiny with Ava when she had announced she would not be returning to college her senior year. With no children of her own, Ava took seriously her role as Florina's godmother.

Ava transferred the leftover chicken to a metal pan, and put the pan into the oven. The pot of water she set on the boil began to cry. She poured two cups of tea and joined Florina at the table. "The chicken will be warm in a few minutes. Ava set the cups of tea on the table before Florina answered. Ava said, "In the meantime, tell me what's happened."

Florina lowered her head, felt herself about to cry then Ava's forefinger lifted her cheek. "You're not the first woman who's left her husband and you won't be the last." The light in Ava's eyes dimmed.

They were eating Ava's chicken and string beans when Florina said, "I'm afraid I've made a mess of things."

"That's not what Hammond says," Ava quipped.

Startled, Florina lowered her fork onto the side of her plate.

"You met Redmond out on my patio," Ava said. "Carolyn and I saw the whole thing. My two crates of strawberries would have gone to waste if Redmond hadn't rushed to you and caught them."

Florina breathed in.

Ava said, "Hammond and I speak each week after church." She sipped her tea. "I heard about your house guest." Florina lowered her gaze. "You mustn't let Agnes Elder shake you."

The name Agnes Elder sounded horribly strange to Florina. She didn't think of Agnes as Macon's wife, but simply as Agnes. "She doesn't love her husband," Florina said.

"But Redmond loves you."

"Are you so certain?"

"Men are not like us women. We have many ways of loving many people. Men, they love only one way. And only one person."

"Then why are they unfaithful?"

"Are you saying that Redmond's been unfaithful to you?"

Ava's words shook Florina back into the reality of truth from which her emotions distanced her. "He slept with Agnes after she married Macon."

"When he was not married to you, nor had he even met you."

"Why is it I feel everyone knows Agnes better than me?" Florina said.

"Because we do? And she doesn't frighten us. We're also older and we've seen a little more than you. Or Redmond."

Florina resumed eating her string beans. Ava had eaten her last slice of chicken when Florina asked, "Did you ever stop to think that Redmond's past might cause trouble for our marriage?"

"Everyone enters marriage with hidden baggage." Ava's eyebrows lifted ever so slightly. Florina considered her secret marriage to Ennis. "The question is whether the secrets in those bags are of equal proportion--both in size, scope and the nature of their problems."

"In that case, I've been outsized."

"Are you so sure about that?"

She can't know about Ennis. Florina thought. *How could she?*

Ava said, "Your mother said you've re-entered college."

"Agnes was surprised Redmond had married me without my having graduated," Florina said.

"She would be--not that having a degree did much for her. But Redmond needed a wife. And as you've demonstrated, one can always return to college."

Florina fixed Ava with a stare. "Why did you push us together?"

213

"I don't know that we pushed you and Redmond together. We instead cleared the way for you to meet."

"And afterwards?" Florina asked.

"Your and Redmond's parents did for you and Redmond what their parents did for them, what my and Bill's parents did for us."

"Daddy's parents hated Momma's parents," Florina shot back.

"Don't attribute the envy and foolishness of your father's sisters to his parents."

"Well they raised them."

"Children are their own separate people. We are all a product of the society in which we live," said Ava.

"Don't tell me you think it's okay for light skinned blacks to look down on dark skin blacks?"

"Accepting it as a part of life, a reflection of people's fears is not the same as liking it." Ava said, "Your Grandpa George was eager for your father to marry your mother, once he and your grandmother Ruth met your mother, and learned what she was about." Ava's words shocked Florina. "Your Grandpa George liked that your mother had graduated college. None of his five children, and that included your father, had achieved what she had. Your aunts barely graduated high school. All his land and education couldn't buy what your mother had earned. This brought him great shame. He respected that. He didn't care that your mother's skin was dark. She was educated. That's why your aunts despise her. She has something they'll never achieve."

"And Grandma Ruth?" Florina asked. George Gavin's words and beliefs ruled her thoughts. How sad, Florina concluded. "I'm determined to have my own thoughts and ideas," she said.

"Then don't let your fears stop you from completing college this time."

Ava's words, ' ... *this time* ... ' stayed with Florina during the ride to her parents' farm outside of Laurel. What had Ava meant? Florina recalled Ava's statement concerning the state in which people enter marriage.

"We all have regrets. Whether those regrets are linked to actions casting irreparable damage to ourselves and others determine our ability to move forward with another."

On arriving home, Florina pleaded weariness due to the bus ride from Poinsettia and went straight to her room. Ava remained for another forty-five minutes or so speaking with Helen and Gavin, and then Helen alone.

Florina felt herself back where she had been upon returning home from college that May of '66 when Melinda had informed her of Ennis' death. Florina lay upon her bed, and looked out the window at the setting sun. Melinda had held the death of her son for nearly a month before telling Florina.

"You were so close to finals. I didn't want to upset you, mess up your junior year," Melinda had said, her apology for not having delivered the news sooner. Florina had been too full of shock and despair to have considered the heavy burden then weighing upon Ennis' mother.

She wondered of Melinda now. After returning home for the summer Florina had written her each month--sometimes twice, or three times. Florina had been careful not to write too much. She had not wanted to alert her parents, less they think the letters were to someone who knew Florina's secret, why she had chosen not to return to college.

She had also wanted not to beleaguer Melinda with her pain and sadness. Then the letters had become burdensome. Florina could not remember when she had come to feel that writing them had become an obligation, rather than an act wherein she could speak freely.

Staring at the sun, nearly dissolved in the western horizon, Florina realized that at some point carrying the memory of Ennis had become heavy, a task of which she had wanted to relieve herself. And yet nothing had presented itself to replace his memory. This had dominated her thoughts the afternoon she had headed out from her parents' farm with the strawberries for Ava. The strawberries would serve as dessert for the house guests she entertained each year, Austin and Carolyn Hammond.

Ava had known Carolyn as a child. They had reunited when Ava married Bill Reynolds and moved to Washington, D. C, where Bill, worked as medical resident with Hammond Austin, then married to Carolyn. Bill and Hammond Austin had studied medicine together at Howard University.

Ava Reynolds might know Robert MacIntosh, Florina concluded. The idea that more than simple friendship existed between Carolyn and MacIntosh had never left Florina. Ava's statement about the secrets and baggage with which both men and women, husbands and wives, entered marriage had removed the disquiet that had otherwise prevented Florina from considering the roots of Carolyn and Robert's relationship.

The sun completely gone, darkness descended. Florina drifted into sleep knowing that despite whatever secrets lived between Redmond's mother and Florina's English professor and mentor, she would need to face her mother the next morning. Unlike when she returned home that tortuous summer of 1966, Florina would not have two months to ponder her decision regarding her act of leaving Redmond.

———————————————————

Chapter 27

Florina was sitting the dirty breakfast dishes in the sink when her father, Major, entered the kitchen Saturday morning.

"This is a late breakfast for you," said Major Gavin. He poured himself a cup of coffee.

"Would you like me to make you a fresh pot?"

"I'm fine with this." Major took a sip and sat to the table.

Major's smooth and comforting voice reminded her how much she had missed him the past two months. She turned on the faucet and made ready to wash her dishes.

"Leave that for your mother," Major said. He crossed his legs and patted the chair next to him. What seemed a spacious kitchen during Florina's childhood now felt small. The knick knacks and ceramic figures--cows, ducks, chickens, a farmer, his wife and children appeared to turn their eyes upon Florina. "On second thought," Major stood. "Let's go for a walk." He took his cup to the sink and then getting their coats, they left.

Florina and her father headed across the hardened and bare field against the February cold and entered the woodlands where Florina had played for hours upon days as a child. Some distance into the forest, she said, "This path looks fresh. Like someone's been walking here." She nodded down at the footsteps.

"I come here often," Major said. "You didn't think I'd let you roam these woods without searching out your old haunts."

But Florina was now an adult, a widow into her second marriage. Florina then said, "So that's why you always told Momma not to worry."

"It's my land and it was my job to know about it, keep it safe." He grasped Florina's hand and the cold fear that was threatening to overtake her dissipated. Again, she eyed the fresh footsteps along the path. Her father glanced down too. "You may be Mrs. Redmond Austin," he said, "but you'll always be my daughter. I've missed you."

Some distance along Florina said, "There's a woman. She and her husband are our next door neighbors. Her husband and Redmond grew up together. Macon's the other doctor in Poinsettia after Redmond's father, Hammond."

"You mean after Redmond and his father," Major corrected.

Florina considered the implication of Major's statement in light of recent events.

They both went to Howard Medical School. Redmond and Macon," Florina said. Macon, though, is older than Redmond." She felt herself avoiding the true nature of the story she was sharing.

"Redmond dated Agnes before she married Macon." A wave of relief passed over Florina. Yet even as she spoke the words, heaved a sigh, a heaviness descended upon her heart. She heaved a sigh.

"What part of their relationship, Redmond and this Agnes', remains alive?" Major asked.

"I don't know." Florina turned to her father. Another wave of relief washed over her. She felt understood. "Redmond says he loves me," said Florina. "I feel he's telling the truth. But--"

Major fixed his gaze upon her.

Deeper within the forest Florina explained. "Some weeks ago, Agnes left without a word to anyone. One night when Redmond and I were eating dinner, a white woman came pounding on the door."

Major Gavin's eyebrows assumed a soft arch. Florina relayed the story of Agnes' arrival. "She'd had an abortion, was bleeding heavily." Florina told of Agnes' recuperation in their home. "She left after three days."

Florina and her father walked further. "Macon says Redmond made Agnes have the abortion to save our marriage."

"He's accusing Redmond of being the father," Major clarified. Florina nodded.
"Do you believe him?"

"Macon or Redmond?"

"Which one do you believe?"

Once more Florina examined the fresh footsteps along the path she and her father trod. "There's truth in what both are saying?"

"You believe Redmond fathered Agnes' baby," said Major.

"No!" Florina said, shaking her head violently, then calming, "Redmond says it wasn't."

"And Agnes?"

Florina observed her father's eyes inspecting her face. "She keeps going on about how evil I must think she is for having killed her child."

"Interesting thing for a woman to say who's supposed to have had an affair with your husband." Major Gavin clasped his hands behind him. "Sounds like she looks up to you."

Florina torpedoed her father with a hard stare. Major's perspective left Florina stunned, provoked her into rigorous thought.

On their return towards the cleared field he asked, "How would you feel towards Redmond if the baby Agnes aborted was his?"

"I don't rightly know." Florina tried to remain open to her father's questioning. She strolled along side Major. "It would hurt terribly."

"Is that to say you're not hurt now?" Major asked.

Florina lowered her gaze once again, and observed the fresh set of footprints, hers and her father's, intermixed with the single set she had noticed when first entering the woodlands.

"I don't hate Redmond," she said. "I don't believe the baby Agnes carried was his. But why would Macon lie?"

"There's some element of truth in what he accuses Redmond of." Though not a question, Major's statement, offered no answers.

"Why would he accuse Redmond of such and then seek out his help for one of his patien--" Florina caught herself thinking aloud. She explained of the emergency caesarean Redmond performed on Rose Thornton--how he save mother and child. "It could have all been avoided," Florina said. "Macon admitted he could have sent them to Poinsettia General, that someone would have seen them. But instead he called Redmond to prove that Negro doctors are just as good, even better, than white doctors."

"Macon believes in what he's doing," Major said, " ... however wrong he may be. Perhaps this is the only way he can accept that his wife didn't want his child or any child, and that the woman he's married can never love him."

Again, Florina beheld her father in awe. How could he know these things, not that she completely believed them? Major's gaze, brown and sturdy like Redmond's, ran soft. Florina felt her heart cracking open. Major opened his arms. She entered her father's embrace and released tears onto his thick, wool jacket. "Oh, Daddy, what's happening?"

"I don't know," Major patted her head. "But our hearts never lie."

"I love Redmond," Florina sobbed. "Truly. And I believe he loves me. I feel it."

"Then let it be," her father whispered. Again he patted her head. "Let it be."

Florina closed her eyes and sobbed some more.

220

On clearing the forest Florina spied a nineteen sixty-seven Mustang parked in the driveway. From nearly a thousand yards away the black convertible glistened in the winter sunlight.

"Well someone's got a nice car," Gavin said with his hand providing shade to his forehead.

"Who is that?" Florina said.

"I thought you might know?"

"Redmond would never buy a car like that. Too expensive and flashy."

The two started across the bare field towards the house.

On reaching the yard, Florina's mother, Helen, greeted them. "You have a visitor," she said to Florina. A young man wearing a blue army uniform descended the steps from the back porch. The gold braids on his shoulders caught Florina's attention. She tried not to gasp, forced herself to breathe.

"Clifford," she said approaching him, " ... is this yours?" Again she looked to the green Mustang convertible. "Isn't it a bit cold to have the top down?"

"I'm just so glad to be home." The army officer reached out to Florina and she embraced him. "It's so good to see you," he said then whispered, "Ennis loved you unto the end."

Florina closed her eyes and wiped away tears. She then made introductions. "Daddy, this is Major Clifford Matthews, US Army. Clifford this is my father, Major Gavin."

"Did you serve, sir?" Clifford asked. He shook hands with Florina's father.

"No, son," Major said. "My father's best friend was in World War I, always wanted to be a Major. He died, a Negro man, never achieving his goal. My father gave me the name to remember his friend. He warned me never to go to war. Fortunately I was able to steer clear of the military."

"I'm sorry to hear that, sir," said Clifford.

Florina cringed at the thought of how her father might have reacted to Ennis had Florina's husband lived and attended her graduation as he had planned.

"Not to worry, son. It seems you've accomplished the dream of my father's friend. Both he and my father would be proud of you."

"Thank-you, sir. Not a lot of people feel that way," Clifford said. He straightened his stance, threw back his shoulders.

Florina's breathing calmed in the wake of her father's last words.

"It's not your fault you're over there fightin' in Vietnam. Our government sent you there. We just pray you and others like you come home safe." Major patted Clifford's shoulder, then turning to Helen, her eyes alert and inquisitive, said, "Let me get back to the house and help you cook lunch."

"I've already prepared lunch," Helen retorted.

"Well, I'm sure there's something that needs to be done. Let's start dinner." Major grasped Helen's arm and ushered her back towards the house.

Florina marveled at the skill with which her father directed her mother away from Florina and most particularly Clifford.

The two had barely begun their stroll down the one-lane road when Clifford said, "Thank God you and your father came back from your walk. I don't know how much longer I could have staved off your mother's questions." A small sigh of relief escaped his lips. "When she said nothing of Ennis I figured you never told them. And then she said you had married." Clifford's smile dissipated.

"The day after Christmas," Florina said. She pulled the collar of her coat tighter around her neck.

"Your mother says he's a surgeon."

"He wanted to enlist, work in a MASH unit in Vietnam."

"Don't let him come," Clifford said.

Florina turned to the man who'd been Ennis' closest friend. The two had enlisted together. "Maybe if someone like Redmond, a Negro surgeon, had been with Ennis he wouldn't have died," Florina said.

Tears flooded Clifford's eyes. Red engulfed them.

Florina felt herself grow weak. She slumped to the cold pavement. Clifford knelt before her. "He loves you, Ennis. Right now," he whispered and looked to the sky. "Always will." Florina wept some more.

She described the town of Poinsettia to Clifford, how she had met Redmond, and all about his work and his family.

"He seems like a good person," said Clifford. "And the town where he lives seems nice."

"I miss home." Florina said nothing of Agnes, Macon and her trials with Redmond.

"Your mother said I was lucky to have found you home this weekend."

"This is my first time back since we married," Florina said.

"She said you're back in college, Johnson C. Smith."

"My mother-in-law introduced me to a wonderful professor. He liked what Dr. Drayton wrote about my writing," Florina said.

"Ennis talked about your poems all the time," Clifford said. "He read one every night when he got the chance." He reached into his army jacket, took out a large manila envelope, and handed it to Florina.

Staving back tears, she lifted her gaze to Clifford, and said, "What happened? I want to know everything."

Clifford sighed, looked into the distance. They were more than two miles from the house. "Nothing could have saved Ennis," he finally said.

"Still, I want to know."

⋅•⋅•⋅•⋅•⋅•⋅•⋅•⋅•

Chapter 28

⋅•⋅•⋅•⋅•⋅•⋅•⋅•⋅•

Florina and Clifford began their journey back to the house as he explained.

"We had been fighting for what seemed like weeks, really only a day or so. The jungle felt exceptionally thick and hot that morning, like there'd never been a morning, but that we'd woken up to a swollen noon. Everybody was sweating and out of breath." Clifford was describing what he had identified to Florina as The *Battle of Xã Cam My* fought April 11th and 12th, 1966. His gaze retreated into the memory where the experience remained alive.

"Ennis and I had been given our orders. We were set to take our men into the forests of a nearby rubber plantation and draw out the enemy."

"The Viet Cong?"

Clifford nodded. "We had lost a lot of soldiers over the last few days," he said. "There weren't even a hundred and fifty of us. We, Charlie Company, were the bait." Again he gazed out towards the sun moving into the distant west.

Strangely enough, Florina wondered about Redmond, what he was doing the in the wake of her having left. *Where had he eaten dinner last evening--at Carolyn and Hammond's? Had*

225

he told them of her leaving? How had he felt coming back to and empty house, waking up in an empty bed? She felt horrible. Florina had for intents, behaved like Agnes.

Clifford continued. "Gun fire wasn't that heavy until around two-o-clock." He frowned as if pained by what he recalled. "One of my men reported having seen Viet Cong officers. We knew that heavy fighting would soon begin. But that was our job. We knew the mission." Florina clenched her hands and forced herself to breathe. "Two other divisions were supposed to show up once we got the Viet Cong out in the open. That's what we had been told. With them on one side and us on the other we would have had the Viet Cong surrounded." Clifford grew silent. His lips trembled.

"What happened?" Florina whispered.

"They never showed. Better yet when they did, it was too late. Nearly forty of us were killed. We fought into the night and the next day. They never let up. Instead of us surrounding them, the Viet Cong encircled us."

"What happened to the two other divisions?"

"The thick jungle. *And the heat.* It was too much. They had to cut their way through vines and over growth. No path had been laid out like usual. It was native tropical forest, untouched. They had been through their own war." Clifford lowered his head.

He teared up, redness swallowing the whites around his irises. "Towards the middle of the night the Viet Cong heated up their firing. We thought it was all over, that in the next moment their entire company would descended on us. I lost track of Ennis. Like me he was trying to keep focus on his men amid the fighting and keep them alert. Firing died down about one the next morning. We began to hope. Then one of my men reported seeing a soldier dragged off. By morning twenty-five men lay with their necks slit."

Florina gasped, brought her palm to her lips.

"Not more than ten yards from me, Ennis lay dead."

"Oh, no."

"He couldn't have lingered," Clifford said. "It's the only thing that keeps me sane. We both said that when it happened we wanted it to be fast and quick. No time to think. Or even pray."

Florina considered Clifford's words, " ... *when it happened* ... " Ennis had never spoken of the eventuality of death in his letters, rather, " ... *when I get home for your graduation and you introduce me to your parents* ... "

"I never got to say "Good-bye," Clifford said, barely audible.

Neither had Florina.

The chimney of Florina's childhood home loomed in the distance as they entered the last leg of their walk back down the one lane road where she had lived Ennis' death in Clifford's telling.

"How were you able to go back into battle?" Florina asked.

"It was the only thing I could do. Every time I want to stop and get angry or feel sorry for myself, I think of the hundred or so guys who either didn't make it or were wounded."

"Do you stay in contact with them, the ones who survived?"

"We don't fight with anyone else," said Clifford. "Ten guys under my command survived. All we have is each other."

"Are any of them married?"

"Eight were during the battle. Two others have married since then."

"How do their wives deal with the possibility of them ... "

"Dying?" Clifford finished Florina's sentence. "Some of them are like you, they have no idea what the man they love has gotten himself into."

Florina took a long swallow, the innocence with which she had married Ennis, one day after he had enlisted, making its way down her throat.

"Others, like my wife," Clifford said "... have their own personal way of coping. Shelia believes that God allowed me to live to meet her. Because of that she says He won't take me away."

"Is that what you believe?" Florina's heart pounded.

"I have no other choice."

"Tell Shelia I believe the same thing."

Clifford smiled. Again Florina embraced him. The two held each other for a long time.

On nearing the driveway to her parent's house, Florina spied the familiar black 1966 Buick Riviera parked behind Clifford's green Mustang convertible. *Redmond--* she thought.

"Looks like you've got visitors," Clifford said. They started up the driveway. Florina looked inside the Riviera. "You know the person who drives this?" Clifford asked.

"It's my husband's." Florina led Clifford towards the back of the house from where they had started out. They stepped onto the porch when the door opened and Redmond came out. He was wearing his usual blue wool coat and looked smarter than ever in his black suit, white shirt and red tie.

Florina's mother Helen joined them on the porch and stood beside Redmond. "You two were gone forever," Helen said. "I had begun to worry."

"We had a lot to talk about," said Florina.

"I should say," Helen quipped. She said to Clifford, "This is Florina's husband, Dr. Redmond Austin."

"I've told Clifford about Redmond," Florina sought to quell her mother's anxiety. The two had yet to speak since Florina's arrival. Florina said to Redmond, "Clifford and were students at college. He's now a major in the army."

"Pleased to meet you," Clifford said and extended his hand to Redmond.

Florina's father, having come onto the porch said to Redmond, "Clifford's achieved a mighty high rank in a short time. The two of you could talk a lot about your accomplishments." Major patted Redmond's shoulder despite the hard glance Helen shot him.

"I'm more eager to hear what you have to say about the fighting in Vietnam," said Redmond.

"Stay away," Clifford said. "And I don't mean any disrespect."

As Redmond appeared shocked Clifford explained.

"This war is a mess--has taken a downturn since the TET Offensive back in January."

Florina recalled that several of the flurry of newspapers surrounding Agnes held articles questioning the purpose of the Vietnam War in light of the surprise attack launched by the Viet Cong during what was to be a cease fire in celebration of Asian New Year.   Television news journalist had begun echoing the same refrain, also raising questions as to whether the United States could secure a clear victory. American military forces had yet to recover from the TET ambush, what military officials had initially described as a few rounds of bullets fired, but reports now clarified had resulted in a watershed of casualties that had continued amid the increased fighting.

In the wake of this Dr. King had become more vocal in his criticism of the war.

Clifford looked to Florina, said, "We don't need to lose any more good men, particularly Negro men in a war that's about nothing but power and greed."

Redmond's eyes lost energy.

Clifford then said to Redmond, "If everything Florina says about you is true, we need you here."

Redmond turned to Florina. He looked as if buffering back tears.

Clifford addressed Florina's parents. "Mr. and Mrs. Gavin," he reached towards Helen then Major, thanks for your hospitality."

"Won't you be staying for dinner?" Helen asked.

Florina eyed her mother, aware of her anxiety concerning Clifford's presence, and knowing that Helen had not wanted Clifford to remain any longer than needed. Florina lamented that Helen could be as coy as her sisters-in-laws, Florina's aunts.

"I'll see you to the car," Florina said.

"I'll move my car," Redmond said to Clifford.

Florina walked Clifford to his green Mustang aware of Redmond inside the black Riviera observing her. "Thanks so much for coming," Florina said to Clifford. He had yet to get inside the convertible. She absorbed the image of Clifford in his dress blues and wondered what Ennis might have looked like in his. Had he ever worn them?

"How long will you be here?"

"I'm on leave for a month," Clifford said. "My first since we shipped out." He'd been away for nearly two years.

"Ennis and I promised each other that if anything happened, we'd go to the other's family as soon as we got a chance." Florina felt herself again about to cry. "I'm driving to see Ennis' mother tomorrow."

"Melinda," said Florina. "But you should have gone to see her today."

"She told me to come here first," Clifford said.

Florina felt sorry for having stopped writing Melinda.

"She's been worried about you," Clifford said.

"She doesn't know I've re-married."

Clifford glanced back at Redmond sitting in the Riviera then down upon Florina holding the envelope of letters he had given her and now tucked within her coat. "Ennis would have wanted you happy," Clifford said.

Florina lowered her head ashamed of having grown to love another.

"Redmond seems like a nice guy." Clifford opened the car door and got inside.

Florina looked to Clifford once he was inside the convertible. "Like you, I never said "Good-bye.""

"I know." He started the ignition. Florina closed the door and stepped back.   Clifford rolled down the window and said, "Melinda will understand. Write her."

"Will you tell her, I say, *"Hello,"* when you see her tomorrow?"

"Those are my orders," Clifford said. "And I always carry them out." He saluted Florina.

Florina waved to Ennis' friend in college and in battle. With Redmond's Riviera out of driveway, Clifford pulled the Mustang into reverse and left.

Chapter 29

Last rays from the sun filled the winter sky as Florina and Redmond headed out across the field. Dinner had been quiet and tense at best, downright nerve racking at worse. Wanting answers and having yet to speak with Florina, Helen was both relieved and frustrated. With Clifford having refused dinner, Helen had been able to focus her energies on making Redmond comfortable. Yet his presence prevented Florina's mother from interrogating Florina as to why she had returned home without her husband.

Redmond's request--"Florina, will you join me for a walk?" provided Major the perfect opportunity to occupy Helen once again. "And we'll clean up the dishes," chimed Florina's father.

"It'll be the third walk she's taken today," Helen said.

"And as my father said," Major spoke, "walking is good for the soul."

Major gave Redmond a lantern, "Sun's settin'. You might need this to guide you," and then patting Redmond's shoulder, sent him and Florina   through the front door.

Walking across the yard, Florina said, "I've never seen my father help with meals and dishes as much as this weekend."

"He's worried about you," Redmond said.

Florina turned to her husband, his face growing dim in the fading sunlight.

"I promised to make you happy."

"What did you say to them?" Florina asked.

"The truth."

"You told my parents of having slept with Agnes? That you fathered her child?"

"I didn't father Agnes' child," said Redmond. "And even if I did, it's absurd that I would have performed an abortion on her."

"That's what Macon is asserting," Florina said.

"And you believe him."

Florina's cheeks ran hot. She was angry at her disloyalty to Redmond and doubts about his faithfulness. It had been so clear with Ennis, their love ... who they were, their lives before meeting each other. But Redmond, five, nearly six years older than Florina, had a history. *As did she.*

"I'm a surgeon," Redmond said. "I certainly have the skills to perform one."

"But you wouldn't--certainly not on the woman carrying your child," Florina said. She lifted the collar of her coat, tucked it around her neck.

"I slept with Agnes. But the child was not mine. We were together in June," Redmond said. "Any child that I might have given her would have put her at five or six months pregnant. No sane doctor would have performed an abortion on a woman over four months. Agnes could have died."

Florina recalled the heavy bleeding Agnes had experienced. Days prior to her having gone missing Agnes' waist had been nearly paper thin.

"She would have had no bleeding had she not traveled so soon after the procedure. My father concluded that when examining her over the three days she spent with us."

232

Florina looked at Redmond's bare hand, holding the lantern against the growing cold. "Let me take that." She took the lantern with her gloved hand.

Redmond pocketed his hands. "You can ask my father if you don't believe me."

"I believe you," Florina murmured.

They continued across the field, its soil hard against the night and cold.

"Clifford seems like a nice guy," Redmond started. "You knew him in college?"

"He says the same of you. He was two years older than me."

"Your mother said she had never met him. That she and your father knew very few of your friends from college."

"I introduced them to my dorm mates."

The two continued walking, darkness enveloping them and illuminating the lantern's glow. "I'm sorry for everything," Redmond said. "Mother said my first mistake was not having apologized, but instead defending myself."

Florina turned to him. "Had you done that I might have wondered if there was more you weren't telling me."

Surprise mixed with caution and hoped glowed upon Redmond's face against the light of the lantern scattering the darkness. "That's what Grandmother said. Of course we were alone when she told me."

"I like your grandmother."

"Mother and father are worried. They like you very much."

"And like them. They're good people." Florina lifted the lantern, drew close to Redmond. She spoke softly and deliberately. "I'm sorry for having lied to you. It's been difficult to trust you, not simply because of what's happened between you and Agnes, that you two had a previous relationship, but because I too-- " Florina paused, and then meeting Redmond's gaze, said, "I was with someone before meeting you."

Redmond sighed, a halo of his warm breath encircling him and Florina.

233

"I married someone in the fall of my junior year in college. His name was Ennis. He went to Vietnam right after we married. Six months later he was killed. Clifford was his best friend. Only Ennis' mother knew we married. Ennis must have told Clifford after they reached Vietnam."

Redmond stared at Florina.

She felt free and at peace for the first time ever.

Chapter 30

Daybreak had yet to arrive, the sun having yet broken through the clouds of winter, when Florina placed her suitcase in the car. Her mother met her on the porch.

"We haven't spoken since you arrived," Helen said.

Florina and Redmond had returned from their walk last evening a few minutes past ten and had gone straight to bed. "I'm sorry about that," Florina said. "Things have been difficult."

"I should say. Two men visiting you in one day. One your husband, the other we're yet to truly understand who he is and why he came to visit you." Helen frowned and seemed perturbed. She got that way when worried.

"This is Clifford's first time home since going off to Vietnam."

"He seems like a nice enough young man, but--"

"Don't worry, Momma, I didn't date or promise to marry him before he left," Florina said. Wearing but a sweater, Florina rubbed her palms together and headed towards the door to return inside.

She was barely past her mother when Helen said, "You may not have held feelings for Clifford, but you gave your heart to someone." Florina turned around. "And I don't mean Redmond." Florina's lips trembled. "Three times you left this house yesterday. The first was with your father. The two of you headed into the woods, where you always go when something's troubling you. Your second journey was with Clifford. Men don't cry for no reason. His eyes were red and glassy when you both returned. Your face was dry, but your cheeks were red and swollen." Florina marveled at how well her mother knew her. Helen continued. "Redmond came back with you last evening looking like a little boy someone had punched and who was refusing to cry." Florina loved her mother and would not speak disrespectfully to her. "You're not the only person who's lost their first love," Helen said.

Helen's words left Florina feeling strange. She went into the house. Helen followed. Some aspect of Helen had emerged, a hidden part that tugged at Florina in conflicting ways.

"I was a young woman, just like you when I met your father," Helen said. "And before that, I had been girl, a seventeen year old girl who had loved a man much too old for my own good. Still, I had loved him. Just like we don't choose the people who love us, neither can we choose the ones we give our hearts too."

Florina's chest ran full. She felt as if her heart would drop from her chest and crash onto the floor, breaking into a million pieces--most of which she could never gather.
She replayed her mother's words in the car during the four-hour journey back to Poinsettia. Each time Florina turned to Redmond driving beside her. Interspersed between considerations of all Helen had stated, and the intentions of her mother's self-revelations, Florina found herself recounting the many Friday evenings Redmond had driven from Poinsettia to Laurel, where he had stayed with Ava and Bill Reynolds, so that he might visit Florina on the weekends. He would leave on Sunday after services at Laurel A. M. E. Zion. Torn by his hesitancy to leave, Florina urged him to start back for Poinsettia.

"The drive is long and you're alone," she would always say. She had wanted him to be safe, as had Helen.

"Don't keep him here too long," Helen had said that first weekend Redmond had returned after he and his parents had vacationed with the Reynolds that last week in July and first in August.

Heat and social unrest had encapsulated the summer of 1967, riots erupting in the cities of Newark, Detroit, Baltimore, and Cairo, Illinois. Paratroopers sent to quell the maelstrom of violence in Maryland, along with General Westmoreland's claims of victory in Vietnam, and his request to deploy forty-five thousand more troops in Vietnam, catapulted the country into a time warp demanding change.

Twenty weekends Redmond had driven to Laurel and then back to Poinsettia after preventing two crates of strawberries, Florina had brought to Ava Reynolds, from slipping out of Florina's hands. Strawberries--ripe, red and luscious--picked and delivered in the heat of summer and violence.

Florina and Redmond arrived back in Poinsettia just as parishioners were descending the church steps. He drove into a space in the church parking lot and turned off the ignition. "I need to speak with my father about a patient," Redmond said. He left the car.

A few older women waved at Florina as they headed towards their cars. John and Jeanne Cartwright came to the Riviera. Seeing as they intended to speak to Florina, she opened the door and got out.

"We missed you this morning," Jeanne said with a smile that looked as if she willed it upon her face as pale as the dead of winter they were experiencing.

"I went home for the weekend," Florina said.

"My, my," Jeanne sighed. "Agnes goes away only to return feeling severely under the weather, and you go to visit your parents. Your poor husbands. I suppose the wives of today don't adhere to the same rules that governed my generation."

John Cartwright looked to Jeanne as she continued. "Your parents are well, I trust." Jeanne's alert gaze gave the impression she was searching for an answer to the question hidden in the probing mind of her statement. Or perhaps it was an opening.

"They're fine. How is Cynthia?" Florina asked. "Will she be coming home for Easter?"

The animated curiosity in Jeanne's gaze lost steam. "I would suppose." She left John and drew near Florina. "Then again regarding those in our town, it's so sad about Agnes," Jeanne said. "It appears as if she's taken ill again. I would imagine that Redmond told you." In the silence of Florina's shock, Jeanne then said. "Or perhaps he hasn't."

"I left on Friday," Florina said. "Redmond arrived yesterday at my home."

"Perhaps in the rush of things, he didn't mention it," said Jeanne. "Then again, he might have wanted not to worry you. Being that you and Agnes are neighbors and such good friends."

"I trust that you are well," John Cartwright said, "that you're settling into life here in Poinsettia."

"I am," Florina said, wondering how on earth anyone could have posited she and Agnes as good friends. She recalled how Redmond had accorded Agnes' coming to them after her abortion as her seeking solace from Florina as much as medical care from Redmond. "She *trusts* your discretion," he had said.

Now having relieved herself of that which she sought to confess, Jeanne Cartwright said to Florina, "I'm told you've returned to college."

"Yes, I'm taking courses at Johnson C. Smith."

"I think that's absolutely wonderful that you've chosen to better yourself," Jeanne said. "So many women would think that having married a surgeon, they need not acquire any education."

It angered Florina that Jeanne Cartwright, like Agnes, expressed a similar surprise in Redmond having married Florina who possessed no college degree, but that also and unlike Agnes, Jeanne assumed Florina had never even attended. "This is my senior year," Florina said.

"You were at another school?" Again, the sparkle of curiosity in Jeanne's gaze dimmed.

"North Carolina Teacher's College, where my mother and godmother, Ava Reynolds graduated. They're both teachers."

"Oh my, I suppose the gift for teaching flows in your veins."

"I'm not quite sure. I'm studying Literature."

"You share the same interest as Carolyn's father, Redmond's grandfather," said Jeanne.

"I believe he was a professor at Howard," John Cartwright added.

"He was the head of the English and Literature Department," Florina said.

"Too bad you won't be able to continue like him-- your being married and all," Jeanne said.

"I don't know about that," Florina quipped.

"Well it must be difficult changing your course of study." Jeanne said. "That's why you stopped and are now going back to school."

"I've always been an English major," Florina said. She marveled at how Jeanne could tease out the story of people's lives. Angered yet again she moved to set Jeanne straight. "It was never my intention to become a teacher. I took time away from school for another matter." Then before Jeanne could pry and ask why, Florina said, "To mourn the death of my husband."

Both Jeanne and John's faces fell, her glee and his half-mocking appeal floating away in the gray cast lent by the clouds.

"You were married previous to meeting Redmond?" Jeanne spoke as if she had seen a ghost, that each word might be her last, and that uttering every syllable required all her strength.

"My husband was killed in Vietnam."

John lowered his head. "I'm so sorry."

"Well, I never would have guessed," Jeanne said and gave a sigh. "You're so young."

"He was twenty-three when he died," Florina said. "His name was Ennis. Ennis McCreary."

239

Chapter 31

It felt good to speak Ennis' name, to say he had died in Vietnam, with honor, and that she, Florina, had been his wife.

Florina had not asked her mother about the person she had loved before marrying her father. She had not been ready to hear Helen's story. Yet in knowing that it existed, that Helen had undergone a similar experience, delivered Florina a life raft from which to escape the lies and guilt binding and encasing her heart, imprisoning Florina in a sea of shame and self-recrimination for having loved and married another.

She breathed with calm as Redmond drove them home. Her chest no longer labored to decipher when and how she might reveal her secret and how others might respond upon learning it, or that they might discover Florina's lies by some other means. Approaching their house, Florina grew concerned for Agnes, whom Redmond had yet to speak about.

"Jeanne and John Cartwright came to the car while you were speaking with your father," Florina said.

Redmond stopped the car in front of their house, and turned off the ignition. They were out of the car and half way up the steps to the verandah, Redmond carrying her suitcase and his, when Florina said, "It seems that Agnes has left again."

Redmond stepped onto the verandah, unlocked the door and carried the bags inside. He set them down, removed his coat and placed it in the closet. Florina did the same with hers. They had not spoken during the drive from Laurel.

"Jeanne and John know that I was widowed before marrying you."

Redmond turned to her. "I told them," Florina said.

"Do you miss him?" Redmond asked.

"Yes. But I also love you."

Redmond's gaze intensified. "I love you as well," he said.

"And Agnes?"

"I feel about her the same as you feel for Ennis," Redmond said.

But how could that be? Florina found herself growing angry and enraged. *The two were not the same. She and Ennis had been married. Redmond and Agnes had not been so. Redmond had slept with Agnes* after *she had married Maco--"*

"I know it's not the same. But my feelings for Agnes, what I had with her, is now dead. It can never come alive again," Redmond said. "Not even if I wanted it to. And no matter what she says, or does, there's nothing she can do to resurrect it."

"Then why did you sleep with her after she had married Macon?"

"I was hoping, wishing ... " said Redmond. A gust of anguish swept across his face. He clenched his fists. "If I could go back and change things, believe me, I would. I had no idea that meeting you was around the corner, or things would have gone differently. I would never do anything to hurt you. I'm sorry for seeming to have misled you. That was never my intention. Meeting you changed my life. I needed to save those strawberries not just for you or Mrs. Reynolds."

The image of strawberries spilling onto the driveway, as Florina had feared, blazed before her. She saw Redmond, not herself, scrambling to gather them.

Florina's heart now ached for Redmond too, and all that he had desired and yearned to have with Agnes. Florina accepted she may never know the entirety of what had lived between Redmond and Agnes. Perhaps neither he nor Agnes comprehended it.

In the light of her father's counsel, and now once again, Redmond's words and Agnes' actions toward Redmond seemed failed attempts at salvaging that, which was already lost. Like Florina's future that had died with Ennis--his neck slashed and body slaughtered on that dank, hot night in the jungle of Vietnam, on April 11th, 1966, the connections that once bound Redmond to Agnes had drowned in a sea of unknowing that neither of them possessed the skill, abilities or will to decipher.

Tuesday morning Florina felt fortunate that Redmond had come to Laurel and that she had returned with him to Poinsettia. Though desperate to evade her mother's interrogation, Florina had not the strength to endure a second bus trip within days of having arrived in Laurel. Had she remained in Laurel she would have missed her Tuesday, and most probably her Thursday classes.

Florina greeted Robert MacIntosh following her Tuesday class. Unlike on previous meetings she brought with her an awareness of how much energy, both emotional and physical, writing poems required. Remaining emotionally connected with the world and those in the world around you was integral to practicing the craft of writing whatever the genre. But that took strength and courage.

Florina had eaten the last of her ham sandwich. MacIntosh sipped his tea, then after commenting on the recent days of freezing cold, asked, "How was your weekend?"

Florina considered what you might say and if in telling the truth of what had occurred, how far she would go. "I went home to Laurel," she said.

"Back so soon?" MacIntosh appeared surprised, sounded interested in why she had not stayed longer.

"I wouldn't have wanted to miss class," Florina said. She had not thought of that when leaving on Friday. Though four days in the past, the five-hour bus ride felt as if it had occurred months ago. "But that's not why I came back Sunday. Redmond came on Saturday and asked me to come back ... with him."

MacIntosh lowered his cup onto the saucer. "Am I to take it you left without his knowledge?"

"I took the bus home not knowing when I'd come back," Florina said. She looked at her notebook lying on the coffee table beside the sofa. The notebook contained poems she had written. The pages also held notations MacIntosh had written in red ink. *What could I have been thinking when I boarded that bus?* She chided herself. "I supposed I'm not that different from Agnes," Florina said.

"I hear that she has left Macon once more," MacIntosh said. "Redmond was worried that she had coerced you into joining her."

Florina frowned. "Why would I do that?"

"Agnes can be very persuasive." MacIntosh arched his eyebrows, focused his gaze as if to indicate that Florina understood this aspect of Agnes all too well.

"I wouldn't leave Redmond to go anywhere with Agnes."

"But you did leave him to go back home."

"He slept with Agnes, admitted so, after she had married Macon."

MacIntosh drew still, his brown gaze retreating as if comprehending something he had hoped would not occur.

"Why didn't Redmond marry Agnes?" Florina said. "I know he loved her, at least at one time. He refused to serve as best man at their wedding. That much I've figured out. You stood in for him. He never showed."

MacIntosh stole another moment to reflect. "Whatever Redmond loved about Agnes, it did not exist."

"Love is not poetry. It either is or isn't," Florina said.

"Love is never that simple. You'll see as you grow older." MacIntosh lifted the tray from the coffee table, stood and headed towards the kitchen in the back of the house.

Frustrated that her mentor had delivered no more clarity about Redmond and Agnes, the invisible and elusive ties that bound them, Florina surveyed the study and into the hallway where stood the grandfather clock ticking as if it had kept time immemorial.

Again, Florina observed her surroundings, this time with purpose. Like the relationship between MacIntosh and Carolyn, his study held a familiarity that eluded Florina's grasp.

After glancing back to the swinging door that led from the study into the kitchen she walked into the hall, and observed the grandfather clock standing to the right of the entryway into the front room. Made of maple, it seemed to not only indicate the time, but hold it. on the left of the doorway. The dining room where MacIntosh had first hosted Florina with Carolyn beckoned her. Florina brushed her hand across the smooth cherry wood surface of the table and six chairs surrounding it. And then it hit her, the chairs and table were identical to those which graced Hammond and Carolyn's dining room.

Florina recalled the tablecloth she had received as a wedding present, ivory with intricate stitching. The doilies at the center of MacIntosh's dining room held the same pattern of stitching, as did the curtains shading the windows. She gazed past the grandfather clock across the hall, and noticed that every table covering held the same stitching.

MacIntosh returned with the tray, this time carrying a fresh pot of hot water. Florina held the oval, ivory doily that usually lay at the center of the coffee table when he lowered the tray on to the table's surface.

"Redmond and I received a ivory table cloth as a wedding gift. With no name attached to it I was unable to send a note of thanks," Florina said.

"You could have asked Carolyn from whom it came," MacIntosh said.

"I never said I thought it came from a person in Poinsettia."

"I would assume you'd know who gifted you from Laurel, and would have ways of deciphering what they gave--

should there be any confusion," said MacIntosh.

Florina's mentor had again become elusive.

She handed him the doily from the coffee table. "The table cloth we received has this same pattern." Florina pointed to the stitching. "It's like none I've ever seen, nor my mother or Ava Reynolds."

MacIntosh's eyes widened at the mention of Ava Reynolds. "She's my godmother. Then again, you would know that. You would also know her. She was friends with Carolyn when Father Hammond and Uncle Bill were in medical school at Howard."

"The doilies and the curtains, everything here with that stitching was Carolyn's, or I should say, her mother's."

Robert MacIntosh's statement left Florina stunned. "Why is it here and not at Carolyn's?"

"It was the only thing she could give me. In that she had married Hammond ... while pregnant with my child," Robert MacIntosh said.

"You're Redmond's father?"

"I'm surprised he hasn't told you. Along with how much he hates me."

Florina's chest rose then sank, as if punctured.

"If I'm correct," MacIntosh started, "Redmond slept with Agnes in June, two months after she and Macon married."

Florina nodded.

"Redmond and I had a rather heated discussion last June, around the middle of the month. My guess is that the incident with Agnes occurred sometime after we'd had it out."

Florina clasped her hands and stared into the lap of her dress. Her diamond shone through the interlinking of her fingers. She could make no sense of what MacIntosh had revealed.

"Carolyn married Hammond Austin knowing that I loved her, as did Hammond, but afraid that I wouldn't be around, wasn't as dependable as Hammond," MacIntosh said. "She was right. The worst thing I did was let her think that I had died in the Port Chicago fire. Then ten years later I returned wanting to see my son."

246

Florina forced herself to breathe.

MacIntosh continued. "Redmond was sixteen. And not getting along with his father. He was going through the usual things that teenage boys experience. But my presence made it worse. And then there was Macon Elder who worshipped Hammond, all that he did and how the entire Negro community and even some whites looked up to him."

Slivers of answers to questions plaguing Florina landed and slid into place as Robert MacIntosh explained.

"As Redmond rebelled, Macon drew closer to Hammond sought to please him. He volunteered at Hammond's office, sought his counsel on applying to medical school, became the son that Hammond always wanted, the son Hammond had been to *his* father, Lucius Austin." MacIntosh sighed.

"At the height of their battles, Redmond declared he had no love for medicine; that it had kept Hammond away from Carolyn too many nights. Hammond was hurt. He set his mind to help Macon achieve all he could. He wrote letters to old friends at Howard University and then to the medical school. Macon was two years older than Redmond, but you would have thought they were the same age."

"Carolyn was at her wits end when I appeared and wanted to meet Redmond, see how he was doing. She was afraid of losing Redmond. Hammond was angry. By then he had pretty much figured out, and by Carolyn's own admission that we'd slept together, that I was Redmond's father."

Florina found it both awesome and daunting that she had not recognized the resemblances of father and son, Robert MacIntosh and Redmond, which she now beheld, clear and sharp, in the light of MacIntosh's story.

"It was an April afternoon when we told Redmond. He went to his room. What seemed a desire, almost an outright intent, to anger Hammond disappeared. He grew studious," said Robert MacIntosh. "And silent."

"Two years later he entered Howard with no need of help from Hammond. Of course we all knew that Redmond was the grandson of Dr. Whitley. I had returned to Howard and was teaching English Literature." MacIntosh frowned as if in pain, perhaps even tortured.

"He met Agnes two months after he'd completed medical school. Macon had been a resident for two years. The two had been dating. He'd been attending Reverend Julius's church. Agnes had been in many ways, as rebellious as Redmond. She was twenty-four two years younger than Redmond, four younger than Macon. Her behavior had become a problem for Reverend Julius who lived to maintain his image. *His persona is his capital.* And Agnes was doing everything possible to destroy it. If she wasn't running off to a civil rights rally or protest it was to hear Malcolm X or Martin Luther King Jr. speak, or to a anti-war rally. Each time she'd disappear, Julius would send some of his minions, thugs from the community that he paid, and quite well, to bring her back. They'd never hurt her. With Julius, his wife and Agnes able to pass for white he'd have had them lynched," MacIntosh said. "And then came Macon."

"He'd begun attending Julius' church as an intern working at Howard Hospital. Julius' wife, Hannah, didn't care much for Macon. I suspect Julius didn't either. He couldn't pass for white as they could. But they were desperate. And Macon was a doctor.

"Julius was as determined to have Agnes marry Macon, as Carolyn was at forcing herself to remain practical and marry Hammond, the responsible one, versus me who followed my passions." Somberness overtook MacIntosh. A look of melancholy washed over his face. He stared at his hands.

"It was hard standing in as best man for Redmond at Macon and Agnes' wedding," the English professor said. "Throughout the entire service, listening to the vows, over which, I might add, Reverend Kensington officiated, I felt as if I had witnessed everything that was occurring. I had seen it. I had felt it. I knew its stench. The betrayal, the disloyalty, the hurt, the lies. I knew it. And yet it was so human."

Florina considered all the reasons she had not told her parents of Ennis, of having met and fallen in love with him, and then that they had married. *Mama won't like him. His skin is too light. He looks like my aunts ... is lighter than me. She will feel that I have betrayed her.*

Florina cold have never imagined that Helen might hold the slightest amount of understanding. She felt horrible, that she had misjudged her mother, had behaved as badly as her aunts.

Florina said to Redmond's biological father, Robert MacIntosh, "Does Carolyn feel that she made the right choice?"

"You'll have to ask her. As for me, I'm certain she did."

MacIntosh's words surprised Florina, opened her to viewing her own actions anew. She no longer felt regret for having done that which she held so recently held guilt and shame. There is no need for remorse in the absence of confusion, humiliation, and blame.

Florina no longer blamed herself for Ennis' death. He died a man having married the woman he loved and who loved him. Her poems had given him solace.

He read them every night. Clifford had said.

Florina had given Ennis the ability to make peace with what had he concluded would be his eventual death in war.

Florina lifted the doily and fingered it, noted the intricacies of its pattern, mimicking the human condition, the comings and goings of life. "We all have secrets," she said. "And I have mine."

Florina told of Ennis, their marriage, and what she had confessed to Redmond that previous weekend.

"How is he taking it?" MacIntosh said.

"He came after me on Saturday, brought me back on Sunday."

"And you're here this afternoon," said MacIntosh. He observed Florina's notebook lying on the table, asked, "Have you anything for me to read?"

Florina lifted and opened the notebook to the last page on which she had written. She handed MacIntosh the notebook. "I wrote this on the bus to Laurel."

Grabbing his red pen, he slipped on his glasses, and began to read with an intensity fueled by a life Florina better understood. *Only those who know the pain of secrets can appreciate what gifts liberation from their claws deliver ...*

249

All of which Florina felt privileged to be privy.

———————————————————

Chapter 32

Robert MacIntosh's revelations further confirmed Florina's growing recognition that very little in life was as it appeared. Every situation consisted of at least two perspectives, most often created and furthered by two or more entities. Concerning relationships, human individuals comprised those entities.

Despite Redmond's protestations of love and commitment to her, Florina, until now questioned only the fidelity of his heart. Learning that Robert MacIntosh was Redmond's father, and that Redmond's mother, Carolyn, had been unfaithful to Hammond Austin, opened an entirely new dimension to Redmond's personality and inner struggles.

Complicating matters was Julius Kensington's insistence that Agnes marry Macon whom the Kensington's deemed suitable primarily because of his profession.

But why had Redmond not sought to marry Agnes? And if he had, would Reverend Julius have approved? Clearly Agnes held more than a fondness for Redmond.
Hers was an abiding love that nothing or any person could change or alter. In spite of herself, Florina understood too

251

clearly why Redmond would have sought solace from Agnes--if indeed he had gone to her after the row with Robert MacIntosh as MacIntosh had suggested.

Had *Redmond* told MacIntosh of Florina's leaving?

"He was afraid Agnes had turned you against him, and taken you with her," MacIntosh had said.

What had Redmond discussed with MacIntosh? Florina turned the question over in her mind as she drove back to Poinsettia. She could only imagine how Redmond must have felt when at sixteen he learned MacIntosh was his father, and not Hammond Austin. The backdrop of Macon fulfilling Hammond's desires to be looked up to, what Hammond wished to experience with Redmond, must have exacerbated the situation to a point of rawness injuring all.

Florina could not decipher where she might begin a conversation with Redmond on the topic. She was not supposed to know any of this. Robert MacIntosh's revelation carried a level of intimacy that went beneath anything Florina had imagined.

She had asked a question, and he, as her biological father-in-law, had given an answer. Florina had found truth in the least likely, but, not most, unexpected place. She would anticipate no more from MacIntosh. That her mentor held the answers and gave them so freely, almost as if unburdening himself, awed her.

Florina spoke with MacIntosh after class on Thursday.

"How's Redmond," the English professor asked as he walked Florina to her black Riviera.

"I've said nothing to him." Florina held her books close. Writing now meant more to her. Life had taken on a heaviness, and while not carrying a pain same as her loss of Ennis, delivered another somberness. "I'm not supposed to know any of this. I don't know how to explain how I learned," she said to MacIntosh.

"Tell him the truth."

252

"Our marriage has about as much of the truth as I think it can hold for right now," said Florina. They had reached the Riviera. She unlocked the door and placed her books in the back seat.

"You'll know when to raise the subject and tell him."

Florina was about to enter the driver's seat and then she remembered. "Your wife, Ingrid," she said. "Did she know about you and Carolyn?"

"I told her everything."

"Ingrid knew Redmond was your son," Florina said.

"She liked him," MacIntosh said. "They grew close. Redmond came home and was with me when she died."

Florina felt another layer of the intricacies defining human interactions enwrapping her.

Thursday Redmond spent the entire night at Charlotte Negro Hospital, operating on two patients, both suffering from appendicitis and needing surgery. His nurse, Clara, rescheduled morning patients leaving him only Friday afternoon appointments. Saturday he slept.

Sunday arrived and they attended services at St. Andrews.

Reverend Mitchell's sermon, unlike his others, felt more woeful. Speaking from Jeremiah, he appeared relaxed and calm, confident of his words.

"Jeremiah was an indomitable prophet. We owe him much. Yet, I fear we in the clergy do him an injustice. You will hear few, if any, sermons from the Book of Jeremiah." Mitchell pulled at his black velvet robe. He gripped the lectern, and lowered his head.

Florina sensed he was crying. She was holding back her own tears.

"Jeremiah suffered. No one wanted to hear what he had to say." The sturdy forty-five year-old minister looked out upon the crowd, and said, "Jeremiah urged the Israelites to go into exile. And yet he warned them to leave some things, for when

253

they returned. 'You'll be back,' he said. 'You'll be back.'"
Mitchell again pulled on the sides of the lectern.

At the outset of one of his previous sermons Reverend Jeremiah Mitchell had explained that his wife had given birth to their daughter, Katherine, when they were fifteen. They'd married six months prior.

Jeremiah Mitchell took a sweeping view of the congregation. Florina with Redmond to her right, occupied their usual places at the end of the pew beside the aisle. The name, Austin, stood engraved upon the window at the end of the other aisle across from their pew. Hammond, and Carolyn Austin sat to Florina's left. Mother Austin had chosen not to brave the immense cold of late February and had remained home.

Mitchell again pulled at his robe, took a breath and spoke. "Our people know about suffering. An awful lot. And yet, there are others beyond us who suffer too." His voice dipped. "Sometimes they suffer more. It takes great insight to realize this. To see beyond the pain that grips you. Better yet, to use your pain as a lens to connect with others in their tribulations."

A low gasp swept across the audience then folded into thick silence.

"Dr. Martin Luther King is a lot like the prophet Jeremiah," Mitchell said. "Dr. King has suffered. He *is* suffering right now as I speak—as we—you and I—" Mitchell pointed to his chest and then the audience, "—experience refuge in this warm, comfortable sanctuary." Mitchell steadied himself at the lectern. He hung his head. "People don't like Dr. King's stance on the war. This country doesn't like it. *And he is at war with this country.* We, Negroes don't like it." The minister paused. "Dr. King is against the war. He's against this country sending our boys, our Negro men that this government and its leaders and white citizens mistreat—he's against this country sending them halfway around the world to fight people who have done no wrong to any of us."

Mitchell's voice took on a solemn tone. Tears sparkled in his eyes. Florina, amidst the audience that lacked Agnes and Macon, recognized a new aspect of her pain, an ache through which she now better understood Redmond. She reached for her husband's hand. Her loss of Ennis and the truth of Redmond's parentage revealed sore spots in both Redmond's and her own spirit—a bridge over which they, if able to cross and meet the other half way, could connect.

Mitchell said, "We are all suffering. But a lot of us don't know it. For some of us our pain is apparent." He raised his hand. "We here in the congregation usually know when someone is sick or ailing. We definitely know if a family has a member who's dying. But what if the ache doesn't involve death? What if our ache isn't attached to something so tangible? What if it's rooted in something we can't attach an object or price to?" Again his voice dipped. He leaned into the lectern and towards the congregation. "What if our hurt comes from what's invaluable—something whose presence isn't so clear—but when it's lacking we sure feel it's absent?"

Mitchell stepped from behind the lectern, descended the pulpit steps and approached the congregation.

Florina gave way to the tears pulling at her. She had spent the last two days thinking of how she could make sense of the hidden truths, some of them secrets that had alienated Redmond and her from themselves, and each other. Florina turned to Redmond, his eyes fixed on Mitchell swaying and exhorting the congregants to contemplate their pain and link it with that of what he was certain Dr. King was experiencing.

"I'm told there are times when Dr. King feels alone— that God has truly forsaken him. Of course we know that God has not. As Christians we must believe so. But even Christ wondered. Do you doubt?" Mitchell's gaze swept over the congregation.

Redmond remained attentive. *What was he thinking?* Florina again looked to him.

Mitchell returned to his imperative. "Some of us feel that our parents don't love us. They say they do. But we see or experience no evidence of it. And so we feel alone. Our hurt cries out for balm."

Redmond's stillness appeared to solidify, as if he was

255

willing himself to remain open to Mitchell's words while at the same time steeling his resolve to receive their truth.

"Some of us are lost and our parents, brothers, sisters—wives and husbands—have no clue to find us. They have expectations that we can't live up to. Every morning we wake up hating ourselves, and to the reality that we don't love those closest to us, those who don't love us as we wish, or perhaps we don't love them the way we once or ever did. Worse yet, we see that what we fell in love with doesn't, or perhaps, never existed. But we've become so attached. We can't live without what was never there, what we never had. We're caught up in an illusion, bound by a desire for that which never was or can be. Despite ourselves and against everything in our hearts we yearn."

Redmond's solemn austerity gripped Florina's attention. He was holding her hand. Yet even with eyes open, and his chest expanding and contracting, Florina felt life quivering within him.

Jeremiah Mitchell interwove his fingers. He lowered his head. "The prophet Jeremiah warns that we all have our exile. And that when it ends God calls us to return, or rather returns us unto Him. Just like he called the Hebrews back to their homeland."

Redmond's palm slid open. His fingers gave way. He released Florina's hand.

She began to cough.

"What if—" Mitchell's words faded into the distance.

Florina coughed again. She had felt it coming on all week, but now in the church's stuffy warmth she could not escape the need to clear her throat as she had the tears pushing for freedom. She stood, and with hand to her mouth, hurried down the aisle towards the back of the sanctuary. Passing the ushers seated on the back pews, she pushed open the doors and on entered narthex, where she released a series of coughs. Hacking overtook Florina. She stole breaths in between each rasping cough. Tears followed.

She started towards the door leading outside. It opened.
Agnes.

Chapter 33

"What are you doing here?" Florina spoke in a scratchy whisper.

Agnes walked past her and peered through the window into the sanctuary. "I need Redmond."

"Where've you been?" Florina said as she regained her breath. "The Cartwrights were talking about how you left again. Macon isn't at church. He must be worried."

"Not so much that he was at home when I came back this morning." Agnes turned around. "Go get Redmond. Someone's been shot." Her lips were pursed. "Two people." A look of terror overtook the coldness in her eyes. "We need Redmond to take out the bullets."

After absorbing Agnes' blunt confession, Florina walked past her, entered the narthex and sent one of the ushers for Redmond. "It's an emergency. Someone's been hurt. Tell him to hurry."

The usher, wearing a white dress, nodded and with a hurried, but calm gait, walked down the aisle to Redmond sitting on the third pew from the front. Other congregants, including Hammond and Carolyn, had gathered at the altar for prayer. Redmond had remained seated.

257

He exited the sanctuary and stared at Agnes as if awakening from a meditation initiated and sustained by Mitchell's sermon.

"There was a march over by Charlotte," Agnes explained. "Sheriff Tucker and his men came. Then Klansmen appeared."

"How many were shot?" Redmond asked.

"Two. They're on their way to my house—may already be there," Agnes said.

"I need to get some things from my office." Redmond looked to Florina. "Go with Agnes. I'll be along."

Florina ran back inside, retrieved her purse, and joining Agnes in her car, they left.
Agnes parked her sedan between their houses. A brown ford four-door sedan drove up behind them.

"That's them," Agnes pulled her eyes from the rear view mirror, and hopped out of the car. Florina followed.

A lanky, young man ran towards them. "We came as fast as we could, Miss. Elder."

Agnes made introductions. They young man's name was Elmer.

"How are they?" Agnes said.

"Tyson's okay, but--" Elmer rushed back to the other car.

Agnes and Florina joined him.

The lanky young man looked to the man in the front passenger seat, gripping his shoulder. "Tyson caught one in the shoulder." Looking to the back seat he added, "They shot Innis in the stomach."

Agnes pulled open the back door. Elmer pulled the wool coat from Innis and displayed the full extent of crimson staining his shirt. Blood covered the floor and seat where a young white man lay.

"What did you call him?" Florina drew near.

"Innis," said the young man Elmer, now without his coat.

Innis looked up to Florina. She met his blue eyes. Florina gripped her stomach, tried to remain standing.

258

"Florina." Agnes and Elmer caught Florina just as her knees were touching the dead grass of winter.

Florina surveyed Agnes' face as she had when first spying her, cigarette in hand, sitting on the steps leading up to the verandah.

Macon appeared. And then Redmond. As Macon attended Innis lying in the back seat of the sedan, Redmond knelt across from Agnes, lifted Florina and took her inside. The lanky, Elmer, assisted Macon in lifting Innis Halpern from the car and onto Florina and Redmond's kitchen table. Redmond had taken Florina to their bedroom, but she refused to remain there. "I need to see him," Florina said, as she fought to stand.

"Redmond and Macon are with him," Agnes said.

"But he needs me." Florina walked past Agnes to the kitchen.

Having extracted the thirty-eight caliber, from Tyson's shoulder, while Macon had administered Innis an anesthetic, Redmond frantically applied more gauze to Innis' wound.

"The bullet's just below the diaphragm--probably pierced his stomach," Redmond sighed. "But here's too much bleeding? Why didn't you take him to Charlotte Memorial, Poinsettia General?" He glimpsed Agnes.

"We did," Tyson said with speech slurred due to the drowsiness brought on by the anesthesia Redmond had given him.

"Innis screamed at the nurses in the emergency room—the doctors too," Elmer explained. "Called 'em racists. Wouldn't let 'em touch him."

Redmond stared at the two men not believing that was the end of the story.

"Innis said that if they wouldn't treat me, and Elmer, they couldn't touch him," Tyson said. He touched his bandaged arm and looked to Elmer. "The doctor walked out of the emergency room."

"The nurses didn't know what to do," added Elmer.

"That's when we call Mrs. Elder," Tyson said.

Macon grimaced and turned to Agnes.

She rushed to kitchen table, and helped Redmond apply gauze to Innis' swollen stomach, an increase of blood flowing from it. "We have to do something," Agnes screamed.

Mesmerized by Innis lying on the table, Florina was unable to move. Moments earlier his eyes had exhibited slow movements. They now lay closed.

Redmond, careful not to press too hard, felt the man's abdomen. "His belly's hard and distended." It was growing bigger. "I can't do anything without stopping the bleeding." He ran his finger around the bullet's entry point.

The country had become a battlefield.

Innis pulled opened his eyes, and lifted his hand to Redmond who lowered his head to Innis. The injured young man whispered into Redmond's ear. The light in his blue eyes dimmed as his lips fell still. Redmond stood up. A faint smile took shape upon Innis' lips. His body began to shake.

"He's going into shock." Redmond grew angry as he clamped the man's shoulders to prevent him from falling off the table. Macon searched through Redmond's bag, extracted a bottle and syringe. On filling the syringe with the liquid from the bottle, he injected the medicine into Innis' arm. His body settled into a peaceful calm. Redmond's face grew hot. He rubbed his palms as if fire gripped them and lowered his ear to the man's lips that were losing color.

Florina felt her body growing cold.

Again Innis opened his eyes and again reached for Redmond. In a low, weak rasp he spoke so all could hear. "Thank ... you. I'm sorry ... for what ... my people ... to yours." His breath grew shallow, his words light, with each syllable. "Very ... sorry."

Redmond grasped his hand. "All is forgiven," he said looking into Innis' eyes.
Innis attempted a smile, but instead exhaled. His pale lips fell still. A cold and heavy silence settled within the room.

His hands once more awash in blood, Redmond lifted his wrist, "One-forty-seven pm," he read his watch then wiped his brows with the back of his palm.

Florina lowered her palm to the white man's eyes held open by the rigor of death and smoothed his eyelids closed. She then ran her fingers alongside the edge of his chin, cheek and forehead growing cool. With each movement she felt him come alive—not Innis Halpern—rather Ennis McCreary, her husband. The eyes she had closed opened. They were blue-gray and filled with joy evidenced by the smile of his thin pink lips. Unlike Innis Halpern, his skin was the color of buttermilk. A neat mustache overlay his lips.

Florina lifted Ennis McCreary's hand. His fingers tightened around hers. She smiled. He sat up, his legs dangling from the table. Florina placed his hand upon her stomach, then lowered her head, and rested her lips on his.

A hand landed upon her left shoulder. A second one settled on her right.
She turned.

Redmond. My husband.

Florina glanced back, stole one last look of the body stretched upon the table. *He's dead.* She reminded herself.

Agnes drew near. Her lips mouthed unintelligible words. She reached out and took Florina's hand. Redmond took the other.

"Get away from me!" Florina pulled back. "I want him! I want my husband!" But he was dead. Both Ennis McCreary and Innis Halpern. Ennis McCreary had gone. The body of Innis Halpern lay sprawled upon the kitchen table on which Florina sat and ate meals with Redmond.

Redmond eased Florina onto the bed, "You're a doctor," Florina said. "Save him!"

Redmond's despair and confusion thickened upon his face.

Florina feared him growing angry. Again she pulled away. "I shouldn't have married you."

As if to decipher Florina's madness, Agnes turned back to the kitchen where the corpse of Innis Halpern lay on the table.

"You took him away!" Florina screamed at Redmond.

Macon approached her, softly said, "We did all we could." His grey eyes held the sadness that had filled them

261

when he had said he yearned to be with Agnes and have peace in their marriage.

"I need him to live," Florina said, her emotions pouring through. And yet a calm descended.

"We're sorry," Macon said as if he knew her story.

"You killed him!" Florina turned to Redmond and pounded his chest. "You could have saved him, but you didn't!" Florina unleashed onto Redmond her rage pent up for nearly two years. She hit him several times more until Macon wrapped his arms around her.

By then she was screaming wildly. Agnes brushed her forehead as Macon held her taut. Redmond having lifted a syringe and bottle from his bag filled the syringe with the sedative that had eased Innis Halpern's suffering as he approached death. Florina was not dying, but she needed peace, if only for a short while. Florina felt a slight prick. Ennis McCreary's voice emerged in the descending darkness. She felt herself being lifted as she moved through the echo of his words.

I'll be back.

He had returned for a momentary stay.

I promise.

Florina felt a heavy sleep settle upon her.

––––––––––––––––––––––––––––––

Chapter 34

Florina awoke to Redmond sitting on the sitting the bed beside where she lay.

Caution and fear roamed his eyes. She gripped her temple against the dull ache in her head. She closed her swollen eyes and recalled Tyson shot in the shoulder and then blood pouring from Innis' pink belly. She had given Redmond angry words, her fist pounding his chest.

Save him! Save him! Isn't that what you're supposed to do? You're a doctor! Florina had said.

The two faces—those of Ennis McCreary and Innis Halpern—one light beige, the other pinkish white—hung before her. Florina wept.

She opened her eyes, said to Redmond, "I'm sorry."

"He'd lost too much blood."

Florina lowered her eyelids again and held them shut.

"Did you know him?" Redmond asked. He lifted her hand on receiving no answer.

Florina snatched it back. *Where was his anger?* Redmond had every right to be cross with her. And yet--

The two faces of Ennis McCreary and Innis Halpern refused to exit the stage of her mind. A wave of guilt rallied within Florina. The images then merged, that of Innis Halpern subsumed into the memory of Ennis McCreary that lived within, and superimposed, upon Florina's memory. Florina wished to banish them from her thoughts. Rage overtook her.

"Where is he?" she asked Redmond.

"It's over and done. Agnes and I cleaned up the kitchen while Macon went for the coroner. You were asleep when they took him away. It's done and finished," Redmond said.

Florina recalled pushing closed Innis Halpern's eyes that had been staring out, as if searching, wanting, longing for his soul to return to its body, regain his life. He, Innis Halpern, had been her Ennis, Ennis McCreary. She had felt Ennis McCreary's spirit trapped inside Innis Halpern's body, and speaking to her. Ennis' spirit had called out, and awakened Florina, where upon she had opened her eyes to Redmond sitting upon the bed, and entered his arms that now held her.

"I shouldn't have let them bring him here. Agnes asked too much this time," Redmond said.

"They had been shot, were suffering."

"I'm suffering. You're suffering."

"We're all suffering," Florina said. "That's what Reverend Mitchell was trying to get us to see in church this morning."

Redmond stood and walked to the window opening onto Agnes and Macon's house. He pocketed his hands. His back was to Florina. "Do you love me?" Redmond spoke back to Florina lying upon the bed.

"Yes." Florina observed her hands and the wedding band upon her left finger.

"I mean as much as him, Ennis, your first husband."

Florina maneuvered out of bed, steadied herself against the dizziness and walked to the window by which Redmond stood. She eased her arms around Redmond's waist.

Redmond turned around. His eyes seemed to say, *It was like you knew him*--about her response to Innis Halpern's death-- *—like you loved him.*

264

Florina reached past Redmond grasped the cord to the window shade and pulled, but the cord wouldn't give way. It was jammed. Florina pulled again. Despite herself she looked across to Agnes and Macon's living room, saw Agnes to her writing desk by the window behind the couch. She was sliding a manila envelope into the drawer of the desk.

As if she knew Florina had been watching, Agnes lifted her head. She smiled and waved. Florina pulled the cord a third time. The shade fell.

"Forgive me," Redmond said.

"I do." Again she lowered her eyelids.

Redmond kissed her, then reaching behind Florina, unzipped her dress, slid it from her shoulders. It dropped to the floor.

Florina unbuttoned his white shirt. It held only a smattering of blood. She would wash it out with cold water the next morning, hang it on the line to dry then iron it. Unlike the one Redmond had been wearing when delivering the Thornton baby, this shirt would be good as new by tomorrow evening.

Florina and Redmond walked to their bed. She lay back down. Redmond slid underneath the covers beside her. Again took her into his arms. And with more tenderness than during their previous lovemaking--a greater sense of awareness of all that life encompassed and exacted than Ennis McCreary--his junior--had gathered, Redmond entered Florina and delivered and ever depth of passion and thanksgiving.

When all had come and gone amid the vicissitudes of emotions, and that which remained everlasting had solidified its place, Florina looked to Redmond, and saw only his face, with eyes that mirrored none but her.

Chapter 35

The lingering sensation of Redmond's warm kiss dissipated from Florina's cheek, as she watched him descend the verandah, also observing Sheriff Tanner emerge from his car parked on the street.

"I need a word with you, Dr. Austin," Tanner said. He started towards the steps, met Redmond, on his way to work, at his black Riviera.

Florina descended the steps and joined them.

The sheriff's hazel eyes glistened against the early morning sun at the outset of that last week in February. Barely twenty hours had passed since the coroner had arrived and collected Innis Halpern's body. A brief exchange had passed between Redmond and the medical examiner. Redmond had ended the discussion insisting he needed to see to Florina.

Redmond placed his bag inside the car and closed the door then reached for Florina's hand. "What is it you want to know?" Redmond said to the lawman, Tanner.

The portly sheriff lifted a small pad and pen from his shirt pocket. "You say that the Halpern boy refused care at the Poinsettia General?"

"That's what Mr. Andrews and Mr. Baker said."

"That would be Elmer and Tyson." The sheriff, whom everyone in Poinsettia knew to be a part of the Klan gave Redmond a sideways glance.

The pace of Florina's heartbeat increased.

"Yes. Elmer Andrews and Tyson Baker said they took Mr. Halpern to Poinsettia General. He refused to let the nurses administer him care in the emergency room. He took the same stance with the doctors."

"You know of any reason why the boy would do such a thing?" Tanner pursed his lips.

Redmond breathed in and considered his words. "Mr. Halpern said he didn't want any racists touching him."

Sheriff Tanner's cheeks reddened. Florina took in breath.

A shade nearly as crimson as the blood spilling from Innis Halpern's blood spread across the sheriff's face. "Elmer and Tyson told you this," Sheriff Tanner said.

"No. Mr. Halpern."

Tanner squeezed his pad. Then with hands upon his waist the portly white man gazed up the street then in the opposite direction. "You expect me to believe that?"

Florina put her hand to Redmond's back. A white man had died in Redmond's care. The witnesses were three other black men, Elmer Andrews, Tyson Baker and Macon Elder. The two women, Agnes and Florina didn't count.

"I suppose you know why he was shot?" Tanner's terse words took on an angry bitterness. He was out for retribution and more blood to avenge that, which had been spilled.

"I was told he was at a civil rights march."

"I guess you weren't there. Too uppity for that," Tanner said. He scratched the back of his neck, beet red. "A bunch a gang busters causin' problems and stickin' they noses where they got no business!" Tanner's nostrils flared, sandy hairs extending from them. He took in breath and exhaled.

"I don't know what went on—"

"Looky here—Austin." Tanner leaned in and released the smell of Jack Daniels he was known to love. I got a dead boy on my hands and his Daddy wants to know what happened.

Now you can either tell me the truth or--" He reached for the revolver in his holster.

Redmond grasped Florina in an effort to shield her. She stifled a scream.

A voice rose. "Dr. Austin is speaking the truth."

Florina turned to see the chief of staff at Poinsettia General, Dr. Schaeffer, approaching.

Tanner leaned back, returned the gun to his holster, and straightened his stance.

Schaeffer spoke again. "Innis Halpern refused our care." Schaeffer extended Tanner a folder. "The physician's note corroborates Dr. Austin's statement."

Tanner snatched the chart, and flipped it opened, missing Schaeffer's wink to Redmond.

"Good morning, Mrs. Austin," Schaeffer acknowledged Florina, offered his hand which Florina shook.

Tanner fired Schaeffer a hot stare. "This signed by you?" Despite his ever-present pad and pen, rumor held the Sheriff could not read.

"He refused to let anyone touch him," Schaeffer said.

"I can see why—you being a Jew and all."

"I wasn't at the attending physician in the emergency room," Schaeffer said. "What *could* save others who are injured, like Mr. Halpern, is to have physicians like Dr. Austin on staff at Poinsettia General."

"That ain't got nothin' to do with why he didn't get no care." Sheriff Tanner stood his ground. "And long as they ain't runnin' with the wrong crowd--"

"It has everything to do with it." Schaeffer arched his back and brows. "You call having a baby associating with the wrong people?"

Tanner frowned. Lines spread across his forehead.

Florina grew ever more intrigued.

Schaeffer explained. "Even if Mr. Halpern had accepted our care, I doubt we would have been able to save him. We had no general surgeon available to do the surgery he needed. Mr. Halpern was shot in the stomach."

"There's Doc Hanley," Sheriff Tanner said.

269

"And if I'm correct he was on his way to meet you for your regular Sunday afternoon card game out at Emma Munson's near the county line—that is until you were called away for the shooting that took place involving Mr. Halpern, Mr. Baker, and three other men."

Florina grew tense.

"I suggest you tell Mr. Halpern's parents the story relayed in the envelope you now possess. And if gets lost, I have copies that I'll be glad to personally deliver." Schaeffer lifted a card from his breast pocket and extended it to Tanner. "Have them call me any tim--"

"That won't be necessary," quipped Tanner. Again he flared his nose, exhaled sharply. The smell of Tennessee whiskey remained ever more pungent. The Sheriff tore a glance at Redmond, snatched Schaeffer's card and shoved it inside the folder before leaving.

"You did not come a moment too soon," Florina sighed.

"Thank you," Redmond, this time, extended his hand to Schaeffer.

"I thought you might be needing my help." Schaeffer took Redmond's palm. "Several of the nurses said Tanner questioned them for over three hours last evening. They called me this morning afraid of what he might do."

Florina raised her eyebrows as did Redmond.

"You seemed surprised," said Schaeffer.

"I didn't know they cared," Redmond said.

"The nurses--that is," Florina chimed.

"Your husband saved Rose Thornton and her baby. They haven't forgotten."

"I wasn't very nice to them." Redmond pocketed his hands.

"You'd just performed a caesarian—inside the back of a moving car." Paul Schaeffer extended Redmond his card. "On second thought I'll give this to you." He handed the card to Florina. The chief physician in charge of Poinsettia General said to Redmond, "This may be hard to believe, but Poinsettia General needs your services."

Redmond lowered his gaze, in an effort, Florina surmised, to ingest Schaeffer's statement.

Schaeffer added, "Your father's worried that you're going to leave Poinsettia, and with what happened yesterday so am I."

Redmond frowned, glanced at Florina.

"Everything I told Sheriff Tanner is true. Richard Hanley is the only general surgeon we have at Poinsettia General," Schaeffer said. "He's used his relationship with the board of trustees to deny admitting privileges to other general surgeons. When he's not drinking and playing poker with Sheriff Tanner, he's rushing through surgeries, for which he's handsomely paid, all so he can cover his gambling debts. The number of surgeries Richard Hanley's botched in the last five years has been atrocious. Hanley refused Rose Thornton because her husband had not paid *him*, not Poinsettia General, for having performed her last three deliveries that required Caesarean."

Schaeffer continued," I left New York and accepted the position of chief of staff at Poinsettia General with the understanding that I'd bring on more general surgeons. The best I could find."

Redmond and Florina each took in a deep breath.

Schaeffer extended his hand once more. Having revealed the intricate nature of his desire to bring Redmond onto the staff of Poinsettia General. "Consider what I said on your way to work."

Schaeffer then gazed down the street in the direction the lawman had driven. "And don't worry about Sheriff Tanner. He's got his hands full with Innis Halpern's father."

"I'm told Innis Halpern was from Mississippi," Redmond said.

"By way of New York. His mother's Jewish and his father is a long time civil rights advocate—an attorney," said Schaeffer.

"Does Tanner know?"

"He'll find out soon enough." Schaeffer turned and left.

Again Florina touched Redmond's back. He pulled her close. She leaned her head upon his shoulder and closed her eyes.

Chapter 36

Florina had been returning breakfast dishes, dried and washed, to the cabinet when Agnes knocked on the front door. Florina let her in and they returned to the kitchen.

"Sheriff Tanner surely took his time coming," Agnes said.

She's always snooping. Florina thought. Angry, she turned from having set a pot of water on the stove to boil and glared at Agnes.

"It's not every day that Poinsettia's Sheriff visits our neighborhood, not that I welcome it," said Agnes. She gave a weak and shameful grin. "A white boy dies in a black neighborhood and eighteen hours pass before the law arrives. Now that's a record." Agnes stood. "Let me do that." She assumed the process of making tea. "Yesterday was difficult."

An image of Innis Halpern lying upon the kitchen table overtook Florina. Feeling as if she might collapse, she forced herself to the table and sat in the chair she normally assumed when eating with Redmond.

As during Agnes' previous visits the casualness with which she lifted two cups and saucers from the cabinet where

273

Florina had but a few moments earlier placed them caught Florina's attention. "You know this house very well," Florina said.

Agnes closed the cabinet, pulled out the drawer containing flatware, and picked up two spoons.

"Did you and Redmond make love in our bedroom here, or at your house?" Florina asked.

Agnes lifted the two saucers each bearing a cup a spoon, and brought them to the table. "He hadn't met you," Agnes said.

"How did Macon learn about the two of you?" Florina pursued. She was on a mission, not simply to escape memories of Innis Halpern, but to also save her marriage.

"Macon needed to renew his medical license," Agnes said. "He had left the envelope with the form at home." Her gaze receded. What began as a sneer, "Always forgetting things--Macon," assumed petulance.

"He's your husband."

Agnes whipped Florina a hard stare. "That doesn't mean I have to love him. I wouldn't be the first. I dare say your mother probably, and mine most definitely, had a first love. But marriage is a business."

How can you know these things? The confidence with which Agnes spoke what bordered on aphorisms--her ability to read people, sense their vulnerabilities--left Florina once again feeling exposed, yet also in awe.

"Whatever may have happened prior to meeting each other, my parents love each beyond their pasts." On this of which she was sure; Florina regained emotional footing.

"You're lucky," Agnes said.

The pot of boiling water began to cry. Agnes extinguished the flame, filled each cup with water and joined Florina at the table. Florina lifted a teabag from the crystal dish upon the table, as did Agnes.

Agnes took her first sip of tea, then as if waiting for her mouth to cool, said, "I've got to give it to Redmond. He chose well when he went for you."

And yet, Florina wondered. "Why didn't he marry you?" she asked Agnes. "Better yet, why did you marry Macon?"

274

Agnes stared into her cup of tea, moved to take a sip then, "He wouldn't have me."

Agnes' statement made no sense. "You mean Redmond wanted to wait?" Florina said. *Why would Redmond refuse to marry Agnes, and yet be intimate with her?*

"My father forced me to marry Macon."

"You kept this hidden from Macon?"

"He knew," Agnes said. She pursed her lips. Her petulance returned full force. "Macon is a social climber, and of the worst kind, if you haven't already figured it out. He desires what others have, what those he worships possess. He justifies the pursuit of his desires by fooling himself into believing his goals are for the betterment of mankind."

Florina frowned. And yet she understood Agnes' explanation all too well. "But if his desires are based upon what others have, their lives, who is Macon? And what does he want?" Florina said.

"And so you have identified the conundrum?" Agnes gave a pithy smile.

"As for why I married him," Agnes then said, "I had become too much for the Right Reverend Julius Kensington to manage. He was tired of sending his deacons to retrieve me from events that didn't reflect his view on life. When it became obvious that I would not become Mrs. Redmond Austin, he turned to Dr. Macon Elder, to assist him in settling me into the respectable role of wife and mother. Macon, ever ready to become like Redmond, was too eagerly accepted the role."

Astonished, Florina parted her lips. "Did Macon know you had dated Redmond?"

"Now, see you're forgetting," Agnes said while waving her finger. "This was Macon's way of one-upping Redmond. My father lied, claimed to Macon that I had fallen out with Redmond, had come to prefer Macon to Redmond." She laughed and arched her eyebrows. Her voice took on a dark tone as she smirked. "Imagine what he must have thought when discovering me and Redmond in bed just two months after our wedding."

275

Florina tried comprehending Agnes' confession, if indeed that had been her purpose in sharing it. "Quite frankly, I don't care," Agnes said.

"He's your husband," Florina said of Macon. "You married him. Your father performed the ceremony."

"You speak as if reciting vows casts a magic spell. '*For better, for worse. For richer, for poorer. In sickness, and in health.*' They're just words." Agnes arched her brows.

"Then why say them?" Florina said.

A tortured look gripped Agnes' face, pale and nearly white. Florina sensed the pain coursing through Agnes ran deep. "I will always love Redmond," Agnes said.

Agnes' words stabbed Florina. "He says he doesn't love you," Florina quipped. She believed Redmond.

"Certainly not like he loves you."

Evermore puzzled, Florina asked. "How *did* he love you?"

Agnes lowered her gaze, again stared into her cup of tea. "Like a brother to a sister, siblings," Agnes said. "Siblings lost and trying to find our way home."

Agnes' statement defied understanding. Yet one lay entangled within the words, a meaning she tried to grasp, their echo rattling through and commanding her to awareness.

"But you were intimate, slept together," Florina said.

"You're not so pure yourself."

Despite Agnes' sharp tone, Florina sensed her once again reaching, and probing for some string of Florina's vulnerability. "I never said I was."

"You lie by omission," said Agnes. She raised her cup of tea to her lips and drank.
"You were truly moved when Innis died." Agnes sipped more tea. "I can't imagine Redmond was too pleased to have you blaming him for that white man's death."

"He was a person. A *human being.*"

"But unless you knew him from some previous time, my guess is that he reminded you of someone." Agnes eyes became alert. She said, "But that complicates things. Innis Halpern was white. And you're Negro. I'm stunned as to how you could have so much sympathy for a whit--"

"I was married before ... " Gripped with pain Florina paused. "I was married before meeting Redmond," Florina forced the words. She refused to look at Agnes, meet her gaze. "He was a Lieutenant in the Army." It was all so hard to say, but all so very true. "I never told my parents," Florina said. "He died in Vietnam."

The kettle cried out a second time. Agnes was refilling her cup with hot water when Florina left the graveyard of wilted memories amid dead hopes and wishes she had held for her and Ennis McCreary. She stood. "I'd like you to leave," she said to Agnes.

"Is that what you really want?" Agnes joined her.

"I don't trust you. You've tried to wreck my marriage, kill it from the start and are still doing so."

"I'm sorry," Agnes said. "Redmond is my only friend. And you've taken him away."

"I've taken no one. He chose me after you married Macon."

"You don't listen very well," Agnes spoke with a solemnity that startled Florina. "Redmond loves you. He will never love me the way he loves you. And there is nothing you or I can do about it."

Florina wanted to scream but she spoke with calm. "Then why are you here?"

"I have no one. You won't believe me. But I have no one."

"I need you to leave," Florina said. "See yourself out. And don't come back."

On hearing the door close, Florina slumped into the chair and for a minute she imagined Ennis McCreary lying upon the kitchen table. Reaching out she touched his head, then moving around the body covered in battle fatigues she came to see his throat slit and drained of blood. She touched his chest, cold and hard. The truth of Ennis' death seeped throughout Florina, spread throughout her body.

She lowered herself onto the chair Agnes had occupied, laid her head upon Ennis' corpse and sobbed.

Chapter 37

Florina was lying on the bed, no memories of even going to the bedroom, when Redmond arrived home. He lay down beside her, touched her shoulder.
Florina turned to face him.

"You've been crying. Your eyes are puffy," Redmond said.

Florina touched her cheeks then stood.

She was through the door and on her way to the kitchen when Redmond said, "I'm not angry at you."

Still in the throes of confusion and unable to absorb his words Florina set about preparing dinner. Redmond joined her in the kitchen. Florina began peeling potatoes.

"I'm sorry about Ennis," Redmond said. "That you felt you couldn't tell your family."

Florina turned to Redmond. "He's dead."

"But he was your husband. And if he hadn't died I most likely would have never me--"

"You're my husband. I'm married to *you* ... now. Ennis is gone. He's not coming back, if that's what you're worried about. Clifford was there with him."

"But *you* haven't mourned."

Florina's hands trembled. She dropped the knife and then the potato. As Redmond moved to gather them from the floor, she rushed past him.

Out in the front room Florina grabbed her coat from the front closet and ran outside.

Down the street and growing cold despite her wool coat, Florina began to cry. Still she walked. Nearing the end of the block she spied a woman with a suitcase. She slowed her pace. The woman waved as if to hail an oncoming car. A taxi approached, stopped at the corner. The driver got out and placed the woman's suitcase in the trunk. He then opened the back door. The woman got inside. It had begun to drizzle, but as the taxi turned the corner and drove by Florina saw all too clearly Agnes sitting in back. She was looking out at Florina. Agnes waved. Florina waved back. Her heart ached. For what Florina yet could understand.

She walked back home. Starting up the stairs Florina looked up and saw Redmond standing on the verandah. He walked down, met her half way, embraced her.

"I'm sorry," Florina whispered. "I should have told you, but--"

"It doesn't matter." Redmond held her tight.

As he walked her up to the verandah Florina recalled Agnes in the car, and their waving to each other. Agnes words, "*I have no one*," refused to leave Florina.

The following afternoon, Robert MacIntosh led the class through examination of two poems, *Ode to a Nightingale* by John Keats, and *Death*, by W. B. Yeats.

Lines in the next to the last stanza of Keat's *Ode to a Nightingale* gripped Florina.

Thou wast not born for death, immortal Bird!
No hungry generations tread thee down;
...
Perhaps the self-same song that found a path
Through the sad heart of Ruth, when, sick for home,
She stood in tears amid the alien corn;

Ennis, her *immortal bird*, had loved life. And yet all who live must die.

But why did it have to be so soon? Florina's heart ached.

Amid the trials of her and Redmond's marriage Florina longed for home. And yet unlike Ruth of Moab, Florina had not upon Ennis' death, cast her lot with her mother-in-law, Melinda. She had instead taken the path of Oprah and returned home.

Redmond was alive and vibrant. The house in which they lived had become not simply a home, but the refuge in which Redmond despite their struggles, took her into his arms and introduced her to a new world of soul making.

Florina yearned for her father's farm where she had gone and remained for the eighteen months following Ennis' death. Long walks in the woods had brought momentary peace, a temporary quietness of mind. Florina had walked alone during those months following Ennis' death, unlike the one taken during the weekend she had fled Poinsettia, her father, Gavin, joining her.

Florina he had felt like *alien corn* that weekend she had sought escape from Poinsettia. And yet the secret of her marriage to Ennis and his death living within her had become unbearable. She had confessed her truth to Redmond. Florina had grown comfortable and safe living with him. She had come to like her place beside him, lying in his arms at night after their intimacies.

MacIntosh's reading, during the last half of the class, of W. B. Yeats' poem, *Death* stirred Florina even more.

Nor dread nor hope attend
A dying animal;
A man awaits his end
Dreading and hoping all;
Many times he died,
Many times rose again.
A great man in his pride
Confronting murderous men
Casts derision upon
Supersession of breath;
He knows death to the bone –
Man has created death.

Florina had read what little she could about *The Battle of Xã Cam My* in which Ennis had died. It had taken place on the fields of Vietnam, between the capital of the French colony, Cochin-china--Saigon--and the coastal city, Vung Tau. Caught in the heat of battle, bullets swarming around them, and no one had been able to attend Ennis' wounds.

Clifford, like, Ennis, had enlisted, hoping to serve his country, a nation that hated Negro and Native American men. They had hoped to survive the Vietnam War, return home and with the strength they had gathered, make a better life for them and their families. But even the words dispensing their desires did not come easy.

Of Ennis' death, *"They slit his throat,"* Clifford had explained when Florina demanded to know what had killed Ennis.

"No dread or hopes attend a dying animal. A great man ... confronting murderous men.

By her accounts, and Clifford's confirmation, it had been a suicide mission.

Looking back on it, they never expected any of us to get out. Those of us who did were lucky. Clifford had said.

A man awaits his end dreading and hoping all.

Clifford had said, "I saw him, his body, before we left. We had no time to bring our dead with us when leaving. But I

282

aim to go back and get whatever is left. I will find Ennis'
remains."

Florina could not understand how Clifford continued to
fight.

Many times he died. Many times he rose again.
Perhaps that's all he now knew.
But Redmond, though at home, was fighting a battle too.
He knows death to the bone--man has created death.
He had seen so much blood in the last month.

Florina was nearly to the black Riviera when Robert
MacIntosh caught up with her. Nearly out of breath he said,
"You walk fast when the need strikes."

"I was thinking," Florina said. She opened the door,
pushed forward the driver's seat of the two-door Riviera and
placed her books in the back seat.

"I hope you didn't find the poems too morbid."
MacIntosh was now breathing easier.

"They're honest, left me with a lot to think about."

"Now that you can think openly," MacIntosh said.

Florina looked to the English professor and mentor.
"Ennis died in a suicide mission," she said.

MacIntosh lowered his gaze as if in reverence.

"Redmond says I haven't mourned. He told me that this
morning."

"Five years passed before I mourned Ingrid's death,"
MacIntosh said.

Florina frowned, then realized she knew few, except the
elderly, who had lost a spouse.

"When the hurt is too great it's easy to escape into
work," MacIntosh said.

Later when they were again walking behind his house,
Florina explained of the months after she refused to return to
college. "I rarely left the house. August had come and then
December. I was ashamed. Everyone wondered why I hadn't
gone back to Durham."

"And you had no baby." MacIntosh gave a broken spoken smile. "I don't mean to be flippant."

"I'm sure many wondered," Florina said. "Some even concluding I'd had an abortion."

"And then you married Redmond."

She followed MacIntosh onto a path behind the hot house. Florina considered his hydrangeas, more specifically the orange one.

He said, "Carolyn was a great help to me." Having reached a door to the back of the hot house MacIntosh pulled open a door.

Florina followed him inside. Like him, she pulled off her coat then noticed the windows covered with fog. "You spend a lot of time here," she said.

"Almost as much as I do in my library." MacIntosh was now at the table where three potted hydrangeas stood. All were orange and encased in an arched house of square glass panes.

"This was Ingrid's idea--had one of the art students make it," MacIntosh said. He carefully lifted the house and placed on the table down from the hydrangeas. "'*Orange hydrangeas are an oddity,*' she said. 'They need to be protected.'"

Florina sensed the specialness of Ingrid's creation, the orange hydrangeas that MacIntosh's wife had cultivated, and the awareness of their vulnerability. "Sometimes I feel like an orange hydrangea," Florina said.

"*We're all orange hydrangeas,*" said MacIntosh. He extended to Florina the uniquely cultivated orange hydrangea, beckoned her to touch it.

She touched the soft petals and began to cry.

During their trek from MacIntosh's house to the Riviera parked in the student's lot, MacIntosh handed Florina a small paper bag. "It's a hydrangea root bulb."

"But I know nothing about growing flowers," Florina protested.

"You and I'll be learning together. Ingrid could grow them during winter, inside the hot house, something virtually impossible to achieve, but never the garden outside-- sunlight with a bit of shade--which is what they prefer along wt

Again, Florina touch, this time marveling, the orange petals.

As for the color," MacIntosh said, "that's dependent on the ph of the soil. How she accomplished that is a mystery. I'm still trying to figure it out."

Florina inspected the bag with the hydrangea root bulb and saw a folded paper. She lifted it out.

"*The Charge of the Light Brigade*," said MacIntosh. "Like *The Battle of Xã Cam My*, those at Balaclava, were never meant to return."

Again, Florina looked into the bag holding the hydrangea root bulb. "I hate for things to die."

"*Flowers are the beautiful hieroglyphics of nature with which she indicates how much she loves,* Johann Goethe," said Robert MacIntosh.

Florina returned the paper containing the poem, *Charge of the Light Brigade,* into the bag, folded the bag closed and got inside the Riviera. She placed the bag holding the bulbs for growing orange hydrangeas in the seat beside her.

MacIntosh closed the door and she rolled down the window.

"'*Honor the charge they made, Honor the Light Brigade,*' MacIntosh quoted the last lines of *The Charge of the Light Brigade*. "Their glory shall never fade." His eyes brightened.

Though not grasping the full meaning of his words, Florina drove away understanding a wisp of his intentions.

She would strive to do the same.

Chapter 38

Florina entered the kitchen and found Redmond sitting at the kitchen table.

"How'd you get home?" she asked while checking her watch.

"I hitched a ride with Father."

After classes on Tuesdays and Thursdays, Florina usually came home, and while Willa Mae finished up her work, started dinner. Florina would then drive to Redmond's office and bring him home.

"Have you been here long?" Florina put on her apron, went to the range and began lifting lids from pots.

"About an hour. Willa Mae cooked dinner."

Florina turned to see plates and silverware laid out upon the table. "She should be resting. I told her not to worry about dinn--"

"You mean you didn't want her worrying about us," said Redmond.

Willa Mae had made it all to clear her awareness of the strained relations between Florina and Redmond.

Since Agnes' surprise arrival in January, Willa Mae had given Florina several warnings, some subtle, some not so understated. "Men can be weak sometime," she had said. "My Thomas has certainly faced his temptations. But Dr. Redmond, he's a good man, even when we were children he always did the right thing."

And then one day when she had been ironing sheets, "Miss Agnes is a sly one. She's given Dr. Elder a sure run for his money. Everybody wonders why she married him." Willa Mae had then begun to fold the newly pressed sheet. "'Course we all know what he saw in her. Too bad it's tarnished. And so quickly."

Florina turned back to the range, said to Redmond, "I'll have to thank Willa Mae," and began placing the food in large bowls.

"What's this?" Redmond opened the paper bag containing the root bulb for the orange hydrangea.

"It's for growing hydrangeas. Orange ones," Florina removed the baked chicken from the oven, placed it in the center of the table next to the bowl of rice and green beans.

"Where'd you get it?"

"Robert MacIntosh gave it to me," Florina explained. "His wife, Ingrid, cultivated them, orange hydrangeas, that is. They're quite a delicacy when it comes to flowers." She sat down to the table.

Redmond stared once more into the paper bag, and then folding it closed, said, "You might want to put it in water."

Florina nodded.

Redmond lifted a envelope from his pocket and handed it to her. Wiping her hands with her apron, Florina accepted the envelope that was from a Major Clifford Matthews.

"I spoke with him. I called Clifford," Redmond said. Florina inspected the back of the unopened envelope. "I wanted to know why he was writing you," said Redmond.

"What did he say?"

"They found Ennis' body."

Florina gasped, brought her hand to her mouth.

"They'd been in such a hurry to escape the battle he and his men had had to leave the bodies."

The Battle of Xã Cam My, Florina thought.

288

"He told me," Florina said. Her cheeks ran warm, then hot. "But how do they know its him--Ennis?"

"He said they're certain. In either case, he saw Ennis dead." Redmond sighed. Florina knew that too.

"Clifford said it was the hardest thing he's ever done-- leaving Ennis' body. The second hardest was writing this letter to you."

Florina lifted the spoon from the rice and began scooping some onto her plate. "What does he want me to do? If they know it's Ennis' body then--" She stiffened.

"They're bringing Ennis' body home. Clifford wants to give him a proper burial."

"This is insane." Florina couldn't believe her words. And yet she continued to speak them. "He's dead. Ennis is dead." She stuck a fork into a piece of chicken.

"Clifford needs your permission to hold a memorial service. He's informed the military that Ennis was married, so has Melinda, Ennis' mother."

Florina turned to Redmond. Her eyes began to burn. Hot tears filled them.

"You need to mourn," Redmond said. His eyes were red. "I love you," Redmond whispered. "And I would never wish Ennis' death upon him. But if he hadn't died I--"

"You would have never met me."

"You loved him. And he loved you," Redmond said. Florina hardened her stare.

"I love you," Redmond said. His voice cracked. "But we need to make a place for him. *You* and *me*. We need to honor Ennis' life." Florina began to cry. Redmond grasped her trembling shoulders. "Your love for Ennis ... it's sustained you ... through all the turbulence here." Florina's tears turned into sobs. Redmond embraced her. "You trusted that life would bring him back from Vietnam. And when it didn't you hung in there. Call it fate or whatever, but when it didn't you kept going."

Florina strained to understand the meaning of Redmond's words, wh
at he was trying to say.

289

"You didn't give up," Redmond continued. "If you had, you would have never let me come back to see you after my parents and I vacationed at the Reynolds."

Redmond lifted Florina's hand. A consoling warmth filled her chest. She breathed in, and asked, "Where are they bringing Ennis' remains?"

Redmond lifted the letter beside Florina's plate.

Florina took the envelope, slit it open and read Clifford's words.

February 20, 1967

Florina:
It was nice seeing you last weekend. For the first time in months I sensed Ennis' presence. It felt good. And yet something was lacking.

I hated leaving him, felt guilty. He was my friend. I should have saved him.
Perhaps that's why it's been difficult for me to feel Ennis nearby.

The service we held for Melinda was but a memorial. We gave her a flag, but nothing else, no gun salute or military honors.

I promised you I'd find him, and I have. I need to put Ennis to rest, and in the right way.

It pains me to tell you this, but I've been informed that we've found Ennis' body, what remains of it. I don't mean to intrude into your life with Redmond. He seems to love you. And for that I know Ennis would be grateful. He only wanted you happy.

For this reason I'm asking that you let me give him a funeral, the home going that he and others like him killed in battle, but their bodies not always recovered, deserve.

As Ennis' wife I can't do anything without your permission. ...

Florina folded the letter, returned it to the envelope in which it had arrived, and went to their bedroom. She was lying on the bed, palms under her cheek and facing the window that opened onto Agnes and Macon's house, when Redmond lay down beside her.

"He's not doing this to hurt you," Redmond said of Clifford. "He said he'll take care of all the arrangements for the service."

Florina was clutching Clifford's letter Florina began to cry. She closed her eyes. Sobs overtook her body as they had in the months following Melinda telling her Ennis had been killed in action. They had been her only way of feeling close to him, her attempt at maintaining intimacy with, and keeping alive a memory she feared losing.

Redmond touched her trembling shoulder, said, "Like you, Clifford is trying to put this behind, move on with his life."

Florina sobbed. Part of her wanted to rip Clifford's letter into shreds and flush it down the toilet. Another stood in awe of Clifford's loyalty, was incredibly thankful that he had been with Ennis. "I don't know if I can do this."

"You're not alone. Let me help you."

She turned over to Redmond.

"I love you," Redmond said.

In the past she had heard Redmond's saying those words as an utterance, an attempt to hold on to a truth whose honesty threatened to flee at a moment's notice. Now as he said them, a clear commitment to the vows he had made rang through, "*For richer, for poorer, better for worse, in good times and in bad, sickness and health ...*"

Redmond stroked her cheek.

Florina thought of the root bulb for the orange hydrangea. She would need to get it into the ground soon, plant it.

Redmond drew Florina close. "I will love you until death. And beyond," he said. He brought his lips to hers. They lingered there delivering balm to her loss resurrected in Clifford's request.

Chapter 39

The five-hour drive to Ennis' home left much time for Florina to think.

She had met Ennis during a sophomore English class. When she asked why he, a junior, was taking a sophomore English class, Ennis explained, "I like poetry. I'm also in ROTC."

That a man preparing to become a soldier would also value poetry puzzled, as well as, intrigued Florina. Following class that afternoon, she accepted Ennis' invitation for a hotdog and soda at the malt shop near campus where students often socialized.

"Sorry I can't buy you a better date than this," Ennis had said while observing Florina squeeze mustard and ketchup onto her hotdog.

"What's wrong with eating hotdogs?" she had asked.

"Plenty of girls would find it cheap. It if weren't for ROTC, I wouldn't be here."

Though she had found it a bit daunting, Florina had liked Ennis' honesty. She had said, "I'm from the country, raised on a farm. Eating anything you don't grow or raise yourself is considered *eating high on the hog*."

Both had laughed at her turn of phrase *eating high on the hog*. The laughter had broken the ice, and had presented an opening through which Florina saw the beauty of Ennis' genuineness, something very few of her girl friends would acknowledge a young man of Native American, Negro and white ancestry.

"You're the first Negro girl to give me the time of day," he said to her some months later.

"If that's the way you feel then why'd you come to a Negro college?" Florina didn't like the tone of truth she sensed in his statement.

"Don't get me wrong--I can understand why your people distrust us." Ennis had flashed his palms in defense of whatever else Florina might fire his way. "I know I look white."

"But you're not. Anyone can see that."

Ennis had knitted his brows, answers peering through his eyes.

"You're no more white than I am," Florina said.

Awareness sparkled within Ennis' blue-gray eyes. He laughed. "Some of girls in your dorm say they thought you were white, that is until they saw your mother and father." Florina had lowered her gaze. "Like you with me," Ennis said, "I knew the minute I laid eyes on you that you were Negro. And proud as they come."

"So what gave you the impression I'd give you a minute of my time?"

"You are nice and kind," Ennis said. "Your poems speak to me."

After that Florina began reading all she wrote to Ennis. Where she distrusted others, and would not share the secrets of her heart entombed in her poems, Florina found in Ennis a safe haven wherein to hear herself read and breathe.

294

What is it, I wonder, that makes us hope and yearn,
tick and kick at life,
keep pace with its difficulties and daunts?
What keeps us bound to the precipices of mountains threatening
our death?
Their jagged edges jutting into our breasts, drawing blood and
angst,
pain and despair.
Like buttons upon a blouse that we slide through the holes that
keep them straight,
we ease from our mother's wombs into these turbid waters called
life,
and reach for a rock, a stick, a rambling bush or weedless vine,
something to hold onto,
something to entrap or encase us,
something to imprison us with hope.
So that we don't give up, let go, drop and fall.
Why the need to go on?
Why not let go, give in, surrender, submit?
Why?
And if not, how?

Ennis had been crying when Florina stopped reading. "What's wrong?" she asked and touched his cheek.

"I love you," Ennis said. "I love you and I promise to always be faithful. To take care of you all my days."

Florina knew then that she had found the man she loved, the one person with whom she wanted to spend the rest of her life.

Chapter 40

Clifford stepped down from the pulpit and instead of returning to sit beside Florina, he left the church. As she watched him leave Florina gave thanks for Clifford having arranged the funeral.

Reverend Herring returned to the lectern, laid open the Bible, and read aloud. "Ecclesiastes tells us, ' ... *there is a time and season for everything under the heavens; a time to be born, a time to plant and a time to uproot, a time to speak, and a time to be silent, a time to scatter stones and a time to gather them, a time to laugh and a time to dance, a time to love and a time to build, a time for war and hate, a time to kill, a time for peace, and a time to embrace, and a time to die ...,* 'and for those left, a time to mourn those we have embraced, and who have held us not simply with their arms and hands, but with their hearts."

Reverend Herring gazed upon the flag-draped casket then looked to Florina and softly smiled. "I've known Ennis McCreary since the day he was born. His mother called me hours after she gave birth to him. Asked me to come and bless him. Seeing him wrapped in his little blanket I knew he was destined to do great things. When she told me he had been killed

I was sad. I hurt even more when she said that while the Army knew he had been killed, they didn't have his body. How do you have a funeral without a body? You can do it, *but* ... That was eighteen months ago." Herring gripped the lectern. Anguish, tempered by restraint, flooded his face. "*Well*," the Cherokee minister paused, tears glistening in his eyes, "We held a service. But a lot was missing." Reverend Herring again looked to Florina.

Florina observed Melinda sitting on the front pew across the aisle and recalled how she had delivered the news of Ennis' death.

"*We've had a service,*" Melinda had said. "*I knew you would be in finals and I didn't want to upset that. Your education was so important to Ennis. He wanted you to get your degree.*"

Melinda had spoken truth, and Florina appreciated her concern. She would not have been able to enter or complete final exams knowing Ennis had been killed. During the ensuing months Florina grew even more grateful when she realized she did not have the strength to return to college her senior year. And yet she felt horrible. Looking back, Florina felt heartily sorry for not having told her parents about Ennis.

What must Melinda have felt, alone, and enduring the death of her only child and son, with only the half-truth of a service? Melinda explained the truth in a letter that Florina received when she was home during the summer of 1966. That the Army had not recovered Ennis' body, placed him in purgatory. He was dead, but the ghost of his loss remained with those he had loved, neither at peace. The reality of what had occurred left Florina feeling even more depressed, and sealed her decision not to return to college for her senior year.

Florina now sat in awe of Melinda.

Reverend Herring continued the eulogy. "Ennis McCreary brought great joy to our community. We were happy to see him go off to college. Melinda kept use abreast of how well he was doing in his classes at college. She also told me when he decided to marry."

Once more he turned his gaze upon Florina. "Ennis loved you. He told me that. And I saw it. I also saw that you loved him as much as he loved you, perhaps even more. It's hard to let someone you love go away to a place that you know he might not come back from. But you did that. You married Ennis, knowing that he had enlisted. In doing that you gave him a gift that neither I, nor his mother or anyone except God could provide. He knew that if he died, he would not be forgotten." Reverend Herring looked upon his black leather Bible and back to Florina. "You have moved on. Ennis would have wanted that." The Cherokee minister turned to Redmond by her side. "I don't know you, but I am glad that you have entered Florina's life. She's a good person. You are lucky to have her. You bring Ennis peace. He is thankful."

Reverend Herring then said to Florina, "Paul tells us in Ephesians, '*to be strong in the Lord and rest in the strength of God's might.*' Our minds can do wicked things to us when we are in mourning. But remember God loves you, as do I, and our entire community." The Reverend gestured his hand towards Melinda. Then grasping the Bible, Herring opened his arms. "Though many of our tribe have not come to know you, did not even know that Ennis had married, they love you as much as we love Ennis. You, like Ennis, will live forever in our hearts. You loved one of our own. And for that we are thankful.

"So I tell you as said the Apostle Paul, put on the whole armor of God, Florina. Let Him shield and support you in the following days, that you might know that God loves you, and that Ennis has found peace and is at rest. We do not wrestle against flesh and blood, but against the rulers, against the authorities, against the cosmic powers over this present darkness, against the spiritual forces of evil in the heavenly places." The minister spoke with greater force. "Take up the whole armor of God, that you may withstand the evil in this day. Stand strong, fastened to the belt of truth, knowing that you gave all that you had. God will bless you for it."

Florina jumped at the first volley of shots. Reverend's Herring's closing words of the eulogy had shaken her, provoked her to thought. The last months had been difficult.

But what could Reverend Herring know about the recent events of her marriage to Redmond, or the tension of watching and listening to Agnes and Macon's arguments?

Redmond gripped her hand. She turned to him. His lips formed a broken smile against the honor guards' second volley of firing shots. The third round of shots fired. A blanket of silence settled as the waning sun glistened upon the casket bearing the American flag.

Florina regarded the dark hole beneath the Ennis' casket. A solemn chill settled upon her shoulders amid the winter cold enwrapping them all.

Displaying the most solemn of attention, Clifford, and two soldiers all in dress blues, marched in perfectly metered rhythm to the casket. As Clifford looked on the two soldiers lifted the flag from the silver casket, stepped away from the pall, and with synchronized movements, folded the flag into a triangle. The two soldiers turned, and with Clifford, saluted the casket.

Florina's eyes hands trembled. Warm tears rolled down her cheeks, sore and stained from crying. Again, Redmond tightened his hold upon her palm.

The soldier holding the flag then marched to Clifford and extended him the flag. Clifford turned, and walked to Florina sitting beside Redmond. He knelt. Florina closed her eyes. Unable to stave off the finality of the moment, she opened her eyes and lifted her hands. Clifford placed the folded flag upon trembling palms. *Oh, Ennis.* She had yet to plant the hydrangea root bulb. An enormous ache filled Florina's heart. She brought the flag to her chest and wept.

Florina spent her last moments with Ennis kneeling at the casket yet lowered into the ground. *"I love you so much,"* she whispered. Her head lay against the pall, cold and hard.

Redmond and Clifford grasped her arms when she moved to stand and helped Florina to her feet. Her lips and cheeks trembled with tears when she in a hoarse whispered to Clifford, "Thank you ... for everything."

"I made a promise and I carried it out," Clifford said. "I appreciate your permission allowing me to do it."

"This was beautiful." Tears flooded Florina's throat. She shook her head. Sobs filled her chest. Again she clutched the flag to her chest. "I miss him so much," she whispered.

"So do I," said Clifford. "So do I." He embraced her.

The pent-up pain of her Florina's loss came forth in sobs racking her body ... and *soul*.

Redmond turned to Florina when they reached the black Riviera. "Melinda is hosting a repast. If you're too tired I can tell her--"

"No. We need to go. I need to go," said Florina.

Moments later Redmond turned out of the cemetery, and Florina directed him to Ennis' home--the place where they had married. Redmond had turned off the highway and was half way down the dirt driveway towards Melinda's house when Florina noticed a familiar blue 65' Chevrolet Impala parked amid the torrent of cars filling the yard.

"It can't be--my parents? That's their ca--"

"I called them," said Redmond. He brought the Riviera to a halt beside the Impala, turned off the ignition and removed the key.

But what could he know of why I didn't tell my parents about Ennis? Florina bounced the question back and forth as Redmond, then out of the car, came around and opened her door.

"You need to put this behind you." Redmond lifted her hand. They started towards Melinda's house. The front door opened as they reached the steps leading up to the verandah. Ava Reynolds stepped out along with Florina's mother, Helen.

Florina's chest froze. Air flowing in and out of her lungs halted as if held in purgatory, then weeping, she looked to her mother she whispered, "I'm so sorry."

301

Helen opened her arms and embraced Florina. Ava Reynolds placed her arms about mother and daughter.

Chapter 41

Despite Ennis' absence Melinda McCreary's home held the same warmth as when Florina and her son had wed. Florina regretted not having invited and made their marriage known to those who now filled the house. She lifted from the bureau a picture of Ennis as a little boy and riding a wooden pony, and brushed her finger across the glass encasing the image. A hand came to rest on her shoulder. Florina turned to Melinda standing next to her.

Melinda touched the picture. "He was so cute," she said.

Florina gazed back upon the image of Ennis. More tears filled her eyes. She placed the picture back upon the bureau and forced herself to look at Melinda. "I should have written." Again, she began to weep.

Melinda caressed Florina's trembling shoulders and shoulders, and as Helen and Ava had done moments earlier, embraced her. "Redmond is a nice man. He loves you," Melinda whispered. "I'm so glad you let Clifford do this."

Later as they were away from others and sitting on the sofa in what had been Ennis' room Florina explained. "I never meant to stop writing. Things happened so fast."

Melinda's eyes glistened as Florina spoke. "My mother told me to drive to crates of strawberries to the Reynolds one afternoon." Florina's thoughts traveled back to that day in July, '67, seven months earlier. "It was so hot. I didn't want to go. My mother and father, the Reynolds--they had no idea why I hadn't returned to school. Ennis was gone. Our plans ... "

"And then you met Redmond," Melinda said. Florina turned to Ennis' mother, the woman who until December had been her only mother-in-law. "Mrs. Reynolds and your mother explained. I called them."

Florina parted her lips to speak.

"When Clifford called to say you had given permission for the funeral, I decided it was time for the truth," Melinda said. "You loved my son. I wanted your parents to know that my son had loved you. That I loved and respected you. "

"I should have told you about Redmond."

"You needed to move on," Melinda said. "I was so happy when Clifford told me you had remarried."

"I abandoned you," Florina said.

"My son died knowing that you loved him," said Melinda. Again her eyes glistened. "You forget that I witnessed you saying your vows to each other." Ennis' mother lifted Florina's hand and brought it to her chest. "The memory of my son lives in the love you held for him."

"*I ... still ... love ... him,*" Florina whispered.

" I know." Melinda patted the back of Florina's palm. She drew close, brushed Florina's cheeks red and wet with tears. But you must go forward. Love Redmond. And by all means, let him love you." Florina closed her eyes and sobbed. Again, Melinda embraced her.

Melinda had gone out to speak with guests at the repast when the door opened to Ennis' room. Florina, still in the throes of emotion, stood thinking that Redmond was about to enter. Instead a white man entered. He had sat with Melinda throughout the funeral, had accompanied her to the interment. The man had also witnessed Florina and Ennis marry. Florina knew that Melinda worked as his personal secretary.

"Please sit," the man said. He approached Florina. "May I join you?"

"You're the mayor," Florina said. "Melinda works for you."

"I saw you marry Ennis," the man said.

"I remember," Florina began to feel anxious. *What did this man want?*

He surveyed the area. "I don't know if Melinda told you my name. I'm William Masterson." He extended his hand.

Florina accepted it. As with the stitching of the doilies and curtains in Robert MacIntosh's home matching that of the tablecloth Florina had received as a wedding present, she recognized the same blueness in William Masterson's eyes that reminded her of Ennis'.

"You're Ennis' father?" Florina said.

Masterson gave a sad smile. "Yes, I am. May I sit down next to you?" Florina gestured to the space beside her. Masterson lowered his tall body onto the sofa. Again, he observed the space. "I've seen this room many times ... mostly without Ennis."

Florina looked at the elder white man, then to the walls bearing pictures of Ennis throughout his childhood as well as his drawings. Her eyes settled upon Ennis' rendition of what seemed like a cowboy and Indian.

"That's how he saw us--me and him," Masterson said. "The Lone Ranger and Tonto."

"He knew you were his father, that you could never marry his mother," Florina said.

"Ennis was no fool." The white man sighed. "He saw me. I saw him. But we never truly met." Masterson's cheeks reddened. He lowered his head. Tears dropped from his eyes. "I came here at least twice a month." Masterson made a fist. "My way of checking on him. I hope he understood." Masterson spoke in a soft, penitent voice. He turned to Florina. "Did he speak about me, ever say anything?"

"He said you were good to his mother. But that you could never marry her, openly acknowledge him."

"What about me as a person? You were his wife. Surely he said someth--"

"No." Florina shook her head. "It was I who asked about you. Ennis had emphasized that he was part Cherokee and Negro until I saw you the day Reverend Herring married us."

Masterson gave a soft laugh laced with what seemed irony. "I always thought you wanted to hide the marriage from your parents because Ennis had told you he was half white."

Florina lowered her gaze.

"Your people are no different than us," said Masterson.

"We all have families. And we're all afraid, I suppose."

"On that you are correct," chimed Masterson.

Yet Florina had never considered white people experiencing fear, an emotion common to all humankind. Yet Florina had never connected *fear* with whites. They always appeared so confident. Now looking at Masterson she realized an aspect of their frailty that left her feeling ashamed for how she had viewed them. "I think," she forced herself to speak, "that Ennis felt you were doing as best you could considering the circumstances."

"And by circumstances you mean segregation and supremacist beliefs that whites are better than everyone else, so much so that we can't even acknowledge our own children?"

His statement left Florina lost for words, and yet she could not judge William Masterson. "I regret not having told my parents about Ennis, that we had met, that I loved and wanted to marry him. Even after he died, I let them think I may have been pregnant, as the reason why I wouldn't return to college my senior year."

"Melinda came to me when she received news of Ennis' death," Masterson said. "She felt you should know, but she didn't want to do anything to upset your exam schedule. She said your parents very much valued education, that your mother was a teacher. I told her you would need to hold onto school as a way of getting through the next year."

"I returned to school in January," Florina said.

"I'm told your husband is a surgeon."

"He's a good man."

"Melinda says he's a lot like Ennis." Masterson again regarded the drawing of the cowboy and Indian.

Florina noticed that the Indian was wearing a black mask.

"It's amazing," Masterson said, "what a young man can do when he has a father, knows that father, knows whose bloodline he carries." *But says nothing,* Florina thought.

Florina considered Robert MacIntosh, not Hammond Austin, being Redmond's biological father. Despite the hurt of learning the truth, Redmond had two men fighting to be his father, while Ennis had had no one willing to claim him. "Life is unfair," Florina said.

"And yet in time it all balances out." Masterson added. "I never acknowledged my boy, and now he's gone."

"You don't think Ennis enlisted because you never claimed him as your son?"

"He needed to prove he was worthy. That I know. Even if he didn't. It's how we men are. We need to make our way in the world. The presence of a father in our lives tells us we can do what we set our mind to. When that's absent we have to be our own father, prove it to ourselves." Masterson lowered his head. His wife was dead and their marriage had borne no children.

"Did you know your father?" Florina asked.

"Yes, but we weren't close. I'm mayor. I run a city. But I can't tell you who my father really was. I never came to truly know him as a person. *Or love him.*" The redness in Masterson's cheeks deepened as if he sensed what Ennis lacked in knowing him, and what he, his father, wished to be known by his son about himself by in this life to which Ennis was now gone. "Ennis was my only child," Masterson said. "My only hope for immortality."

Florina's heart grew heavy. She wanted to learn more of this man. She had never spoken so intimately with a white person--certainly not a white man.

The door opened. Redmond entered. Masterson stood. On gathering himself he walked to Redmond, extended his hand and said, "Melinda and I appreciate you bringing Florina,

307

allowing her to be here." Masterson glanced back at Florina then to Redmond. "Take care of her. Ennis loved her very much. She was good to my son." Masterson looked to Redmond, met his gaze.

"I will." Redmond shook Masterson's hand with what seemed a calm he had not exhibited all day. Redmond joined Florina sitting on the couch, said, "This room reminds me of mine back at home."

"I haven't seen your room at your parents' house." Florina smiled for first time that day.

"I'll have to show it to you," Redmond said. He lifted her hand. "There's so much I want to shari--"

The door opened and Florina's mother entered. "Redmond," Florina said, "I didn't mean to interrupt." She turned to Florina, "Your father, the Reynolds and I were getting ready to head home." Darkness had settled outside.

Florina started towards her mother.

"You two talk," Redmond said. "Thank you and the Reynolds for coming," he left Florina and her mother alone to talk.

Florina and Helen entered into a conversation, the territory of which they could not possibly cover in the remaining minutes leaving.

Helen lifted Florina's hand and placed it upon the lap of her black dress. "Give yourself time to heal."

"I don't know where to begin." Florina's eyes moistened. "I thought this was all behind me and I was going to make good on my marriage to Redmond."

"He loves you," Helen whispered. "Very much."

For the first time in almost two years Florina met Helen's gaze empty of the haze of shame, and fear of disappointment she imagined Helen would feel should she learn of Ennis, and their marriage. "I didn't tell you about Ennis because I thought you would think I was behaving like Daddy's sisters. Ennis was Cherokee, and Negro, but he looked white."

"He was your husband. And from all accounts loved you. He didn't push you to tell us what you felt you couldn't," Helen said.

308

"He had planned to come home when I graduated. I figured that with my degree you and Daddy would understand."

"Or if I didn't it wouldn't matter. You'd have graduated college," Helen said. Her lips were firm.

"He was my husband. And I loved him."

"You mean more to me and your father than an education. We wanted that for *you*. *Your life* will be much better with it."

"I'm back in school now," said Florina. She could not decipher where Helen was taking the conversation.

"Your life is different now. I want you to finish college, but things are different."

"Are you saying I'm different from who I was back on New Year's Day and as Redmond's new wife. That I'm soiled goods now that Redmond knows I've was married before him?"

"No." Helen shook her head.

Anger welled inside Florina. "I'm not like Aunt Regina, Christa and Mona or Loretta. I've never liked what they're always saying about you. I may look like them, but you're my moth--"

"You don't get your looks just from your father," Helen interrupted. "I've never told you, but--" Helen turned towards the window, filling with the darkness of the early March night. "You look just like your grandfather." She observed Florina's hand still upon her lap, brushed then lifted it. The darkness of the back of Helen's hand stood in contrast to the pale near whiteness of Florina's. "Your grandfather was white."

Florina pulled her hand from the lap of Helen's dress.

"He died when I was ten. Your Grandma Esther married Grandpa Felix when I was fifteen."

Florina was about to ask why her mother had kept that secret when Helen said, "It's much easier being just Negro or just white in American. People like certainty. Even Negro people." Helen stood. "You don't need my forgiveness. When it comes Ennis you did what all of us do. But your life's different now." Florina frowned. "Redmond knows the truth. And he still loves you. With or without a college degree." Helen leaned down, kissed Florina's forehead. "And so do I." She left.

Chapter 42

Florina sank into dark and ponderous thoughts during the days following Ennis' funeral.

Clifford's words about Ennis and their friendship, punctuated by Reverend Herring's eulogy, set the beginning of a narrative. The middle of this narrative was built upon Florina's conversations with Melinda and William Masterson, and culminated into a climax of Helen's disclosure that her father, Florina's grandfather, was white. Retracing these conversations unfolded further realizations-- the meanings of each would require time to unravel.

Grateful for Helen's honesty, Florina sailed without the compass she had known. Florina's identity had shifted, if but by a degree, reset, and by hundreds of knots, the course of her travel across the ocean of life. Florina's mother had revealed her vulnerability and humanness, her ability for error. Faced with the reality of their sameness, Florina found herself lost.

The house that she had shared with Redmond for the last two and a half months became not only her new home, but also Florina's refuge, the cocoon in which she would dwell in the midst of unknowing change.

Redmond attended Sunday services without Florina.

Although aware of her struggles, he was not privy to their intricacies. Florina did not tell him what her mother had shared. Neither did she share with him her conversation with William Masterson.

Each time she attempted to journal about her experience, the flood of thoughts jumbled with tangled feelings and cast an unmanageable blankness. Her hand refused to move the pen when setting upon the page.

And so she cooked. Florina left the cleaning and other household duties to Willa Mae as usual, and prepared breakfast, lunch, and dinner as if running a restaurant. On completing one meal, she set about deciding the menu for the next. Each day, despite the weekly delivery, Florina journeyed to the Elder's market and purchased the supplies needed. What the Elders did not sell she purchased from the infamous A & P.

The walks and preparing meals brought solace. Florina assumed silence during meals. She gave short answers to Redmond's questions, "How was your day?" and comments, "This fish was good tonight."

Florina did not attend classes that week at Johnson C. State. She would plant the root bulb for the orange hydrangea Robert MacIntosh had given her. Redmond had placed it in water the morning after he had given Florina the letter from Clifford asking permission to carry out the memorial service for Ennis. Now Thursday afternoon, nearly two weeks later, Florina wondered if the bulb was still alive, would take root.

On arriving back from her journey to the Elders' grocery, Florina went to the kitchen table where she had left the root bulb standing in a jar of water and saw it gone. She searched the kitchen wondering where she could have misplaced it.

Maybe Willa Mae moved it. She prayed Willa Mae had not thrown it out.

It was there this morning when Redmond and I ate breakfast.
Florina went to the dining room across the hall where Willa Mae
was ironing. Seeing the dining room table empty she returned to
the kitchen. *I'll start dinner, then search again for it*, Florina
decided

She began unloading the groceries, sank deep into
thought. She did not hear the knock at the door, was unaware
that Willa Mae answered, nor did she hear her greet Carolyn.

Willa Mae's conversation with Carolyn drew Florina
from her reverie.

"You're looking really well," Carolyn said to Willa Mae
as she reached the kitchen doorway. "I've never seen a woman
as excited as your mother to have a second grandchild."

"She feels blessed," Willa Mae said.

Carolyn smiled.

"I've finished all the ironing and done the dusting,"
Willa Mae said as she watched Florina peeling potatoes at the
sink. "I can take over fixing dinner while you visit with Miss
Carolyn."

"You should go home and rest." Florina turned to Willa
Mae, not yet having acknowledged Redmond's mother, and still
silently frantic about the missing root bulb.

"We'll be fine," Carolyn said.

The door out in the front room opened and closed after
Willa Mae. Florina remained peeling potatoes.

Carolyn opened a cabinet beside the sink where Florina
stood, and lifted out two cups and saucers. "My father was good
at making hot chocolate." She took the cups and saucers over to
the table. "No matter how bleak things seemed in winter, hot
chocolate made spring seem just around the corner. I don't
know what helped the most--the hot chocolate, or that my father
took the time to make it."

Anxiety overtook Florina. She needed to find the
hydrangea root bulb. She wished Carolyn had not come, that she
would leave. MacIntosh's words cut a path through the terrain
of Florina's thoughts, "*We're all oddities. Unique and special
like orange hydrangeas.*"

Florina set the potato, its skin gone, into the colander. "I didn't purchase any cocoa at the store today," she said to Carolyn. "I'm using the milk we have for the mashed potatoes."

"I brought cocoa and milk with me." Carolyn lifted out a bottle of milk then set to warming it on the stove.

Tears slid over Florina's eyes and dropped upon the potato peelings in the sink. Carolyn eased the knife and potato from her trembling hands then laid them upon the. Redmond's mother embraced Florina and patted her shoulder as she sobbed.

The cocoa Carolyn prepared warmed Florina in places she did not realize had frozen over. She drank her hot chocolate, both thankful and ashamed of the vulnerabilities the soothing liquid brought to the surface and assuaged.

Carolyn said, "Robert's worried about you."

Florina stared into her cup of hot chocolate. "I'm not going to stop school if that's what he thinks."

"He wants to know if you're writing," Carolyn said. Florina's silence revealed her struggle.

"You must write." Carolyn spoke as if having faced the same challenge.

"My feelings are too heavy for words."

"Perhaps the reason you haven't finished college is because you refuse to write about Ennis; say what's in your heart."

"I love Redmond," Florina said.

"This isn't about Redmond. You loved Ennis first."

Anger bubbled within Florina. "Are you still in love with Robert MacIntosh?"

"Robert told you that he's Redmond's father," Carolyn said.

Startled once more by Carolyn's unabashed honesty Florina gave a slight nod.

"I will always love Robert," Carolyn said.

"How can you love two men?"

"Some people you love. Others you love *and* marry."

"I married both Ennis and Redmond."

"But not at the same time," Carolyn said. The accuracy of Carolyn's statement pushed open a doorway of understanding. "Ennis and Redmond represent different times in your life, distinct aspects of you." Carolyn's words dispensed a truth that comforted Florina.

The two years Florina had known and loved Ennis had transformed her into a different person. Meeting Redmond altered her yet again. "Writing about Ennis seems like a betrayal to Redmond," Florina said.

"Your marriage to Redmond," Carolyn explained, " ... what you share with him, is rooted in your union with Ennis. One could not exist without the other."

Florina recalled the wooden crates brimming with strawberries, about to slip from her hands, she losing hope of ever recovering from Ennis' death.

"In the wake of Ennis' death you found Redmond. There is no Redmond without Ennis."

Florina found comfort in Carolyn's perspective. And yet there remained the issue of Agnes. Florina asked Carolyn, "What is Agnes' hold on Redmond? She married Macon while loving Redmond, says Redmond refused to marry her."

Carolyn assumed a plaintive silence.

"Macon is bitter and angry," Florina said.

"Agnes is very open about her lack of affection towards him." Carolyn spoke with dismay. Her brown eyes retreated.

Florina considered whether Carolyn's love for Robert MacIntosh had diminished her affections for Hammond Austin.

As if hearing Florina's thoughts, Carolyn said, "Love does not always a marriage make. But its absence ensures a union's demise."

"Did you love Father Austin when you married him?"

"Yes. But not as much as I do now." Again Carolyn's gaze slipped back into a past laden, Florina sensed, with heavy emotions. "I always knew Hammond would be a good father. I needed that. I should never have encouraged Robert's feelings, or given him hope. I was lonely. Hammond was busy with his studies. I committed the offense of adultery. That Hammond continued loving me, accepted my child, by Robert as his own, revealed the depths of his love. Until then I don't think I knew what love truly is." Redmond's mother seemed about to cry. "It transformed me.

Redmond realizes he hurt you," Carolyn said. "Agnes is baggage left from his life before meeting you." Carolyn leaned forward, touched Florina's hand to the cup of hot chocolate still warm. "Redmond doesn't want to lose you. He needs you."

Her mother-in-law's statement stunned Florina. She had feared Carolyn came to demand she put Ennis in the past and move on with Redmond in the present. Emphasizing how much Redmond needed Florina, despite her having withheld knowledge of her marriage to Ennis, and then openly discussing Redmond's past with Agnes--displayed Carolyn's willingness to expose her vulnerabilities. *And her lack of hypocrisy.*

"I want my son to be happy," Carolyn said. "That's the most any mother can ask for her child who's alive."

Carolyn's statement reminded Florina of Melinda *and* William Masterson's irreparable loss.

"Redmond has worked very hard to make me happy," Florina said. "Guilt for not telling him about my marriage to Ennis has kept me from seeing that. And a lot of other things." Florina's admission reshaped her view of Agnes. "She's very afraid--Agnes. Bitter like Macon. And unhappy."

"Her parents are very concerned with appearances. Affections don't rank high on the importances of life," Carolyn said. Dismay and sadness again filled her tone.

Florina explained her father's sisters. "My aunts haven't been kind to my mother. They've been downright mean and rude. My mother has been very badly hurt. At the repast following Ennis' funeral she told me ... " Florina shared Helen's revelation with Carolyn. "It's all so strange. Unnerving," Florina said. "My mother's not who I thought she was." *And neither am I.*

"None of us are ever truly who we imagine ourselves to be. As those around us evolve and reveal who they are, so too change the faces we have formed of ourselves and show the world. Those who remain with us, love us throughout this process," Carolyn said " ... are our *true* family and friends."

316

Florina considered Agnes, missed her despite the disruption delivered by Agnes' actions and those things she had shared of herself. "I saw her the night she left," Florina said.

Carolyn lifted her eyebrows as surprise over took her face.

"Redmond had just given me Clifford's letter asking permission to hold a funeral for Ennis. I ran out of the house. It was raining. As I approached the end of the street I saw a cab at the corner. The driver put Agnes' suitcase in the back. She got inside."

"You should tell Macon," Carolyn said. "Then again, I should. He's worried sick about her. Has no idea when she left or where she went."

Florina recognized Carolyn's attempt to assuage Macon's loss. "He's jealous of Redmond, but none of that changes the truth." Florina described the argument she and Redmond witnessed between Agnes and Macon. "She's cruel to him."

"In her defense, much of the anger Agnes gives Macon is meant for her father."

"Why would Macon subject himself to such ridicule?"

"He's as much a victim of Reverend Julius as is Agnes," Carolyn said. Her comment shed greater insight into the intricate machinations of Agnes and Macon's marriage. "Neither Macon nor Reverend Julius or Agnes' mother has heard from her," Carolyn said.   She shook her head.

The door out in the front room opened and closed. Seconds later Hammond appeared in the kitchen doorway. "Mrs. Brooks told me you might be here." Hammond seemed relieved as he spoke. He approached Florina. "How are you, my dear? We've all been thinking about you."

"Better." Florina looked at Carolyn and smiled.

Hammond resumed his serious demeanor, revealing as he spoke, "It seems that Agnes is in Memphis," and what became clear to Florina was intense worry.

"Whatever for?" Carolyn asked. "There's nothing but looting and rioting going on."

317

"Everett Collier says the entire city is wrapped in protest. The police instituted a citywide curfew. Memphis is under siege," Hammond said.

"Everett attended medical school with Hammond," Carolyn explained. "He says, Henry Loeb is as insane as they come."

"Or simply downright evil." Hammond spoke bitterly. "In either case he's determined to not let the striking workers win. Loeb refuses to give into their demands."

"I read that Dr. King has gone once to Memphis, and is planning to return. He's going to march with the sanitation workers," Florina said.

Hammond nodded. "Roy Wilkins has been and marched. Everett said he spoke to a crowd of over seven thousand. The entire Civil Rights Movement seems to have focused its energies on what's happening in Memphis." He scratched his head as his worry deepened. "I have to confess that with Agnes being gone, and Redmond not being available to help Macon with his patients, I lost track of events. Agnes being gone has effected Macon. He's worried and angry."

Chapter 43

Everett's call about Agnes brought home the reality of what was taking place.

"Why would Agnes go there?" said Florina.

To everyone's surprise, Redmond entered the kitchen doorway. "She's always been drawn to protests," he said.

"Oh son," said Hammond. He turned back towards Redmond.

Florina stood. "I'll have dinner ready by the time you shower." She went to the range and began transferring food into serving bowls.

"I don't have time to eat. Macon has three patients I'm attending over at Charlotte Negro. And there's a possible appendectomy," Redmond said.

"Why are *you* also now seeing to Macon's patients?" Carolyn asked.

"He's driving to Memphis to bring Agnes home."

"Thank goodness, she's finally come to her senses," said Carolyn.

"Macon hasn't spoken to her. She most probably doesn't know he's coming. Macon's meeting Reverend Julius at Dr.

Collier's," Redmond explained.

"This won't be pretty," Hammond sighed.

"She's been participating in the protests along with the sanitation workers," said Redmond.

"Oh, my god," Carolyn gasped.

"Macon's been speaking with Dr. Collier," Redmond said.

"Providing daily reports to Macon," Hammond chimed.

"Did you know about this?" Carolyn asked Hammond.

"I suspected as much. Macon was probably hoping Agnes would get tired, see the danger and come home," Hammond added, "The Memphis police shot and killed a sixteen year old boy, Negro.

"Oh, no," Carolyn sighed. She grasped her lips.

Redmond released a sad laugh, shook his head. "Agnes will most likely see that as one more reason to remain in Memphis."

Florina recalled what Cynthia Cartwright had said of Agnes. "*Agnes was at the Audubon Ballroom when Malcolm was killed, saw everything. A week later she came to New York by bus to attend the funeral. Reverend Julius and two of his deacons caught her in Harlem as she was about to enter Faith Temple. They brought her back to Baltimore where one of the physicians at Howard Hospital admitted her onto the psychiatric ward. Reverend Julius has forever been grateful.*" Redmond, by his own admission had been that physician, not Macon.

Florina looked to Redmond, thought, *So why had Reverend Julius sought Macon, and not Redmond, to marry Agnes? And why had Redmond left Agnes?*

She considered Agnes' anger at being forced to marry Macon on April 4, 1967, in lieu of traveling to Riverside Church and hearing Martin Luther King, Jr. speak. "Agnes won't leave--not with Dr. King is planning to come to Memphis and speak the striking workers," Florina said.

"Everett mentioned something about that--that Agnes was excited at the prospect of finally getting to see and hear him speak," said Hammond.

320

"She was not happy the day of her wedding," Carolyn said of Agnes.

Florina recalled Robert MacIntosh describing how MacIntosh had stood in for Redmond who was to serve as Macon's best man. MacIntosh had said, "The event was a miniature fiasco."

"She's never forgiven Macon," Florina said.

"I'm told Reverend Julius chose the day," said Carolyn.

"I warned Macon he should stand up to Reverend Julius, change the date of the wedding, " Redmond spoke. His parents turned to him. "At least let Agnes go to New York. But Macon was intent on pleasing Reverend Julius." *And controlling Agnes*, Florina thought.

"Not the way to endear yourself to the woman who's to be your wife," said Hammond.

"Nor a woman who doesn't want to marry you," Carolyn added.

Hammond shook his head as his gaze retreated. "Macon has always had a need to please, to be accepted. I don't know why."

Carolyn and Redmond exchanged glances against the canvas of regret resonating in Hammond's voice.

"It'll worsen matters for Macon and Julius to again make Agnes leave against her will," Florina said. "The place being Memphis this time."

"Macon's too far in Reverend Julius' debt, too invested in the sham of a marriage to see that," Hammond said. "And now with you and Redmond married, Macon'll never let go of Agnes."

"She doesn't love him," Florina said.

"That's not our fault or problem," Redmond said. "Macon can admit her to the hospital this time." Sadness filled with questions concerning Redmond's last statement overtook Carolyn's face. She looked to Hammond, who, confused like she, shrugged his shoulders, and shook his head.

"Don't wait up for me," Redmond said to Florina as he kissed her forehead then left.

The door out in the front room opened and closed. The deep concern on Carolyn's face eased into a somber silence. Hammond patted her shoulder. "He'll be fine."

Carolyn grasped Hammond's palm to her shoulder and sighed. "Will Agnes ever stop haunting him?" Hammond shook his head. "And what did Redmond mean with, *Macon can admit Agnes to the hospital this time?*"

Florina's in-laws knew less than she regarding what stood between Redmond and Agnes.

"Redmond says he doesn't love Agnes," said Florina. She spoke nothing of Redmond having admitted Agnes to the psychiatric ward at Howard Hospital.

"Then what is it?" Carolyn said. "What could he ever see in her? Agnes is but a walking ball of trouble!"

"Let's not worry Florina," Hammond said.

"Florina has eyes of her own," Carolyn countered. She was angry.

"Yes, and she believes Redmond like I do?" Hammond said.

"Do you?" Carolyn demanded.

"The boy is not a liar," said Hammond.

"There's no telling what he is now that Agnes has had him!" said Carolyn.

Hammond raised his hand, a wash of despair and embarrassment crossing his face.

"I'm sorry. But it's the truth," Carolyn continued. "Redmond slept with Agnes. *After* Agnes had married Macon."

"I know," said Florina. "Macon told me. He found them together." Softly she added, "Redmond confirmed it."

"Good god!" said Carolyn. "Has the boy no shame?"

"He hadn't met Florina, didn't even know of her," Hammond said.

"Still, it's abominable," Carolyn said.

"The boy means well," said Hammond. "And you believe he's been faithful since marrying you? Tell me the truth."

"I do," Florina said. "Then again, it's not like I've been the most forthcoming."

"The two cannot be compared," Carolyn said. "You were married," she said to Florina. "Redmond on the other hand committed adultery, slept with a married woman, a live walking, talking human being who's married to Macon."

"She says Redmond doesn't love her," Florina said.

"Agnes will say anything," Carolyn exclaimed.

"She says that Redmond loves me."

"When did she tell you this?" Hammond asked cautiously yet intrigued.

"About a month ago. I believe her," said Florina.

Redmond's parents exchanged looks.

"What is it that lives between those two?" Carolyn thought aloud of Redmond and Agnes. "It's like they know something about each other, that together they've endured some terrible event."

"The boy's married now," Hammond said. His gaze retreated. He lowered his head.

"A fact that I thought you were reminding him of," Carolyn snapped.

"I have and each time he refuses, or should I say, avoids answering," Hammond said. "Redmond is thirty-years old, has been very clear with me. His time with Agnes is over. She has to endure the life she's created with Macon."

"But he aches for her," Carolyn said. "It's as obvious as one's nose is on your face--and mine." She pointed to Florina. "She sees it."

"I don't know that Redmond aches for Agnes," Florina said, "... as much as with her for what she's suffering through."

Carolyn hit Florina with a stare of befuddlement and incredulity.

"What have you noticed?" Hammond asked.

"Agnes is lonely," said Florina.

"People tend to avoid and ignore those who behave like Agnes," Carolyn said.

"I, like you, was angry and frustrated with Agnes when I first met her. But over time I've come to feel for her too," Florina said.

"You've seen a hidden aspect of her," said Hammond. A hint of recognition about which Florina spoke flickered in her father-in-law's eyes. "Redmond has made similar remarks concerning Agnes."

"Redmond has a wife," Carolyn spoke. "And Macon is Agnes' husband."

"Agnes has described her relationship with Redmond, the love she holds for him, like that of a sister towards her brother," Florina said.

"That's incestuous!" Carolyn said, again declaring the detestation of her son's intimacies with Agnes.

"Redmond accepted me as I was," Florina said. "He knew nothing about Ennis until I told him last month. He demonstrated his love by standing by me, encouraging me to give my permission for Clifford to hold the funeral last week. Secrets reveal themselves in their own time."

Carolyn pursed her lips, folded her arms.

Florina touched her hand. "Redmond will tell me about Agnes when he's ready."

·.·.·.·.·.·.·.·.·.·
Chapter 44
·.·.·.·.·.·.·.·.·.·

During the ensuing days Redmond, busy attending to Macon's patients, entered what Florina realized as similar to her own ponderous reverie.

Like her, he seemed to be revisiting past events demanding he relinquish them.
That Agnes was alive, unlike Ennis, rendered Redmond's challenge more difficult. It was hard watching a life devolve before your eyes.

Heavy footsteps of national events drew close and loud, encroached upon the private intricacies of their personal lives. All was changing as events in Memphis came to a head. Nothing would remain the same.

Florina had laid out dinner when Redmond, already at home, came to the table and handed her the envelope.

"It's from Agnes," Redmond said.

Florina sat to the table and tore open the envelope.

March 13, 1968
    Florina:

I'm in Memphis if you haven't already heard. The city is alive with the demand for change. None of us can escape what's coming. ...

Florina felt thrilled. She continued reading.

... Dr. King is coming to speak. I will hear him this time. ...

Florina prayed Macon and Reverend Julius would not interrupt Agnes' plans.

... Everything brother Malcolm said is being proving true. Dr. King sees that. If only the two of them could have met, that life events and the powers that be had not kept them apart. ...

Just think what our lives would be like, who we could become if only able to speak our truths and without fear of being destroyed. Why does the truth of who we are threaten those who love us? Maybe they don't really love us.

If only we could let go of each other and allow those whom we love be who they are, and we all become the people God wants us to be.

Redmond has done that for me.

I'll always be grateful to him.

You have a treasure in his love.

I love you too. For letting me have time to let go. I saw you the night I left. You're a good and true friend. ...

Florina folded the letter and slid it back into the envelope.

"We should eat," Redmond said.

Florina wanted to ask him about the hydrangea root bulb. Days earlier Willa Mae had said, "I saw it on the kitchen table; I would never throw it out. My mother loves hydrangeas, says they bring blessings and love."

Where could it be? Florina pondered and grew ever more determined to find it.

Later that night, with the last of the dishes put away, Redmond returned to the kitchen. He was standing beside the table when he invited Florina to sit. "I want to talk to you about Agnes."

Florina wanted to ask him about the hydrangea root bulb, but instead joined him at the table. All within Florina fell still as he began to speak.

"Macon has every right to be angry with me. But not for the reasons you think." Redmond continued. "I loved Agnes at one time. But I don't love her anymore. Not the way I did before. That all ended before I met you."

Florina breathed in.

"I proposed to Agnes three years before Macon began dating her. She accepted," Redmond said. He clasped hands. "I loved her. Or at least who I thought her be. The person she presented herself as." He paused.

"And then one day, or rather one night I came home to my apartment earlier than I had intended. Agnes was there. I'd given her a key." Redmond's gaze retreated. "She was there with another woman. I found them in bed."

Florina gasped. Breath escaped her lungs. She strained for air. She inspected the space between her and Redmond, her eyes searched for an understanding of the truth Redmond had revealed.

Redmond's revelations left Florina stunned and quiet.

"She hurt me terribly," he said. "But I haven't been able to hate her." His words floated on a carpet of simple honesty. The larger picture of all that had eluded Florina concerning Redmond and Agnes slipped into clarity. "Finding her there destroyed all bonds of trust. She admitted to having agreed to marry me as her way of escaping her father. And society. Our marriage would have shielded her," Redmond said.

Florina understood the fear Agnes must have felt, empathized with her. The fact that Agnes would have married Redmond knowing her sexual proclivities angered Florina.

"She assured me she would have been the best wife possible, that no one would have suspected," Redmond explained. "Said she would have given me children, that she wanted them."

"But what about being a mother?" Florina asked.

327

"Crazy thing is she would have taught them to respect me."

Florina frowned.

"Agnes loved me. Not the way I wanted in a wife. But perhaps even deeper. She appreciated that I didn't judge her, after I learned, discovered the truth."

"Not many people would keep her secret like you," Florina said.

Redmond eyed Florina with a hard glance. "I tried to warn him. Told him that he shouldn't force Agnes. She didn't want to marry him."

"You were trying to protect her as well," Florina said.

"Reverend Julius knows about Agnes. I think he's known for some time." A slip of anger warped his face. Redmond frowned. "He was furious when I told him that I didn't think Agnes was ready for marriage."

"Why did you go to him, and not her?" Florina asked.

"I didn't want him blaming her. I wanted to keep her secret. Then Reverend Julius revealed that he knew."

Once more, Florina realized Redmond's need to protect Agnes.

"He warned me to not trust any woman, said that there were more than a few women like Agnes, that I should be wary."

"He was angry that you had learned the truth."

Redmond lowered his gaze. "Agnes never intended for me to learn the truth either." Redmond searched the space between himself and Florina. "I loved her. And she loved me. But I couldn't live a lie."

"But you went to her in June."

"I had argued with Robert MacIntosh. He didn't want me to enlist."

"He was afraid of losing you," Florina said. "That you'd be killed."

"Robert MacIntosh said that joining the Army was the biggest mistake of his life," Redmond explained. "He said that had he been half the man he should have been, and settled down

328

my mother would have married him. I would have grown up with Robert, my biological father."

"But your mother was married to Father Hammond when he met her, when she gave birth to you." Redmond hit Florina with a stern look of surprise. "Dr. MacIntosh told me that he was your father some weeks ago."

Redmond's tense gaze calmed. "I'll never know the truth of what happened between him and my mother. MacIntosh seems to think that Mother might had left Dad for him."

"Did your mother love Dr. MacIntosh that much?"

"You've seen them together in recent weeks. What's your guess?" Redmond asked.

"Father Hammond has made your mother very happy. She's told me so. That's why she's remained with him for nearly over thirty years."

Redmond looked past Florina to the refrigerator. "Despite knowing the truth about Agnes, I was hurt when she married Macon. If she could make herself marry Macon, whom she didn't love, I thought that perhaps she could make me happy--me whom she said she loved." Redmond lowered his gaze. Sadness and longing filled his eyes, like when Agnes had reached up and caressed his cheek, the two of them standing on the church yard the following Sunday services at St. Andrew on New Year's Eve.

Florina recalled what she had witnessed. The mixture of confusing emotions that had flowed between Agnes and Redmond now ran clear. What bound Redmond to Agnes also separated him from her.

"Even though it was a lie, their marriage vows, at least on Agnes' part, I envied Macon having her. I felt alone. I wanted someone to call my own, someone who would love me." He touched his chest.

"I knew more about her. She trusted me with her truth, her innermost secret. But Macon was her husband."

"The marriage has brought him pain," Florina said.

"During our childhoods I brought him pain," Redmond said. "He envied my life when we were children. He wished my father, Dr. Hammond Austin had been his father. Macon's ashamed of his parents. I've always seen them as good and upright people. Macon knows who his father is. Learning that Robert MacIntosh was really my father felt like a betrayal, came to see myself as an imposter. *What if people learned the truth?* If I wasn't the son of second-generation doctor, Hammond Austin, then how could I live up to his and his father's accomplishments? I always feared that maybe Macon knew the truth, or would learn it and expose me. That this was the reason he envied me. That his envy wasn't really envy at all, but anger at knowing the truth, but not being able to speak it. And that one day, the whole world would know."

The night I discovered Agnes in my apartment with her friend was like reliving the afternoon Robert MacIntosh told me he was my father. Agnes just stood there--after telling me the gender she was really drawn to--like my Mother and Father had done when telling me Robert MacIntosh was my biological father. Agnes pleaded like Mother, that she loved me. Mother said she wanted me to know the truth, to hear it from Robert MacIntosh with her and Father present." Redmond sighed then softly laughed.

"Agnes on the other hand, said she had never meant for me to know. But that my apartment was the only place she felt safe being who she was. If only I hadn't come home when I did." Again, Redmond looked down.

Florina said, "I was thankful for meeting you. I didn't tell you about Ennis, because I needed to put him in my past. The pain was too much," Florina said. "I thought that if you knew, you'd think I couldn't love you, that you wouldn't want me. I didn't want Ennis or our marriage haunting me, you and whatever might grow between us." She met Redmond's gaze. "I was desperate."

Redmond's face brightened. "Learning you had been married let me know that I wasn't the only one with a past and secrets that I was ashamed of. Telling me about Ennis and your marriage with him, that you hadn't told your parents, gave me hope that if I told you the truth about Agnes, you might come to understand our relationship." Redmond drew near. "What I had with Agnes is gone. It died in the light of my discovering and seeing who she is. I don't hate her for being drawn to other women. But I can't and won't live a lie."

"I understand Agnes' love for you," Florina said. "I don't begrudge her that."

Florina recalled Agnes' letter. ... *Thank you for giving me time to let go, to say good-bye.* ...

Florina lifted Redmond's hand. " Her secret is safe with me."

Redmond leaned forward, and kissed Florina.

...

Florina and Redmond did not make love that night. Instead they lay in bed, each held by the other, their thoughts resting on those whom they had loved first, Ennis and Agnes, and how time with them had made plain the journey leading Florina and Redmond to each other.

•.•.•.•.•.•.•.•.•

Chapter 45

•.•.•.•.•.•.•.•.•

Love does not always a marriage make, but its absence ensures a union's demise.
... You found Redmond in the aftermath of Ennis' death.
... There could be no Redmond without Ennis.

Agnes had set out to attend the funeral of sixteen-year-old, Larry Payne, killed on March 28, 1968, when Macon and her father, Reverend Julius Kensington intercepted her on the steps leading up to the church where a crowd of hundreds awaited the service to begin.

This Florina learned as relayed by Hammond. Macon, and Reverend Kensington and three arrived back in Poinsettia with Agnes the following evening, Wednesday, April 3rd, 1968, before nightfall.

Florina watched from her bedroom window as Macon and the Right Reverend Julius Kensington led Agnes up the steps into their home.

"I wonder whether Agnes got to see Dr. King; hear him speak." Florina said.

Redmond continued undressing across the room at the armoire in the corner. He said, "I read that he led the march to the Clayborn Temple where Larry Payne was killed."

"His name was Larry Payne," Florina said. She thought of how Agnes must have felt when Macon and her father approached her. *Disappointed. Angry. Frustrated. Tired.*

Florina continued looking towards the house next door.

Redmond came to Florina, touched her shoulder. She turned back. The look in his eyes spoke of hunger and the need for them get on with their lives.

As they ate dinner he said, "At some point Macon's going to have to face the truth."

"Surely by now he knows or suspects something." Florina cut into her pork chop.

"If he does, he's too ashamed to face it."

"He's not completely to blame," Florina said.

"Agnes never wanted to marry him."

"Yes, but I can't imagine she told him about herself, nor would Reverend Julius," Florina said.

"Even if she had told Macon," Redmond began, " ... which I wouldn't put past Agnes, Macon would never believe her." Redmond forked a piece of pork chop and placed it in his mouth. After some moments of chewing he said, "Agnes did not want to marry Macon. But he was dead set on making her his."

"I'm sure Reverend Julius stoked the flames." Florina chewed her string beans.

"*He* certainly knew," Redmond said bitterly.

Florina lowered her fork onto the edge of her plate. "I wonder if Macon ever considered why you broke off your engagement with Agnes."

"Agnes and her father are more alike than Agnes wants to admit," Redmond said. His brown eyes glistened with acknowledgement of a reality he had long denied.

"I never thought I'd say this, but I feel sorry for her," Florina said. She met Redmond's gaze, and imagined him thinking the same.

Loud voices rose outside. A loud rapping on their front door ensued. Florina joined Redmond in going out to the front

334

room. Another round of knocking began before Redmond pulled opened the door to Agnes, her hair disheveled and wearing but a white nightgown. Shivering against the early spring chill, Florina pulled Agnes inside. "You're going to be sick," Florina said as she motioned for Redmond to get a blanket. "And bring my socks and slippers."

Florina massaged Agnes' shoulders that were cold as ice. She wrapped Agnes in the blanket Redmond delivered.

"I'm going next door," he said as Florina moved to put one sock then the other on Agnes' feet. Florina nodded. Redmond grabbed his coat from the closet by the door and left.

As she lit the fire in the heater, Florina said to Agnes sitting behind her, "I received your letter." Flames in the burner rose. Florina closed the door to the heater. "The newspapers said a snowstorm kept Dr. King from coming to Memphis on the twenty-second, but I'm told that --" Florina turned back and met Agnes' silent stare.

Agnes had not spoken since Florina had pulled her inside. She knelt before Agnes.

As if requiring all the energy she had, Agnes parted her lips. "Macon only loves my father. He wants to please Reverend Kensington more than he does me."

The front door flew open. A tall and lanky man wearing a black suit and minister's collar stepped inside. "Agnes."

Macon walked from behind Reverend Kensington and came to Agnes. He reached for Agnes, "Let's get you home," barely acknowledging Florina.

Reverend Kensington spoke. "We're sorry to intrude on you and your husband."

Florina saw that Redmond had entered the doorway.

"My daughter is not well," Agnes' father said.

Macon helped Agnes to stand.

"We wrapped a blanket around her," said Florina. She looked at Agnes' feet. "Put socks and slippers on her feet."

"*Whatever you wish that others would do to you, do also to them, for this is the Law and the Prophets*," quote Reverend Kensington, adding, "God will bless you." He turned, shot Redmond a hard glance.

Macon ushered Agnes towards the doorway. They had nearly reached Redmond, when Agnes turned and spit in Macon's face.

"Agnes!" Reverend Julius grasped her arm.

Macon wiped his cheeks. Observing what seemed her calm, he reached for her arm.

Agnes jerked away and said to Macon, "You're nothing but his lap dog!" She nodded towards her father.

Agnes' father tightened his grip upon her arm and pulled her towards the door. Again, Reverend Kensington fired Redmond a hard stare as he and Agnes moved past and through the doorway.

Macon walked past Redmond, giving him as little acknowledgment as he had shown Florina, and entered the cold behind his wife and father-in-law.

Chapter 46

Thursday, April 4th, 1968 started out, like any other day for Florina. She arose at six that morning and prepared breakfast. Redmond came down between six thirty and quarter of seven as usual. The two had started eating by seven.

Around seven forty Redmond stood and made ready to leave for the office. "I'll be late this evening," he said going for his bag. "Two of Macon's patients are still over at Charlotte Negro."

Florina knew that meant Redmond would drive to Charlotte before returning home. Today, he would use Carolyn's car. Five pm traffic on Thursday afternoon would be thick.

"I don't know that Macon will be in the office today. He's got his hands full with Agnes."

Florina's mind refused to let go of the image of despair that remained upon Macon's face as he wiped Agnes' spit from his cheeks. Florina stacked the last of the breakfast dishes in the sink. "I wonder if Leena is coming to clean."

Redmond lifted his black bag and headed out the front room. Observing Redmond retrieve his black wool coat from the closet by the door and slip into it she considered the brief glances that had passed between Redmond and Agnes' father. "I should check on Agnes," Florina said.

Redmond lifted his bag. "You have class today."

Florina imagined for a moment that Redmond had perhaps experienced a change of heart towards his biological father and that he would give a message for her to deliver to MacIntosh. "I've misplaced the hydrangea root bulb that Robert MacIntosh gave me. Have you seen it?"

"As a matter of fact, my mother planted it."

"Carolyn?"

"She has a bit of a green thumb," Redmond said. "I told her when Robert gave it you, how long it had been in water. We'd just returned from the memorial service and you were tired." *Sad and tired*, Florina thought. "I gave it to her that next week. She'd come over to check on you."

Thursday. Florina thought. That's when it disappeared. "Where did she plant it?"

"Outside, just beneath the verandah," Redmond took Florina by the hand, led her out onto the verandah and down the steps. "Here it is," he said and knelt to where the newly dug earth was again settling in. Florina bent over and touched the ground, moist and soft. "It should grow. Just give it time." He stood and looked beyond Florina to Agnes and Macon's house.

"I should check on Agnes."

"Agnes has Macon and Reverend Julius looking after her. *Stay focused*," Redmond said. He glanced back down at the newly dug and replanted earth underneath which the hydrangea bulb lay. Redmond then reached out, drew Florina into his chest, and kissed the top of her head. "Don't get side tracked," he recommended and left.

Willa Mae, six months pregnant, arrived at ten thirty and set about changing the linen after which she would start the wash. An hour later the clothes were drying outside amid the April sunshine as Willa Mae stood ironing a sheet from yesterday's wash.

338

Florina sat her purse on the table. "If I'm late lock up the house and leave." She was preparing to head out for class and knew she would most probably not return that afternoon by four.

"Yes, ma'am," Willa Mae said while nodding as she moved the hot iron across the white sheet, smoothing away the wrinkles.

Florina stacked her books upon the dining room table. "Redmond has to look in on two of Macon's patients over at Charlotte Negro Hospital. I don't expect him home before seven this evening."

Willa Mae brought more of the sheet onto the ironing board. "I see that Dr. Macon and Miss Agnes' father brought her back from Memphis."

"They arrived back yesterday afternoon," Florina said.

Willa Mae folded the ironed sheet and spread another one out. "Have you seen her?"

"No," Florina lied. She went out the closet in the front room and put on her coat. Florina would tell no one of last night's events.

On return she put her purse upon her shoulder, lifted the books and was almost through the dining room entryway when Willa Mae said, "What I should I do if she comes looking for you?"

"Tell her I'm over in Charlotte and you don't know when I'll be home." Florina instructed then turned back. "Say the same thing if she asks for Redmond." Florina then left.

Robert MacIntosh led an animated lecture, one that engrossed and engaged his twenty-five students but left Florina doodling on her note pad. Aware the other students were alert and attentive, Florina heard none of what he said. Her thoughts had remained entangled within the vines and minutia of gazes that Redmond had exchanged with Reverend Julius, as well as the virulent actions rooted Agnes' repulsion of her father and husband.

339

Only with Robert MacIntosh towering over her, his shadow capturing her attention within the emptied room, did Florina realize class had ended.

"Whatever holds your thoughts has no intention of letting them go."

Florina inspected the writings and drawings on her notepad where she still held her pen.

"Anything you'd like to share?"

"Just thoughts," Florina said. "She made no effort to stand.

"The rudiments of poetry." MacIntosh sat across from her.

"I don't know about these." Florina glanced at her writing.

Agnes ... Macon

... tigers ... leopards

civil ... war ... wars ...

The orange hydrangea bulb came to her once again.

"Am I to conclude from your lackluster participation in the class discussion that your neighbor has returned?" MacIntosh asked.

Florina had told him of Agnes' leaving the night it rained, and the daily reports concerning Agnes that Hammond had received from Dr. Everett Collier in Memphis. She took in MacIntosh's brown eyes, the depth of emotion that lived within his face, his cheekbones honed from what she sensed had been hours upon days spent ruminating across and through the underbelly of philosophical questions plaguing poets and sages since time immemorial.

"How did you feel when Redmond's mother made it clear that despite her love for you she would spend her life with Father Hammond?"

Energy seeped from MacIntosh's face. His shoulders slumped. Vigor left his eyes, their light dimming. "I don't think I'll ever get over it. I can never hate her for the decision, choosing Hammond over me, a second generation doctor over a first, and perhaps, only generation poet." There in the empty

340

classroom, MacIntosh looked past Florina to the windows covered in blinds, crying out for a serious dusting. "But I respect her choice."

"Agnes would have married Redmond had he not broken off their engagement," Florina said.

"He told you that?" Seriousness returned to MacIntosh's demeanor.

"He told me why. Or rather what he discovered that made him break off the engagement," Florina said.

"Agnes could never love him the way a husband, a man, wants," MacIntosh spoke cautiously.

"She has conflicting desires."

"She yearns for those of her--our--gender."

Florina leaned into the silence and tone of resignation, linking MacIntosh's words. After some moments, she said, "I'm not so certain that Agnes could not have loved Redmond, that she would not have been a good and dutiful wife to him. I don't think she loved him any less than those of our same gender, and who have vied for her affections, and have loved her. Redmond means a lot to her. She respects him greatly."

"You are probably right. But we men are possessive. Sharing is not our strong suit," MacIntosh explained. "We want to know that we are the one and only."

Florina smiled in the wake of understanding the light his words cast.

They started across the college yard to MacIntosh's house situated at the edge of campus.

"Redmond spends a lot of time over here at Charlotte Negro Hospital," Florina said as they walked.

"You're thinking of our ships, mine and Redmond's, so close, but passing the other in the night."

"I'm speaking of the all the time lost," Florina said.

This time, MacIntosh smiled.

On reaching his house he unlocked the front door, allowed Florina inside. Then lifting his wrist, "Seeing as it's four," he read his watch, "... and that you don't expect Redmond home before seven, why don't you join me for a light dinner? I promise not to feed you too much. And to have you on the road back to Poinsettia by five thirty. Lawrence Mayweather has just returned from having heard Dr. King speak in Memphis last night. He's giving a talk over in Lampert Auditorium in the History building this evening at six. He'll be discussing what he's learned about the sanitation workers' strike, Larry Payne's death and what Dr. King said last evening."

"Macon and Reverend Julius intercepted Agnes as she was going into the Clayborn Temple to attend Larry Payne's funeral," Florina said. "She had planned to attend Dr. King's speech last night."

MacIntosh's gaze brightened. "Perhaps you'd like to join me in attending Lawrence's talk," he said. "Call Carolyn, tell her where you are. She'll inform Redmond not to worry."

The idea of hearing Lawrence Mayweather discuss Dr. King's speech excited Florina. The more she learned of MacIntosh the more Florina gained insight into Redmond. This was something she had been unable to experience with Ennis.

"I would like that," Florina said. "Oh, by the way, Carolyn planted the root bulb you gave me, for the orange hydrangea. I got so busy with the memorial service for Ennis that I forgot about it. But she put it in the ground."

MacIntosh smiled then led her to the phone on a table in the hallway.

"Don't worry about Redmond," Carolyn greeted Florina on the phone. "I'll take dinner down to your place. Hammond and I will eat with Redmond there." Redmond's mother sounded grateful, almost relieved that Florina was forging a relationship with the man whose genes flowed through Redmond. "Give Robert our love."

"I will, and again thanks for planting the hydrangea bulb," Florina said.

Robert MacIntosh prepared three tuna salad sandwiches of which he and Florina each ate one, and split one half of the third.

•.•..•.•..•.•..•.•..•

Chapter 47

•.•..•.•..•.•..•.•..•

Florina considered the nurturing aspect of MacIntosh's personality as he carefully wrapped the remaining half of the third sandwich in aluminum foil then placed the rectangle of foil into a neat, brown bag. "You can share this with Redmond later tonight."

Fascinated by this dimension of his character, she determined to pack the half sandwich in Redmond's Friday lunch.

Florina and the man who was her second, if not true, father-in-law, headed back across campus to Lampert Auditorium. The humid though cooling temperature of early April left her to wonder if the tuna sandwich would spoil.

Dr. Lawrence Mayweather walked upon the stage and began his talk at six pm as planned. Lampert Auditorium, the central theater, comfortably seated three hundred people. Brimming beyond capacity, students, teachers and those interested in Mayweather's work stood against its walls and lined the central aisle, leaving but a thin path towards the front.

"Lawrence Mayweather has been following the Civil Rights Movement since the murder of Emmett Till," Robert MacIntosh whispered as the crowd looked towards the lean and tall speaker, also a history professor at Johnson C. Smith. The graying edges gave the fifty-year-old Mayweather, who was ten years MacIntosh's junior, a distinguished aura.

Mayweather's eyes twinkled as he parted his lips and said, "I'm quite certain we're breaking fire code, and so in anticipation of Dr. Devonshire interrupting me I will be brief." Mayweather grinned, and clasped his hands. The crowd released a hearty laugh. Florina turned to MacIntosh and smiled. Walter Devonshire, the chairman of the History Department, as everyone knew revered rules.

"Those in whom I stir questions," Mayweather continued, " ... I invite to my house tomorrow where I'll be holding a discussion with my students about what I saw and heard during this last week in Memphis."

Everyone clapped.

Lawrence Mayweather held a commitment to not simply tracking and recording events of the Civil Rights Movement, but deciphering and translating the events and their possible consequences for both Negroes, whites, and America at-large. Believing at the outset of the new year, as did Dr. Martin Luther King, that the United States, due to its involvement in Vietnam, had set the country and its people on a trajectory towards disaster, Mayweather had honed his focus the last four months upon studying Dr. King's speeches, both of the past and those given more recently in 1968. Mayweather had tracked Dr. King's movements with intense scrutiny as much as news articles, and personal contacts allowed. He and Dr. King both held great concern for the effects of the cost of America's involvement in Vietnam on the country's poor. They each saw the plight of American Negroes not as separate, but as embedded in the struggle of disenfranchised and poor white Americans, Native Americans and Mexican migrant.

Mayweather began by outlining the events of the Sanitation Workers' strike in Memphis, Tennessee in which Dr. King had become heavily involved during the last three weeks.

"I think we can say that the entry of Henry Loeb into his second term as Mayor of Memphis, Tennessee this past January made conditions ripe for what we have witnessed over the last eight to nine weeks with the sanitation workers strike." Donning a black suit, white shirt and tie, Mayweather moved about the stage, gesturing and speaking with ease. "Mayor Loeb raised the battle cry for an electoral ticket of white unity in 1959. He did this in response to Negroes in Memphis organizing their votes. I've always found this quite puzzling since Mr. Loeb is of Jewish descent. His parents came here from Germany around 1860. Mr. Loeb, himself, fought in World War II, during which time the American military was part of the Allied Forces waging war against Nazi Germany that was intent on eradicating the world of all Jewish peoples." Mayweather's eyes retreated as if trying still to understand the nature of Henry Loeb's stance against Negroes in Memphis seeking to assert their political power.

He turned and started back across the stage. "In any case we know that on Thursday, February first, during heavy winter rains, two Negro sanitation workers, Echol Cole and Robert Walker, were killed in an mishap while working on a Memphis city truck. Cole and Walker were crushed beyond recognition while sitting in the back of the garbage truck because Memphis law forbids Negro workers from seeking shelter from the rain anywhere but on the back of the garbage truck. Never mind this insane law, the truck on which Cole and Walker were killed, was a truck just like the others that sanitation workers operate, and they are not regularly maintained. We also know that white sanitation workers in Memphis receive twice the pay that Negro workers are given. These terrible and unfair conditions led to the Negro sanitation workers going on strike nearly two weeks later on Tuesday, February 12th. Mayor Loeb has not been kind to his city workers."

Florina recalled Agnes sitting amid newspapers and news clippings, one of which included an article regarding the

347

incident Mayweather just spoke about. Similar to Mayweather's remarks concerning Henry Loeb, Agnes had said, "He's Jewish. His own people were oppressed in Germany. But Henry Loeb is acting like Adolph Hitler, himself, treating the Memphis garbage workers like Jews in Europe." Florina remembered Agnes' face was red and swollen from crying.

Florina returned her attention to Mayweather on the stage.

"The deaths of Cole and Williams opened up a long-festering wound."

Heads nodded in agreement in the filled auditorium. Mayweather spoke with vigor and commitment, displaying a desire not only to reveal and highlight the cause and effect of historical events presently unfolding, but also a desire to impact justice through recognizing and understanding the links of certain people's desires set against the wants and needs of others in their efforts to survive.

A flicker of hope illuminated Mayweather's eyes as he spoke. Florina recognized the same look in Agnes' eyes when she had spoken of her determination to hear Dr. Martin Luther King in person. Reverend Julius Kensington was Agnes' experience of injustice. Her wish to see Dr. King, and hear his words in the flesh, constituted Agnes' fight to stand in the presence of the great liberator of their time--Dr. Martin Luther King, Jr.--the drum major for justice, the platoon sergeant for peace.

Lawrence Mayweather did not curtail his talk. The hushed silence of the crowd, bound in rapt attention, opened the floodgates to the full history of what had occurred in the eight or more weeks that had led up to Dr. Martin Luther King, Jr.'s march from the Clayborn Temple. The Memphis police had interrupted the march and an officer had tragically shot and killed sixteen-year-old Larry Payne.

"The first half of February can be characterized as a back and forth between Mayor Loeb and the sanitation workers and their union representatives. Sanitation workers refuse to work. Garbage is lining the sidewalks. Memphis descends into a meltdown of chaos. No one is speaking." Mayweather brought

348

his palms together as if praying and urged the crowd, "Just think if no one in your house was speaking. Your mother, feeling unappreciated, had called it quits and your father refuses to bend." Mayweather lowered his hands to his sides as those who had gathered absorbed his description. "Monday, March eighteenth, over fifteen thousand rally to Dr. King's call for citizens to gather and march. The snowstorm on March twenty second prevents Dr. King from returning as promised. City management meets with union representatives and again try to work out a deal. Dr. Ralph Abernathy comes and speaks to the strikers. Hope flickers." Mayweather surveyed the audience. "By the middle of the following week it becomes apparent these discussions have led nowhere." Mayweather gestured then lowered his head.

Florina marveled at how Lawrence Mayweather transmitted the details of living history in riveting fashion. She grew even more fascinated that he had attained such understanding and clarity of events that had occurred within the recent twelve weeks.

Mayweather spoke of Wednesday, March 28th. "The seven pm curfew is still in effect. Four thousand National Guardsmen are in place. Mayor Loeb has established a siege about the city. Dr. King returns to Memphis and attempts a peaceful march from the Clayborn Temple. Memphis police intercede, and like they always do, begin beating Negro marchers. Police arrest close to three hundred people. The police pull out their full armament of tear gas, mace, bully sticks. Over fifty are injured in the various melees and scraps. A mother, Elizabeth Payne, loses her son to police violence. A Memphis police officer says that sixteen-year-old Larry Payne, pulled a knife on him. This is why the officer says he shot Larry in the stomach."

The crowd moaned, the ache of those who had gathered apparent as they empathized with Larry Payne and his mother, Elizabeth Payne. Florina gripped her stomach, wanting to double over. Her thoughts traveled back to Innis Halpern whom Redmond had fought to save. She recalled her own sense of loss--confusing Innis Halpern, killed in North Carolina, for

349

Ennis McCreary, who had died Vietnam, the two deaths interwoven, and yet distinct.

"Despite what others say, I am certain that Dr. King never meant for the march to descend into the violence that erupted. I'm told he is devastated at the death of teenager, Larry Payne. Still others know this too." Mayweather continued.

"The next day two hundred sanitation workers along with various ministers continue where Dr. King's march left off and arrive at Memphis City Hall. Our president, Johnson, I'm told offered help in getting talks between City Management and union representatives back on track. I'm not quite sure how a man such as Johnson can help, a man who has committed more than four hundred thousand soldiers to fighting people in a country half way around the world from us and who have done nothing to us."

Florina closed her eyes and considered Ennis, his life given in service to a country where his father would and could not acknowledge Ennis having descended from him without experiencing serious detriment to his career.

Mayweather unclasped his hands and lifted his head from heavy thought. "Dr. King cancels his plans to travel to Africa. '*My work is in Memphis*,' Dr. King concludes. He comes back to Memphis on Sunday, the last day of March. February and March have been long months for the peoples of Memphis. Long and hard." Mayweather looked into the crowd. After a long pause he said, "Loeb lifts the curfew on April first. Larry Payne's funeral takes place without the presence of National Guard in the city. I feel fortunate for the ability and freedom granted me by Dr. Davenport to travel and be in Memphis these last two weeks. The culmination for me was being present to hear Dr. King speak last evening. As you can tell, I'm a bit excited. I'm running on adrenaline. I have not slept in over two days." Mayweather for the first time pocketed his hands.

"When Dr. King took the podium last night at the Masonic Temple in Memphis, he looked tired and beleaguered. But just like me, I feel he was excited, thrilled to be a part of a movement whose sole goal is to make the world a better place

350

for all *humankind*. I don't use the word, leader, though for me Dr. King is definitely a leader. But he does not see himself as that, rather a vessel through which God's light and illumination of divine message and intervention shines on us all."

Hands in the jacket pockets of his black suit, Mayweather lowered his head. "It's been a long year for Dr. King, and I don't mean since January. When Dr. King entered the pulpit last evening he did so just shy of a year ago, when he entered the pulpit of Riverside Church in Riverside, New York. Last year, April 4th, 1967, Dr. King made known his stance against America's involvement in Vietnam. This was a turning point in not simply the Civil Rights Movement, but Dr. King's own life."

Florina recalled how MacIntosh, during their walk over to Lampert Auditorium, explained that Mayweather had in the last year focused his attention not simply on studying Martin Luther King Jr.'s statements on the Negro plight in America, poverty, and the war, but also the apprehensive, negative and reprimanding responses of more than a few Negro citizens towards Dr. King's expansion of his message.

Chapter 48

Mayweather digressed again. "Nineteen sixty-five was a glorious year of sorts. We saw the enabling of Civil Rights legislation, which included the Voting Rights Act. January of 1966 brought Julian Bond into the Georgia House of Representatives. Eight other Negroes were elected to similar positions in other states. Last June we saw the legalization interracial marriage. The Supreme Court, in their decision on Loving vs. the State of Virginia, voted to allow Negroes and whites to marry."

Mayweather clasped his hands while the crowd let out a round of uproarious clapping. When silence descended he said, "All this we have seen enacted during President Johnson's administration. Most recently, this past October, we had our first Negro Solicitor General, Thurgood Marshall, take his seat on the United States Supreme Court as the first Negro to hold such a position." Mayweather smiled as the congregants applauded the accomplishments of Negroes in the recent year.

"But may I remind you that while Justice Marshall was settling into his new role, Dr. King was arrested on October 31, yes of this past year, and began a five-day sentence in Bessemer

Jail in Alabama. The charge was that of being in contempt of court."

The history professor, who had made it his work to bring a microscopic lens to Dr. Martin Luther King Jr.'s work and movements, looked directly at the crowd. "Dr. King did not make friends when he took this detour at Riverside Church-- speaking out against the United States' involvement in the Vietnam War. His actions sowed the seeds for enemies in both the white community and in our community—the Negro community. Many of your parents, and perhaps you also, see President Johnson as a friend to Negroes. As I've just listed, we've seen President Johnson enact progressive legislation and make positive gestures for and towards Negroes during his presidency."

Mayweather raised his hand, and forefinger. "But let us not forget. No president is bigger than the presidency into which he is inaugurated. And as such, no one or two actions, however benevolent a president commits, can change what lives and has lived in the hearts of the majority of its citizens for over three hundred years. When Dr. King assumed the podium last night, I felt not only had he, but I too, had lived through a war. The last month of events in Memphis are but a microcosm, a heightened encapsulation of all that has been building since Rosa Parks chose not to move to the back of the bus, and a year before when white men, Roy and J. W. Milam, murdered Emmett Till in August of 1954. These two men reported to a magazine writer that they had kidnapped and killed Emmett, and I believe them. When I listened to Dr. King speak last night of his journey to the mountaintop I knew he had made his way there by traveling untold valleys, deep and wide. I also knew--"

The door at the back of the auditorium opened. A wrenching shriek echoed from the corridor outside.

Dr. Devonshire entered Lampert Auditorium. It was eight-thirty, at least one-half to three-quarters of an hour past when Florina had felt certain Devonshire would allow Mayweather's discussion to continue. "He's come to order us out," she whispered to MacIntosh who said nothing, but instead

354

remained focused upon Devonshire overlooking the crowd and appearing hesitant to speak or move.

A whisper of voices rose from the back, people bending left and right, and speaking to those sitting or standing beside them. Heavy sobs began. Someone released a cry then a wail.

Sixty-five year-old Walter Devonshire began the long trek, winding his way between those sitting in the aisle towards the stage at the front where Mayweather stood silently. A male student, wearing a red v-neck pullover, white shirt and navy pants stood with his hand to Mayweather's ear and whispering. A look of shock and dread slid over Mayweather's face. Cupping his palms, he brought them to his face.

Walter Devonshire joined Mayweather as the student left the stage.
Words passed between the two men. Mayweather nodded. MacIntosh focused intensely on the two men. Devonshire looked out over the congregation and heaved a great sigh. He, like Lawrence Mayweather, wore a black suit, white shirt and tie. Grasping the microphone he parted his lips, and with great gentleness, as if to reverse the set of events that had taken place, make what he was about to dispense untrue, said, *"I'm sorry to announce ... "*

The chairman of the History Department again scanned the room, many in the audience now filled with tears. The young male sitting behind MacIntosh at the end of the row of seats leaned forward and whispered. MacIntosh frowned as if in pain as Devonshire said, *"Dr. Martin Luther King was shot at seven this evening. He was pronounced dead,"* Devonshire lifted his wrist and on reading his watch said, voice trembling, " ... *he was pronounced dead thirty minutes ago."*

A frenzy of emotions and turmoil settled. Tears of denial and chaotic disbelief overtook the crowd.

Florina gripped her chest. Feeling hot and flushed, she leaned forward. MacIntosh placed his arms around her shoulders. "Let's get out of here," he said and helped her stand. Steering her towards the door parallel the stage, they exited the campus where students and teachers stood hostage to shock and grief.

The clamor of voices surrounding them grew louder as Florina, with MacIntosh shielding her from the invisibility of what might come next, made their way to the black Riviera.

"I've got to get home," Florina said.

"Not alone you won't. The streets won't stay safe for long. When the truth finally sinks in all hell is going to break loose." He urged Florina into the passenger's seat then scurried around and got in from the driver's side.

She gave him the keys. "You have to teach two classes tomorrow," Florina said. "How will you get back?"

"That is *if* any classes meet tomorrow," MacIntosh said. "The future will take care of itself. Right now I want to get you safely back to Redmond." He drove them out of the parking lot and down the street. The faces of people standing in their yards came into view as the English professor cleared the college campus and its surrounding neighborhood. Fear and dismay flowing into disgust and anger formed the mosaic. Florina's stomach churned, she knotting her fists. Her thoughts descended upon Agnes.

Loud pops sounded.

"Gunshots," MacIntosh said.

Florina turned to him then hearing the sound once more turned back to the passenger's window beside her. The finality of Agnes never being able to witness Dr. King speak hit the pit of Florina's stomach like a jagged rock.

"*What will she do?*" Florina thought of Agnes, and then of Martin Luther King's wife, children, and the nation, "*What will any of us do?*"

———————————————————

Chapter 49

Robert MacIntosh brought the sedan to a halt in front of Florina's house in Poinsettia. "Well that went easier than I thought," he said and slid the key from the ignition.

Florina looked toward house. "That's strange. It's dark inside."

"What did Carolyn say when you spoke with her?" MacIntosh looked to the house as well.

"She was going to bring dinner down here. She and Father Hammond would eat dinner with Redmond."

"Perhaps Redmond is still over in Charlotte. I'm certain they'll have some extra emergencies with all that's going on."

Florina considered the overwhelming chaos that would envelope the country in the wake of Dr. King's murder. The previous summer had been a firestorm of protests in the face of progress, albeit nil and slow. Dr. King's assassination would signal and symbolize to many the death of a dream deferred long past its time.

"Everything seems quiet here," said MacIntosh. He got out, came around and opened Florina's door.

Florina took in the dark and quiet street of their middle to upper class neighborhood, quite a contrast to Charlotte on their way to the freeway. "All the shades are drawn," she said on closer observance.

MacIntosh closed her door, started towards the verandah.

Florina climbed the steps then reaching the lock inserted the key, and pushed opened the door to an ocean of darkness inside. "Redmond hasn't been home," she said.

MacIntosh touched her shoulder. Sensing his anxiety, Florina stepped aside.

MacIntosh pulled closed the door, re-engaged the lock and gave her the key. "Let's get you to Hammond and Carolyn's." He grasped Florina's arm, and all the while looking out, alert to what she could not see, led her down the steps from the verandah and back to the black sedan. He pulled open passenger's door and a scream reverberated from Agnes and Macon's.

Florina turned back. "It's coming from Agnes and Macon's," she said. A light went on in their bedroom. Florina left the grasp of Robert MacIntosh and started for their house. She stepped onto the porch, and approached the front door. Seeing it ajar she pushed it open, and while entering, called out, "Hello." From behind her MacIntosh lowered his hand upon her shoulder.

Florina walked towards the light flowing from a room midway down the hall. The sound of whimpering clarified as she drew near the doorway through which slivers of light entered. "Agnes," she called out, pushing open the door.

•.••.••.••.••.••.•
Chapter 50
•.••.••.••.••.••.•

Agnes sat on a chair in the corner by the window, the shades drawn as with all the other houses on the street. Her hands lay upon her lap as she whimpered and cried. Her right hand, the one with which she always held her cigarette, trembled furiously.

Macon, sat across the room in a high, wing-backed chair. One arm lay extended along the sidearm. The other gripped a pistol, its long barrel aimed at Agnes.

"You came," Macon said on turning towards Florina. "I was wondered how long it would take."

"What are you doing?" Florina said.

Robert MacIntosh, his hand to her shoulder, gave a gentle squeeze.

"I'm teaching my wife a lesson. *About the importance of lying*. Or I should say, *why we should not lie to particularly those who love you*."

Florina turned to Agnes. "You should go," Agnes softly pleaded.

"Shut up!" Macon commanded.

359

Florina jumped. Robert assuaged her shoulder with another calming squeeze. "What can we do to make this right?" she asked Macon.

"Turn back time." Macon tilted his head to the side then shrugged. "Change a person's heart." He turned directly to Florina. "You tell me," Macon said. He pointed the gun at Florina's chest.

"What do you want?" MacIntosh stepped from behind Florina, moved in front her.

"The truth," Macon said, the gun now aimed at Robert. "Same as you wanted concerning Redmond." Robert lowered his eyelids as if in regret.

"I told you," Agnes started. She spoke with penitence. "Redmond doesn't love me. And I don't love him anymore."

"Not anymore," Macon mimicked her.

Florina stepped from behind Robert MacIntosh. "Redmond and *I* are married," she said.

"He's even thinking of moving to California," MacIntosh added.

"But you see it's too late for all of this now." Macon leapt to his feet, once again made Florina the target of his gun.

Her whimpers growing louder, Agnes lowered her head and clasped her hands, brought them to her lips and began to pray.

"So now we've found that God your father is so fond of quoting," Macon said to Agnes. "You never counted on me figuring out your secret."

Agnes' body was shaking with sobs. "I never wanted to marry you," Agnes pleaded against sobs.

"*You*," Macon aimed the gun at Agnes, " ... led me to believe it was because of Redmond that the engagement ended.

"I loved him." Agnes extended her hands clasped as they had been when praying.

"But not like you loved that woman he caught you with!" Macon said.

Florina gasped, brought palms to her lips.

360

"Don't tell me you didn't know." Macon turned and stared at Florina. She met his gaze. "But then again," Macon said, "... you might not."

Agnes said, "Redmond wanted to tell you, but I begged him not to."

"He kept your secret!" Macon said. He turned back to Agnes.

"I told you," Agnes attempted once more at making her case. She whispered, "I didn't want to marry you. I didn't love you. I told yo--"

Florina winced.

"But you never said it was because you loved women," Macon said as he gestured with the gun. "You and the good Redmond Austin let me think he had fallen out of love with you. And that gave me hope."

Macon wiped tears from his cheeks then turned to Florina. "It's wrong to lie," he said. "And that's what she and Redmond did. They lied to me." Macon aimed the gun at his wife, moved his finger ever tighter against the trigger.

"She hurt you," Florina blurted. "And Redmond too." Macon kept the gun aimed at Agnes. "Redmond thought he was doing the right thing by staying silent. But he was wrong. He shouldn't have lied. But you know the old saying, 'If you can't say anything good, say nothing at all?'"

A bitter frown overtook Macon's face. He stood, came to Florina. "You knew," Macon said. Again he leaned his head to the side and inspected her face.

Florina willed herself not to turn from his gaze. She grasped her hands. "Redmond wanted everything to be clean between me and him," Florina said. "I told him about my first husband, Ennis. Redmond told me about Agnes."

"Only there's a difference between me and him. A big difference," Macon said.

Florina pulled at her knuckles. Her mouth ran dry. She quivered within. Macon drew even closer, aimed the gun at Florina's forehead. MacIntosh slid closer to Florina.

"Your Ennis is dead," Macon said. "And even if he had lived, I doubt you would have left him for Redmond. Even still,

361

now that you've married Redmond, he was never secretly in love with *me*. He's a man. *A real man.* "

Macon's statement confused Florina. She glimpsed MacIntosh beside her.

"Agnes loves you," Macon said to Florina. Agnes wailed as Florina met Macon's stare. "If you don't believe me, ask her," Macon turned to Agnes, sobbing even harder.

"It's not what you think," Agnes said. She lowered her eyelids, squeezed them tightly shut. "All that matters is I don't want to be with you!" Agnes shook her head then opening her eyes and fired Macon with a cold stare.

"You would if she wasn't here," Macon said.

The gun still aimed at Florina, Macon touched its barrel to her forehead.

Florina lowered her eyelids. Tears seeped through. Her hands tightly clasped and to her chest, she drew still.

"You can't get away with this," MacIntosh said from beside Florina.

"And just what is it I'm trying to accomplish?" Macon demanded. "With all your experience of betrayal how would you direct me?" he said to Robert MacIntosh. "Tell me what to do."

Florina would not open her eyes to the gun barrel pressed against her forehead.

"Put the gun down," MacIntosh said to Macon. "You have too much to live for. Life goes on even when we lose the person we love to another. I've lost two women in my life. The ache of those losses will be with me until I die, but--"

Voices called from out front. "Florina. Agnes."

Redmond. Florina tried to remain still against whimpers now rattling through her.

MacIntosh punched Macon knocking him down and the gun from his hand. Sensing herself about to fall backwards, Florina opened her eyes. MacIntosh ran after Macon crawling upon his stomach, and reaching for the gun under the chair.

"No!" Agnes ran towards chair, pushed it aside and reached to lift the gun.

Grabbing it first, Macon whirled around aimed the long barrel of the gun once more at Florina. Agnes pushed the chair against Macon. He fell back. Agnes started for Florina. Two shots rang out. Agnes dropped to the floor. A sharp pain pierced Florina's side.

She imagined the orange hydrangea bursting through the earth, and blossoming, awash in life and vibrancy. Blood oozed forth. *I'll never see it.* Florina despaired against the sound of a third shot ringing out.

She slumped to the floor, glimpsed Macon--*the image of an orange hydrangea canvassed her thoughts*--one half his face obliterated, the other awash in blood.

•.•.•.•.•.•.•.•.•.•

Chapter 51

•.•.•.•.•.•.•.•.•.•

Florina opened her eyes to Ennis standing over her. He was smiling. "You're awake," he said. He grasped her hand and lifted her to stand.

Florina squinted. Bringing her hand to her forehead she took in the sky, surveyed the verdant green fields surrounding them. "It's beautiful," she said of the place in which she now stood.

"Yes, it is," said Ennis donning a pristine white shirt and brown khakis. "They're rice paddies. He gestured to all that encircled them. Lifting her hand to his lips, he kissed the back of her palm. The warmth of safety spread through Florina. They trekked across the field. "It's been a while," Ennis said.

Florina recalled how Ennis had gone away soon after they married. "I wish we'd had more time together after the marrying," she said.

"You speak as if you're having regrets," Ennis said.

Florina tightened her grasp on his hand, tried to understand the meaning of Ennis' statement preceding what felt like an ominous foreboding.

Ennis smiled. "Life is a gift." The light in his eyes dimmed.

Again Florina surveyed the fields, alive and bright green, this time noting brown huts lining the edge of the fields. A thick tropical forest stood beyond the huts.

"It seems like heaven," she said. "Heaven on earth."

"It can appear that way sometime." The ambiguity of Ennis' words again left her perplexed.

"Why am I here?" Florina asked, sensing that she was forgetting something. She looked back from where they had come. Her thoughts reached for an important fact eluding her memory.

"Come," Ennis said. He pulled her forward.

Half way across the field, Florina looked to the line of bamboo huts encircling the field and demarcating where the field ended and tropical forest began. "Who lives here?" she asked.

"People. Villagers," Ennis said.

Phrases lilted across Florina's mind. *The rice paddies surrounding Saigon are alive with joy and grace.* She turned around, and again took in the fullness of the land and sky before her. Another phrase encompassed her thoughts. *Bodies laid waste in a war that divides our country and separates our heart from its soul line the countryside.*

"Where are they?" she questioned. "The bodies."

A mask of sadness slid upon Ennis' smooth face, the color of buttermilk. He released her hand. "You don't want to talk about that."

"But I do." More words of her poem followed.

The spirits of these men live on.

The ghost of a lover wanders the empty field of her father's farm.

"You're not really here," Florina said. "And neither am I."

"But I am." Ennis again lifted her hand. "I'm here with you right now." He pointed to the ground.

"I'm here with all the others." He turned towards one of the huts in the distance.

Fields that in summer yield corn. ...

Florina gripped her head and shook it against the thoughts pouring in. She closed her eyes. "Why is this happening?"

... Corn that in autumn and winter nourish livestock.

"Why wouldn't it be?" said Ennis. He caressed her shoulder. "You're alive." He lifted her chin, looked into her eyes. "You're alive. Don't forget that."

"*But what about you?*" Florina took hold of his hand, gripped his arm.

Clouds formed overhead. Mist filled with darkness descended. The panorama of beauty folded into a hailstorm of loud cries, surrounded by bullets and grenades piercing the night.

The green fields and bright, sun-filled sky no more, Ennis stood before Florina wearing muddy green battle fatigues instead of the white shirt and khakis. An Army helmet sat atop his head. Black earth and sweat covered his face. A machine gun in his one hand, he grasped her arm with the other. Bending over he started them forward. "We need to get to that hut." He pointed towards a hut into the distance. A brilliant radiance emanated from the bamboo structure absorbed in what seemed as bright as sunshine.

Bullets whizzed over around Florina as Ennis led her towards the hut wrapped in light. They hurried on darting past dead bodies and soldiers writhing in pain. Grenades exploded in the distance, releasing orange flames against those still alive and barking orders.

"Come on," Ennis commanded. "We've got to go."

Hope flooding her heart, Florina drew closer to Ennis, grasp tight his free arm.

He fell. "I've been hit," Ennis said. He grabbed his thigh. "Keep going." He waved her on.

"Not without you."

"I'm fine."

"You've been shot," Florina said. Blood poured from Ennis' thigh. She ached to stop its flow. She ran to him, knelt and grasped his leg.

"Go!" Ennis pushed her away.

"I love you!" Florina screamed, trying to make herself heard above the cries of battle in the surrounding darkness.

"I love you too." Ennis' face darkened. Lines formed underneath his eyes and stretched their way across his forehead. His hair that had been cut short, practically non-existent, appeared thick and matted.

"This is too much!" Again Florina shook her head, this time gripping Ennis' hand. "I can't leave you! Not again! I won't!" She remembered the memorial service, Clifford, Reverend Herring, the shots fired during the salute.

"I'm already gone," Ennis spoke.

Florina closed her eyes and held them tightly shut.

"I need you alive," Ennis said. He touched her hand to his leg. His words were calm and firm like the river of blood flowing silently from his thigh. Ennis pointed to the hut glowing with light. "You need to get to that hut over there."

Florina looked back.

"I'm with you all the way," Ennis said.

"You said you're already dead!" Florina sobbed. The fighting grew heavier. An ocean of soldiers moved passed them, some carrying guns, others the limp bodies of those they were trying to save. A soldier yelled then threw a grenade back at a group of men following him.

Ennis turned back. "You need to go," he said.

A man emerged from the mist of fallout from the exploded grenade and started towards Florina and Ennis. She squeezed Ennis' leg as if to will it healed.

"Go!" Ennis yelled. He tried to heave himself up. "Those are my final orders." Decisive and commanding, his voice penetrated the darkness.

Hands took hold of Florina from behind, lifted her from the ground and started towards the hut. She looked up into face of the person whose arms held her. *Redmond.*

Steadily he moved through the mist of gunfire enveloping them, Florina looking beyond his shoulder, and back to Ennis, the man approaching him. The man had no gun. Light flickered off the blade of his knife.

Redmond continued towards the bamboo hut--light glowing through and around it. He had stepped within a hundred feet of the hut when the man reached Ennis, and set his hands around Ennis' neck. Ennis pulled the man forward, threw him over and tried to stand.

The man, whose face Florina could not see, jumped to his feet. Once more he took hold of Ennis, unable to stand, but who battled with all his might. The wiry man snaked his arm about Ennis' neck.

All wars are civil. Because all of us are brothers. The words rang within Florina. A bright light appeared, encapsulating Ennis and the man, his face shades darker than Ennis'. The man brought the knife to Ennis' neck, touched it to Ennis' jugular. Ennis angled his head up, directed the gaze of his nearly blue eyes into brown eyes of the man whose face Florina could yet to recognize. Ennis pulled the man to him. The cuts and gashes on Ennis' face grew ever more pronounced. His eyes ran blood red, life rushing into them.

A third man wearing a black robe trimmed in red stepped from the darkness behind Ennis and man. "Peace I give you, not as the world promises," said the man. She opened his arms and dispensed the circle of light about them.

He extended one hand to Ennis.

Ennis' blue gaze enlivened amid the redness pooling around his irises as he grasped the hand of the black-robed man and stood as if having no injury. The black-robed man, a minister Florina now recognized, turned to Ennis' attacker and stretched out his other hand. The combatant gently placed the knife on the minister's open palm.

Ennis and his foe's gazes remained fixed upon the minister, his black robe glowing ever brighter within the boundary of light encircling them. The minister pulled Ennis, and the man who had once been Ennis' enemy, into his chest and caressed their heads upon his shoulders. Held within the ball

369

of light, Ennis, the man who had been his attacker embraced the minister.

And then the light was no more. Only the battlefield remained, blanketed in darkness and gunfire, its terrain littered with casualties alive and dying, amid voices calling out and others commanding orders.

What seemed the height of the battle descended as Redmond drew near the hut. He walked faster, but not so much as for Florina to miss Agnes standing in the distance and smiling. Soldiers ran to and fro within the distance separating Agnes and Florina who rested in Redmond's arms.

"Dr. King was just here," Agnes said. Her voice carried through the whirring of bullets flying over and past her. Her face brightened. "I saw him. Dr. King," Agnes said. "He was just here. She turned back and pointed to the dark space Ennis and his foe had battled upon. "Just over there. Can you believe it?" She turned back to Florina.

"Yes, I can," Florina whispered from within the safety of Redmond's arms carrying her to the hut. "*I can.*" She began to cry.

Agnes smiled and waved once more.

Redmond pushed open the door of the hut filled with light, left the murkiness of war and fighting behind them and walked to the center of the hut where a beam of light shone down most intensely. He lay Florina on a table standing within the center of the light.

"Close your eyes," Redmond said. "You need your rest." He handed her an orange hydrangea. The room seemed to fill with them.

The energy of the orange hydrangeas filling the room enlivened Florina's body. She looked to Redmond. Her chest grew heavy, her breathing light. She relaxed into the soft warmth of the table.

Her eyelids heavy, Florina drifted into sleep.

Chapter 52

"*My dearest friend is now in the hands of the eternal God. We therefore submit his body to the ground.*

The cemetery is too small for his spirit. But we commit his body to the ground. The grave is too narrow for his soul. But we commit his body to the ground. No coffin, no crypt, nor vault, not stone can hold his greatness. But we commit his body to the ground. We commend his deeds to all mankind, his services and sacrifices to all generations. We commend his legacy of courage and love to ourselves, our children and our children's children. We commend his life to the universe.

We give thanks to God who gave us a leader to heal the white man's sickness, and the black man's slavery. We give thanks to God who gave us a peaceful warrior who built an army and a movement that is mighty without missiles, able without an atomic arsenal, ready without rockets, real without bullets, an army tutored in living and loving, and not in killing. We thank God for giving us a leader who was willing to die, but would not kill.

Peace be to his ashes and rest to his soul.

~~Dr. Ralph Abernathy at the Interment of Dr. Martin
Luther King, Jr.,
     April 9, 1968

Florina's eyelids flickered, she lifting them open, on
Tuesday, April ninth. The voice of Dr. Ralph Abernathy
resounded from a radio in the hall at the nurses' station. This
surprised her when Redmond informed her moments later that
she was in Poinsettia General, and not Charlotte Negro Hospital.
     Realizing the extent of her injury, Hammond Austin
called Mark Schaeffer. On Dr. Schaeffer's orders, Poinsettia
General readied an operating room wherein he, assisted by
Redmond and Hammond, searched for and extracted the bullet
that tore through Florina's spleen and rested just under her
diaphragm.
     "Hello, sleepy head," Redmond spoke softly and smiled.
"You're back with us."
     "Where am I?" Florina strained to keep her eyes open.
     "Poinsettia General," Redmond said.
     "But they don't admit Negro patie--"
     "I think we can say she's now among the living,"
Hammond spoke to Redmond across from him. Both men stood
by Florina's hospital bed.
     Still groggy, Florina had not forgotten the ways of the
American South. "Dr. King," she said. "He's dead."
     Solemnity washed over Redmond as the last memories
of the night of April fourth eked into Florina's consciousness.
     "Agnes and Macon died also," Redmond said. Florina
closed her eyes, the recollection too great, but quite real.

     Reverend Julius insisted upon eulogizing Agnes and
Macon. "She was Macon's wife," he said when speaking at the
funeral. "Macon was her husband." He looked down upon the
two coffins, one metallic blue, the other metallic brown. "*As in*

374

life, so in death," he pronounced. "*They are entwined in the arms of God.*"

Most heaved a sigh of relief that Reverend Mitchell allowed Reverend Julius Kensington to explain away the double deaths that nearly claimed Redmond Austin's new wife, Florina. Reverend Julius had married them.

The reality of the deaths, a murder-suicide, eclipsed by and held within the shadow of the assassination of Dr. Martin Luther King, Jr. stunned everyone in the town of Poinsettia-- more than the somberness of mourning and grief could contain. Those in Poinsettia observed, along with the nation and world, Dr. Ralph Abernathy giving last words to a man whose life would extend beyond those who followed his teachings and whose hearts his words and ideals transformed. They would not understand how within the death of such a man of peace, lay seeds that sowed the fate and deaths of Dr. Macon Elder, and his wife, Agnes.

Florina struggled with this question as she sat among mourners who gathered at St. Andrews on April 11, 1968, a week after Macon's suicide at the hands of the same gun that had commanded Agnes' death, and summoned the dark angel to hover over Florina's body for five days following.

Reverend Kensington opened the eulogy with, Genesis 2:18. "*The LORD God said, 'It is not good for the man to be alone. I will make a helper suitable for him,*' and then moved onto another.

"*Therefore a man shall leave his father and his mother and hold fast to his wife, and they shall become one flesh.*"

And thus, "*He who finds a wife finds a good thing and obtains favor from the Lord.*" Proverbs 18:22

Biblical scriptures in a most literal fashion formed the eulogies Agnes' father delivered of her and Macon, or rather their marriage and they victims of its demise.

"*Let marriage be held in honor among all,*" The Right Reverend Julius Kensington continued. " *... and let the marriage bed be undefiled, for God will judge the sexually immoral and adulterous.*"

"Wives, submit to your own husbands, as to the Lord."
And this is what she did, Agnes, in marrying Macon. *"For the husband is the head of the wife even as Christ is the head of the church, his body, and is himself its Savior."*

And Macon was a *husband who loved his wife, "... as Christ loved the church and gave himself up for her, that he might sanctify her, having cleansed her by the washing of water with the word."* Ephesians 5:23-33

Kensington rolled forward not stopping. In their marriage they learned that,
"Love is patient and kind; love does not envy or boast; it is not arrogant or rude. It does not insist on its own way; it is not irritable or resentful; it does not rejoice at wrongdoing, but rejoices with the truth. Love bears all things, believes all things, hopes all things, endures all things."

And so, *" ... as the church submits to Christ,"* Agnes, Macon's wife *submitting in everything even to death where they are now bound forever in our Lord, Jesus Christ.*

Bewildered, and confused, Florina searched for answers among the same maze of doubts and questions plaguing those of St. Andrews A.M.E Zion Parish. How can he lie? Florina thought as Reverend Julius continued his narrative of untruth at the gravesite crypt that would house the remains of Agnes and Macon.
"Behold, I was shapen in iniquity; and in sin did my mother conceive me."
" ... all have sinned, and come short of the glory of God;" And as it is God has drawn both Agnes and Macon unto Him.

On touching crypt he quoted a Psalm 139, *"Whither shall I go from thy spirit? or whither shall I flee from thy presence? I ascend up into heaven, thou art there: if I make my bed in hell, behold, thou art there. If I take the wings of the morning, and dwell in the uttermost parts of the sea; Even there shall thy hand lead me, and thy right hand shall hold me. If I say, Surely the darkness shall cover me; even the night shall be light about me. Yea, the darkness hideth not from thee; but the night shineth as the day: the darkness and the light are both alike to thee. For thou hast possessed my reins: thou hast covered me in my*

376

mother's womb. I will praise thee; for I am fearfully and wonderfully made: marvelous are thy works; and that my soul knoweth right well. My substance was not hid from thee, when I was made in secret, and curiously wrought in the lowest parts of the earth. Thine eyes did see my substance, yet being unperfect; and in thy book all my members were written, which in continuance were fashioned, when as yet there was none of them. How precious also are thy thoughts unto me, O God! how great is the sum of them!"

"If I should count them, they are more in number than the sand: when I awake, I am still with thee. Surely thou wilt slay the wicked, O God: depart from me therefore, ye bloody men. For they speak against thee wickedly, and thine enemies take thy name in vain. Do not I hate them, O LORD, that hate thee? and am not I grieved with those that rise up against thee? I hate them with perfect hatred: I count them mine enemies. Search me, O God, and know my heart: try me, and know my thoughts: And see if there be any wicked way in me, and lead me in the way everlasting."

Florina looked to Macon's parents, Franklin and Irene Elder, sitting silent and still, perplexed as all others who had gathered in the wake of the bizarre events. Florina felt for them. The Elders carried great shame for their son's actions.

She ached for the truth they would know, that Julius Kensington's well-crafted eulogy would command they adhere to in an effort to preserve what dignified memories remained of their son.

Suddenly, Kensington's voice slowed, he having reached the end of the psalm. "Whither can I go to elude you, your most glorious love?" Taking in his words, the woebegone tone in which wrapped them, Florina realized that in all the Biblical texts he had recited, Agnes' father had not been talking about God and his love for Agnes and Macon, rather the focus of his words, carefully hidden in sacred text had focused upon Macon's adoration and obsession of Agnes.

"I cannot escape you, Not even in death. Not even in death."

And so he committed them to God and then the earth, a web of fantasy serving as the narrative in which he preserved the memory he desired of his daughter and son-in-law, for whom others would whisper the adjectives *troubled* and *greatly distraught* preceding either or both of their names.

Reverend Julius closed his Bible and sprinkled dirt upon Agnes' casket and Macon's lying next it. He walked towards a grey-haired woman, Florina presumed to be his wife, Agnes' mother and grasped her hand.

John and Jeanne Cartwright approached them. Jeanne embraced the woman beside Reverend Julius. John shook Reverend Julius' hand.

"I want to go home," Florina said to Redmond. Redmond helped her to stand, Hammond joining him. They escorted her back to Redmond's black Riviera.

Shards of Florina's dream edged their way into her thoughts, she reclaiming the entire experience, during the drive the drive back to Carolyn and Hammond's. Florina and Redmond were staying at her in-law's home during her recuperation.

"She was there. Agnes," Florina said as Redmond, beside her, looked to the road ahead and drove. "She waved at me." Florina recounted the full extent of the dream as best she could recall. "Agnes was happy and smiling. She had seen Dr. King."

"Where?" Redmond sounded interested.

"There amid the fighting. We were on a battlefield. In Vietnam." Florina turned towards the window and looked at the cemetery beside the Primitive Baptist Church where she had encountered the young minister, Fitzhugh Mason. "All wars are civil because all men are brothers," Florina recalled his words. They had comforted her in battle.

"I thought we had lost you," Redmond said. He tightened his grip upon the steering wheel.

"Ennis was there," Florina said. "He ordered me to the hut. The light was so bright inside. You took me most of the way." She turned to Redmond, still attentive to the road. "I don't think I could have made it without you carrying me."

Redmond released a sigh. His cheeks hung heavy.

Florina said, "I didn't realize it was Dr. King that was in my dream until Agnes spoke his name, told me she had seen him." Again Redmond turned to her. The car sat motionless at a stoplight. "He guided Ennis and the man fighting him out of the darkness and away from the fighting. Seeing him with Dr. King, in the circle of light, I knew that Ennis was okay. Everything would be all right."

"Will everything be all right, okay with us?" Redmond asked. He had guided the sedan through the intersection, but was now driving slowly.

"I died among orange hydrangeas."

———————————————————

······••······••

Chapter 53

•······••······••

Slivers of memory regarding her dream had cut through Florina's consciousness during the days leading up to Agnes and Macon's funeral. The full force of the recollection burst through during the interment.

Florina discussed her memories with Redmond during the drive back to Carolyn and Hammond's house. Florina and Redmond were staying at his parents' home during Florina's recuperation.

"She was there on the battlefield in my dream," Florina said of Agnes, " ... She was standing where Ennis had been fighting the man whose face I could not see." Florina examined her hands, thought of how she had wanted to remain with Ennis and see to his wounds. She recalled the blood on his hands, how she had touched his thigh and it had stained her hands.

Florina turned to Redmond driving and looking at the street ahead. "She waved at me. Agnes was smiling," Florina said. She recalled that, "Agnes said she had seen Dr. King."

Redmond stopped the car at the red intersection light. Florina said, "I didn't realize he was the man in the black robe with red trim until Agnes spoke to me, said his name." The events of her dream took on a realness, became vivid and alive in her mind. "I'll never forget this. It will always be with me. Until I die."

Soft furrows formed across Redmond's forehead.

"I saw Agnes after Ennis had been shot," Florina continued. "He told me to get to the hut at the edge of the field where the fighting was taking place. The hut was filled with light," Florina said.

Redmond drove them through the intersection.

"I couldn't see the soldier's face," Florina repeated, adding, "I always had a feeling it was Macon."

The black Riviera coupe continued down the street.

Lying down at Carolyn and Hammond's, Florina said, "I wonder if Reverend Julius realizes he caused this. Macon killing Agnes and then himself."

"He tried to kill you too," Redmond said. He was over by the closet placing the jacket to his suit on a hanger. "As for the lies he told during the funeral, Julius Kensington, is only concerned with his reputation, how things appear."

Florina sensed the bitterness in Redmond's voice. "He was so dramatic," Florina said. "As if he believed all he was saying."

"He did. For him it is and will always be real."

"His daughter is dead." Florina felt the pain of her wound, touched her left side where the bullet had entered then tore through her spleen. "I miss her," Florina said of Agnes.

"Too miss someone you have to know her, understand her inside and out, at least try to." Redmond turned back to Florina lying upon the bed. "Julius Kensington never knew or even wanted to know Agnes, who she really was. He resisted the truth of her life."

"In that sense he had some sense of who she was." Florina said. "I think he knew her more than we or anyone realizes. He misses battling with her. You said she was a lot like him."

Redmond nodded.

"Reverend Julius may have seen that. If he did I'm sure he misses her." Florina took in breath. "Agnes may have been the only one to stand up to him." And then like memories of her dreaming return, she realized, "Reverend Julius was obsessed with Agnes. Just like Macon. That's what bound all three. Now with Agnes and Macon dead he's all alone."

A thoughtful look overtook Redmond's face. Florina met his gaze, and again observed that the longing that had filled Redmond's eyes when looking down upon Agnes had returned and now reached out to her.

Later as she was undressing, Florina said, I wonder how Agnes' mother is doing. She looked so sad, forlorn, like all life had been ripped out of her. Did you see her?"

"That wasn't Agnes' mother," Redmond said after some moments. "That was Reverend Julius's sister, Clementine." Redmond spoke name as if the person to whom it was affixed held deep history.

"Where was Agnes' mother? Why would she not come? Agnes was her daughter, her only child."

"It was most likely more than she could bear, too painful," Redmond said. "What she had let happen, what she as Agnes' mother had been party to." The sadness in his eyes spoke of what he had described, suggested that he too held regrets for not having told Macon the truth about Agnes' sexual proclivities.

"You did what was right," Florina said. "It wasn't your job to warn Macon. I believe he knew about Agnes. He would have turned on you, had you warned him."

"As if he already hadn't?" Redmond was somber, melancholic despair seeming to overtaking him.

"Exactly my point." As Florina spoke she resolved to end the silence. "I want to visit Mrs. Kensington."

"Agnes' mother?" Redmond appeared almost incredulous.

"It's the least I can do. Her daughter is dead. She needs to know that someone loved Agnes as she was."

Redmond's incredulity diminished into what appeared a strange mix of shock, surprise and awe.

"I want you and Robert MacIntosh to go with me. Drive me to Baltimore." Florina said.

"Are you sure about this?"

"As certain as I have ever been about anything."

Wednesday May fifteenth, 1968, Florina and Redmond set out, with Redmond driving, for Baltimore, Maryland. Robert MacIntosh sat in the front passenger's seat while Florina, at Carolyn and Hammond's insistence, sat in the back of Robert's four-door sedan surrounded by pillows.

"Call us as soon as you arrive," Carolyn commanded in that soft way she had of delivering orders.

Florina thought of how Ennis had ordered her to leave him upon the battlefield of her dreams and seek shelter in the bamboo hut of her marriage to Redmond. That is how she interpreted the dream she had experienced during the surgery to mend the wound caused by the bullet Macon had fired.

"Dr. King's Poor People's March was to have been underway by this time," Robert MacIntosh commented when they crossed into Virginia.

"Agnes would have been there," Florina said. She stared out the back passenger window and took in the fields alive with cotton and pole lima beans and other spring vegetables. *Daddy'll be picking the cabbage,* she thought.

Florina's parents, along with the Reynolds, had set out for Poinsettia late Thursday evening, April fourth after having learned she had been shot. They had remained until she had awakened five days later. They along with Ava and Bill Reynolds had been back at Carolyn and Hammond's home when Florina had opened her eyes. Redmond and Hammond were by her bed. Like others around the country and world, they, along with Redmond's grandmother, Lyla Austin, had been watching the funeral of Dr. Martin Luther King, Jr.

Florina observed once more the fields awash in May sunshine and for the first time, took in the sheer emptiness wrought by Agnes' and Macon's deaths.

384

The houses of the neighborhood in which Agnes had grown up were immense in stature, every lawn was manicured, flowers carefully trimmed.

"This looks like a picture out of *Homes and Gardens*," Florina said as Redmond turned onto yet another street. "I've never seen anything like this, not up close."

"Don't be fooled," Redmond said. "Not is all that it seems."

"And if this is what integration will bring to Negroes, we had all better be warned," said Robert MacIntosh.

"Dr. Mayweather seems to have had a greater influence on you," Florina said to MacIntosh. Mayweather had taken to giving talks, nearly every day since Dr. King's assassination.

"I've attended two and what he says makes sense," MacIntosh said. "Although I'm not sure how much most listening to him can and will make of it."

Redmond brought the car to a stop in front a large white two-story home with green shutters. "Well here we are," he said.

"The grass is so green," Florina said of the lawn spread before the Kensington home. *Like the rice paddies of Vietnam*, she thought.

Redmond got out as did Robert who then opened Florina's door.

"Are you sure you're up to this?" Redmond said to Florina on walking around the sedan to where she and Robert stood by the passenger side.

"They're expecting me." She looked to the house some feet ahead. "Besides, I have to do this." The three started towards the demure porch sheltered by a small awning. Reaching the steps, Florina noticed a row of hydrangeas extending from both sides.

"They're orange," she said to Robert. "Like the one Ingrid cultured."

Robert MacIntosh smiled.

Florina sensed Redmond was going back in time to greet a demon as he raised his hand to knock on the door of Agnes' childhood home. He knocked again. The front door opened.

———————————————————

Chapter 54

The living room of the Kensington home resembled eighteenth century France. A Louis the fifteenth gold gilt sofa occupied the wall next the entrance. Two matching gilt fauteuils stood facing the sofa, a Venetian coffee table between the fauteuils and the latter. Two other matching fauteuils stood about the room, one by the picture window on the opposite wall and a third in the corner down from the window.

The soft, intricate carvings emphasizing curves and personifying the sensuality of the Louis fifteenth era surprised Florina. The Right Reverend Julius Kensington presented more as a Calvinist with a mix of Evangelicalism than worldly Catholicism. And yet the gray and silver cast of the upholstery against the white walls screamed a Puritanical streak that Florina had sensed from the moment she had encountered him after having rescued Agnes, against her will, from Memphis and brought her back to Poinsettia.

Agnes' mother, Esther Kensington, exuded an aura quite the opposite of her husband. Her tea length dress of periwinkle blue and soft chiffon led Florina to wonder if perhaps she and Reverend Julius would be attending an engagement following Florina's visit.

"I hope we didn't interrupt your plans for the evening," Florina said once seated upon the sofa.

"But of course not," Esther said from the fauteuil at Florina's left at the edge of the Venetian coffee table. "Julius and I have begun preparing for your visit two days ago."

Florina smiled at Reverend Julius, standing by the picture window.

"Clementine too, has been anticipating your arrival," said Esther.

As if the sound of her name gave cue for her entrance, Reverend Julius's sister, Clementine, walked in. "It is so nice of you to come," Clementine said. She continued onto the fauteuil by the picture window and sat. Reverend Julius, donning his clergyman's collar, stood behind her.

"I trust you have traveled smoothly," Reverend Julius said.

"Traffic was light," Redmond replied.

"No problems," Robert MacIntosh added.

"That's good to hear," Clementine said. "In light of all that's been happening around the country since Mr. King's death it is a blessing."

Florina bristled at Clementine addressing Martin Luther King as "Mr." instead of the honorific usually accorded, "*Dr.*" She glanced at Redmond and Robert to gauge how this struck them. "We've all suffered a loss," Florina said to Esther. Clementine sat with her hands clasped and lying upon her lap, and her back ramrod straight. Unlike Esther she wore black, emphasizing that of Reverend Julius's ministerial attire. "More the reason I am grateful for you agreeing to see me," Florina resumed speaking to Agnes' mother. "As you know, Agnes and I were neighbors." The reality of the word, "*were,*" evidenced the absence of Agnes that Florina had yet to integrate.

She had moved through the recent months much like riding a roller coaster, spending most of her days climbing out of pits of melancholy, only to reach a height of thankfulness from which she would sink back down and often further into despair when considering the reality of all that had occurred on

388

that fateful evening of Thursday, April fourth, nineteen sixty-eight, or in simply looking to the house next door.

Agnes had been married but one year. The awfulness of the realization hit Florina like a boulder.

"You and Agnes were newlyweds," Esther said and smiled. Agnes' Aunt Clementine sat still and alert. Reverend Julius remained wary and silent. "I would imagine your connection ripe for friendship," she added.

"I don't know if you could describe Agnes and me as terribly close friends," Florina said.

Esther gave a slight frown. Florina clasped her hands, gazed upon the back of her palms. "We did have much in common."

"That's putting it mildly," Clementine said. She released a slight laugh. "You married the man to whom my niece was once engaged."

"Agnes told me about that," Florina acknowledged. She met Esther's gaze and felt the warmth of a shared kinship with the woman who had given birth to Agnes.

"Agnes spoke much of you in her letters," Esther said.

"She wrote of me?" Florina asked. She had not imagined Agnes communicating with either of her parents, certainly not on such an intimate level as with that held in letters.

"Agnes began writing to me in the new year," Esther said. "I believe she met you in December."

"Two days following Christmas," Florina said.

Reverend Julius lifted one eyebrow. Clementine pursed her lips, appeared as if about to speak. Reverend Julius lowered his hand upon her shoulder.

"Agnes was a unique person," Florina said. "Not the easiest to get to know. But once I did, I came to respect her."

"And when was that?" Reverend Julius spoke. "When did you get to know our daughter? How *did* she reveal herself to you?"

Florina struggled to find the right words. Reverend Julius's questions ambushed then sidetracked Florina from her purpose in requesting to speak with Esther. Florina recalled what she had deemed his dramatic performance in delivering both Agnes and Macon's eulogies. As the alpha who had joined them in wedlock, he had also served as the omega, binding them closer to each other in death.

But Agnes' mother had been absent from the event, a fact covered over, and largely missed, Florina now concluded, due to Clementine's presence. They were a team, Julius Kensington and his sister. *How much had their dual actions influenced Agnes, or worse Esther regarding her relationship with her daughter, Agnes?*

"I wanted you to know that Agnes saved my life," Florina said to Esther. "Had she not pushed Macon to the floor and run in between us, Macon would have shot me not once, but twice. I would have died. I'm certain of this."

Esther Kensington's eyes widened. Her face, white like Agnes', ran sad. Yet Agnes' face was not white. Negroes, no matter how fair, held a smattering of color in their skin, hue recognizable to other Negroes, those fair and dark. Florina surveyed Esther's face, strained in her search, and failed to detect a miniscule of color.

Muscles flexed in Julius Kensington's thin neck. Clementine stared into the lap of her black dress and closed her eyelids.

"You're not Negro," Florina said to Esther.

"It is strange the way you speak it," Esther said. She had begun to weep. "But true. I'm white."

"What does this have anything to do with anything?" Reverend Julius demanded.

Florina glimpsed Redmond and Robert beside her, their heads lowered.

"Did your husband tell you the real reason he refused to marry our daughter?" said Agnes' father.

Florina turned to Redmond. He lifted his head. "Agnes could never love Redmond the way he wanted and needed. Redmond was not willing to live a lie."

"He refused to marry Agnes because Esther, her mother is white," Clementine said.

Esther lowered her head and wept more.

"You can say whatever makes you feel better," Florina said to Julius Kensington, " ... speak the truth as you wish it to be. But Agnes, the person she was, saved my life. You may not have liked or approved of that person, but that person, the Agnes that you pulled from Larry Payne's funeral, gave her life trying to save mine."

"You led my daughter astray! You, who are a lover of women!" Julius Kensington walked to the back of Esther's chair, grasped her trembling shoulders. "I warned Esther not to allow you to come, that you would bring only lies and disorder to this house!" Kensington continued. "You destroyed our daughter's life and are now attempting to disgrace her good nam--"

"Julius, please!" Esther said and raised her hand. "Enough."

"But, my dear, this woman is speaking lies. Should you believe them others will t--"

"I don't care who Agnes loved," Esther said to Reverend Julius. "The fact is she gave her life for something... trying to save someone. And for that she'll be remembered."

A broken smile formed upon Esther's lips. "My daughter loved you. She loved you very much."

"I know," Florina lowered her head and began to cry.

•.•..•.•..•.•..•.•..•

Chapter 55

•.•..•.•..•.•..•.•..•

Esther Kensington held Florina's hand as she walked with her to the front door of the Kensington home. On stepping outside she went to the line of orange hydrangeas surrounding the small portico, bent over and plucked the head of one from its stem.

"Oh my," said Florina. She accepted the orange hydrangea.

Esther smiled. She offered Florina an envelope that appeared to have just then materialized.

"Thank you for coming," Esther, said. "Like Dr. King, my daughter knew her time was nigh." Florina frowned. "Don't ask me how," Esther said, "But Agnes knew."

As did Esther, it seemed.

Florina looked at the letter and the head of the orange hydrangea, then at Robert MacIntosh who had given her a root bulb, also for an orange hydrangea. Unbeknownst to Florina-- and quite lucky for Florina in light of recent events--Redmond's mother had planted it.

"*We're all orange hydrangeas*," MacIntosh had said on that February afternoon, days after she had returned from

Laurel, and when she had confessed her previous marriage to Redmond.

Redmond now smiled upon the orange hydrangea. "It's pretty isn't it?" Florina said to him, and then to MacIntosh standing beside him. "An oddity as well."

"Aren't we all," said MacIntosh.

Florina peeled open the envelope at the start of the ride back to Poinsettia in North Carolina.

March 31, 1968

Florina,

Macon won't tolerate me like this for long. I don't love him, never have. You have been a good friend to me. I'm not the person you think I am, nor the one I presented to you that day on the steps of the verandah of your home.
Redmond's a good man. Don't let him fool you. He loves you. You love him. I can see that. Even with Ennis in the background. You've come out of the shadows of the life you had with him, the life you hoped to have had... and you've learned what marriage is all about.

For that I love you. Perhaps in another life I can have someone like you who will love me ... the way you love Redmond. I loved Redmond. But I can honestly now say, I love you more.

Keep tough and honest. Never lose your heart and feeling.
It's what drew me to you.
~~Agnes

Florina folded Agnes' letter then looked up to see MacIntosh, now in the driver's seat and easing the sedan onto Interstate Ninety-five South. She slid the paper holding Agnes' words back into the envelope, observed the orange hydrangea lying beside her, and sighed.

On reaching Poinsettia the late that night, early the next morning Florina thanked Robert for accompanying and helping Redmond with the drive to Baltimore.

"Anything for my daughter-in-law," Robert said. He hugged her then extended his hand to Redmond. "Don't make yourself scarce, son."

"I won't." Redmond shook the palm of his biological father.

That morning before dawn Florina lay in bed and Redmond pulled her close. "And thank you for what you shared with Agnes' mother," he said. "She needed to hear that."

Florina's heart warmed. Her chest filled with peace and contentment. She reached into the darkness, touched Redmond's cheek, and said, "Thank you for taking me to her. I needed to speak those words."

"It was a good thing you did," Redmond said. He kissed her cheek.

Florina awoke the next morning, and prepared breakfast which she and Redmond ate. Later she accompanied him onto the verandah as he prepared to leave. "I wish I could stay here with you, but Father can't see to all my and Macon's patie--"

Florina placed her finger to Redmond's lips. "We'll get through this," she said.

It broke her heart to think of Hammond Austin attempting to explain to Macon's patients that which defied comprehension concerning his life and death. Florina brushed Redmond's cheek, touched his shoulder and urged him to go. "I'll be fine.

He waved while driving away in the black Riviera. The coupe was down the street and had turned the corner when Florina making her way back up to the verandah glimpsed the orange bud that had pushed through the dark earth, and glimmered in the morning sun. The small head of orange hydrangea vibrated with life. Florina grasped her chest, walked to it and knelt.

Ennis, she whispered. And then seeing faded remains of cigarette ashes, barely visible ... *Agnes*. Gently she caressed the petals, delicate like skin, palpating with hope and life.

Florina gazed down the street and into the distance where Redmond had driven, and gave thanks.

———————————————————

www.ingramcontent.com/pod-product-compliance
Lightning Source LLC
Chambersburg PA
CBHW020845090426
42736CB00008B/247